GACE
115
116
615

Health and Physical Education

Teacher Certification Exam

By: Sharon A. Wynne, M.S.

XAMonline, INC.
Boston

Library of Congress Cataloging-in-Publication Data

Wynne, Sharon A.
    GACE Health and Physical Education 115, 116, 615: Teacher Certification / Sharon A. Wynne.
    ISBN 978-1-64239-029-2
    1. Health and Physical Education 115, 116, 615   2. Study Guides.
    3. GACE   4. Teacher's Certification & Licensure.   5. Careers

Disclaimer:
The opinions expressed in this publication are the sole works of XAMonline and were created independently from the National Education Association, Educational Testing Service, any State Department of Education, National Evaluation Systems or other testing affiliates.

Between the time of publication and printing, state specific standards as well as testing formats and website information may change that is not included in part or in whole within this product. Sample test questions are developed by XAMonline and reflect similar content as on actual tests; however, they are not prior tests. XAMonline assembles content that aligns with state standards however, makes no claims nor guarantees teacher candidates a passing score. Numerical scores are determined by testing companies such as NES or ETS and then are compared with individual state standards. A passing score varies from state to state.

Printed in the United States of America   œ-1

GACE Health and Physical Education 115, 116, 615
ISBN: 978-1-64239-029-2

GEORGIA SUBJECT AREA TEST – Health and Physical Education

ABOUT THE GACE

For each GACE (Georgia Assessments for the Certification of Educators) examination, XAMonline has prepared a test framework based on the state subject area competency objectives set forth by the State of Georgia. Each test framework consists of a set of test subareas, competencies, and skills. Collectively, these objectives establish the general set of knowledge that each applicant should possess to achieve certification. All individuals seeking an initial Georgia teaching license must pass the GACE subtest that matches the type of license they are seeking. All GACE examinations are criterion referenced, which means each test measures an examinee's knowledge in relation to an established standard of competence rather than in relation to the performance of other examinees.

TEST ADMINISTRATION

On each test date, prospective teachers can take the GACE Health and Physical Education test in the afternoon session only. Each session is four hours long.

The GACE Health and Physical Education test consists of **two tests**. Each test contains 60 multiple-choice questions and two constructed-response assignments.

SCORE REPORTS

Each score report will indicate whether an individual has passed their respective test. Score reports also include a description of each individual's performance on the major content subareas of the test. The scoring scale for each test ranges from 100 to 300, with 220 representing the minimum passing score.

TEST STRUCTURE

NESINC, the designer of the GACE examinations, describes the test structure as follows:

Test I (Test Code 115)

Subarea Number	Subarea Title	Approximate Number of Multiple Choice Questions	Constructed-Response Assignments
I	Personal Health and Development	22	0
II	Disease and Health-Risk Prevention	22	1
III	Family and Social Relationships	16	1

Test II (Test Code 116)

Subarea Number	Subarea Title	Approximate Number of Multiple Choice Questions	Constructed-Response Assignments
IV	Motor Learning, Motor Development, and Movement Concepts	20	0
V	Health-Related Fitness	20	1
VI	Sports and Lifetime Activities	20	1

Table of Contents

TEST I. HEALTH

TEST II. PHYSICAL EDUCATION

SUBAREA IV. MOTOR LEARNING, MOTOR DEVELOPMENT AND MOVEMENT CONCEPTS

Great Study and Testing Tips!

What you study in order to prepare for the subject assessments is the focus of this study guide, but equally important is *how* you study.

You can increase your chances of truly mastering the information by taking some simple but effective steps.

Study Tips:

1. <u>Some foods can aid the learning process</u>. Foods such as milk, nuts, seeds, rice, and oats help your study efforts by releasing natural memory enhancers called CCKs (*cholecystokinin*) composed of *tryptophan*, *choline*, and *phenylalanine*. All of these chemicals enhance the neurotransmitters associated with memory. Before studying, try a light, protein-rich meal of eggs, turkey, and fish. All of these foods release the memory enhancing chemicals. The better the connections, the more you comprehend.

Likewise, before you take a test, stick to a light snack of relaxing and energy boosting foods. A glass of milk, a piece of fruit, or some peanuts release various memory-boosting chemicals and help you to relax and focus on the subject at hand.

2. <u>Learn to take great notes</u>. A by-product of our modern culture is that we have grown accustomed to getting our information in short doses (e.g. TV news sound bites or USA Today style newspaper articles).

Consequently, we've subconsciously trained ourselves to assimilate information better in <u>neat little packages</u>. If your notes are scrawled all over the paper, it fragments the flow of the information. Strive for clarity. Newspapers use a standard format to achieve clarity. You can make your notes much clearer by using proper formatting. A very effective format is the *"Cornell Method."*

Take a sheet of loose-leaf lined notebook paper and draw a line all the way down the paper about one to two inches from the left-hand edge.

Draw another line across the width of the paper about one to two inches up from the bottom. Repeat this process on the reverse side of the page.

Look at the highly effective result. You have ample room for notes, a left hand margin for special emphasis items or inserting supplementary data from the textbook, a large area at the bottom for a brief summary, and a little rectangular space for just about anything you want.

3. Get the concept then the details. Too often, we focus on the details and don't gather an understanding of the concept. However, if you simply memorize only dates, places, or names, you may well miss the whole point of the subject.

A key way to understand things is to put them in your own words. If you are working from a textbook, automatically summarize each paragraph in your mind. If you are outlining text, don't simply copy the author's words.

Rephrase them in your own words. You remember your own thoughts and words much better than someone else's, and subconsciously tend to associate the important details to the core concepts.

4. Ask Why? Pull apart written material paragraph by paragraph and don't forget the captions under the illustrations.

Example: If the heading is "Stream Erosion", flip it around to read, "Why do streams erode?" Then answer the questions in your own words.

If you train your mind to think in a series of questions and answers, not only will you learn more, but you will also help to lessen test anxiety, by getting yourself used to answering questions.

5. Read for reinforcement and future needs. Even if you only have 10 minutes, put your notes or a book in your hand. Your mind is similar to a computer; you have to input data in order to have it processed. *By reading, you are creating the neural connections for future retrieval.* The more times you read something, the more you reinforce the learning of ideas.

Even if you don't fully understand something on the first pass, *your mind stores much of the material for later recall.*

6. Relax to learn, so go into exile. Our bodies respond to an inner clock called biorhythms. Burning the midnight oil works well for some people, but not for everyone.

If possible, set aside a particular place to study that is free of distractions. Shut off the television, cell phone, and pager and exile your friends and family during your study period.

If silence really bothers you, try background music. Studies show that light classical music played at a low volume aids in concentration.

Music that evokes pleasant emotions without lyrics is highly suggested. Try just about anything by Mozart. It will help relax you.

7. **<u>Use arrows not highlighters</u>.** At best, it's difficult to read a page full of yellow, pink, blue, and green streaks.

Try staring at a neon sign for a while and you'll soon see my point. The horde of colors obscures the message.

A quick note, a brief dash of color, an underline, and an arrow pointing to a particular passage is much clearer than a horde of highlighted words.

8. **<u>Budget your study time</u>.** Although you shouldn't ignore any of the material, *allocate your available study time in the same ratio that topics may appear on the test.*

Testing Tips:

1. <u>Get smart, play dumb</u>. Don't read anything into the question. Don't assume that the test writer is looking for something else than what is asked. Stick to the question as it is written and don't read any extra things into it.

2. <u>Read the question and all the choices</u> *twice* <u>before answering</u>. You may miss something by not carefully reading and re-reading both the question and the answers.

If you really don't have a clue as to the right answer, leave it blank the first time through. Go on to the other questions, as they may provide a clue as to how to answer the skipped questions.

If later on, you still can't answer the skipped ones . . . ***Guess.***
The only penalty for guessing is that you *might* get it wrong. One thing is certain; if you don't put anything down, you will get it wrong!

3. <u>Turn the question into a statement</u>. Look at the way the questions are worded. The syntax of the question usually provides a clue. Does it seem more familiar as a statement rather than as a question? Does it sound strange?

By turning a question into a statement, you may be able to spot if an answer sounds right. thus triggering memories of material you have read prior.

4. <u>Look for hidden clues</u>. It's actually very difficult to compose multiple-choice questions without giving away part of the answer in the options presented.

In most multiple-choice questions, you can often readily eliminate one or two of the potential answers. This leaves you with only two real possibilities, thereby automatically increasing your odds to fifty-fifty with very little work.

5. <u>Trust your instincts</u>. For every fact that you have read, you subconsciously retain something of that knowledge. On questions that you aren't certain about, go with your basic instincts. **Your first impression on how to answer a question is usually correct.**

6. <u>Mark your answers directly on the test booklet</u>. Don't bother trying to fill in the optical scan sheet on the first pass through the test.

Just be very careful not to miss-mark your answers when you eventually transcribe them to the scan sheet.

7. <u>Watch the clock</u>! You have a set amount of time to answer the questions. Don't get bogged down trying to answer a single question at the expense of 10 questions you can more readily answer.

TEST I.   HEALTH

SUBAREA I.   **PERSONAL HEALTH AND DEVELOPMENT**

COMPETENCY 1.0   **UNDERSTAND HUMAN GROWTH AND DEVELOPMENT**

SKILL 1.1   Demonstrating knowledge of patterns, stages, and characteristics of physical, cognitive, social, and emotional growth and development

Physical development – Small children (ages 3-5) have a propensity for engaging in periods of a great deal of physical activity, punctuated by a need for a lot of rest. Children at this stage lack fine motor skills and cannot focus on small objects for very long. Their bones are still developing. At this age, girls tend to be better coordinated while boys tend to be stronger.

The lag in fine motor skills continues during the early elementary school years (ages 6-8).

Pre-adolescent children (ages 9-11) become stronger, leaner, and taller. Their motor skills improve, and they are able to sit still and focus for longer periods of time. Growth during this period is constant. This is also the time when gender-related physical predispositions will begin to show. Without proper nutrition and adequate activity, pre-adolescents are at risk of obesity.

Young adolescents (ages 12-14) experience drastic physical growth (girls earlier than boys) and are highly preoccupied with their physical appearance.

As children proceed to the later stages of adolescence (ages 15-17), girls will reach their full height, while boys will still have some growth remaining. The increase in hormone levels will cause acne, which coincides with a slight decrease of preoccupation with physical appearance. At this age, children may begin to initiate sexual activity (boys generally are more motivated by hormones, and girls more by peer pressure). There is a risk of teen pregnancy and sexually transmitted diseases.

Cognitive development – Language development is the most important aspect of cognitive development in small children (ages 3-5). Allowing successes, rewarding mature behavior and allowing the child to explore can improve confidence and self-esteem at this age.

Early elementary school children (Ages 6-8) are eager to learn and love to talk. Children at this age have a very literal understanding of rules and verbal instructions and must develop strong listening skills.

Pre-adolescent children (ages 9-11) display increased logical thought but their knowledge or beliefs may be unusual or surprising. Differences in cognitive styles develop at this age (e.g. field dependant or independent preferences).
In early adolescence (ages 12-14), boys tend to score higher on mechanical/spatial reasoning, and girls on spelling, language, and clerical tasks. Boys are better with mental imagery, and girls have better access and retrieval of information from memory. Self-efficacy (the ability to self-evaluate) becomes very important at this stage.

In later adolescence (ages 15-17), children are capable of formal thought, however they don't always apply this ability. Conflicts between teens' and parents' opinions and worldviews will arise. Children at this age may become interested in advanced political thinking.

Social development – Small children (ages 3-5) are socially flexible. Different children will prefer solitary play, parallel play, or cooperative play. Frequent minor quarrels will occur between children, and boys will tend to be more aggressive (children at these ages are already aware of gender roles).

Early elementary school children (ages 6-8) are increasingly selective of friends (usually of the same sex). Children at this age enjoy playing games but they are excessively preoccupied by the rules. Verbal aggression becomes more common than physical aggression and adults should encourage children at this age to solve their own conflicts.

Pre-adolescent children (ages 9-11) place great importance on the (perceived) opinions of their peers and of their social stature. They will also go to great lengths to 'fit in'. Friendships at this age are very selective and usually of the same sex.

Young adolescents (ages 12-14) develop greater understanding of the emotions of others resulting, in increased emotional sensitivity which impacts peer relationships. Children at this age develop an increased need to perform.

In the later stages of adolescence (ages 15-17), peers are still the primary influence on day-to-day decisions but parents have increasing influence on long-term goals. Girls' friendships tend to be close and intimate, whereas boys' friendships are based on competition and similar interests. Many children this age will work part-time and educators should be alert to signs of potential school dropouts.

Emotional development – Small children (ages 3-5) express emotion freely and have a limited ability to learn how emotions influence behavior. Jealousy at this age is common.

Early elementary school children (ages 6-8) have easily bruised feelings and are just beginning to recognize the feelings of others. Children this age will want to please teachers and other adults.

Pre-adolescent children (ages 9-11) develop a global and stable self-image (self-concept and self-esteem). Comparisons to their peers and the opinions of their peers are important. An unstable home environment at this age contributes to an increased risk of delinquency.

Young adolescence (ages 12-14) can be a stormy and stressful time for children but, in reality, this is only the case for roughly 20% of teens. Boys may have trouble controlling their anger and may display impulsive behavior. Girls may suffer depression. Young adolescents are very egocentric and concerned with appearance and will feel very strongly that "adults don't understand."

In later stages of adolescence (ages 15-17), educators should be alert to signs of surfacing mental health problems (e.g. eating disorders, substance abuse, schizophrenia, depression, and suicide).

SKILL 1.2　Recognizing factors that affect physical, cognitive, social, and emotional growth and development in childhood and adolescence (e.g., effects of economic factors on child development)

The effect of factors such as gender, age, environment, nutrition and heredity are crucial in understanding childhood and adolescence development. From a physiological standpoint, specifically in regard to the onset of puberty, girls normal range of onset is ages 8-14 in, while boys normal onset of puberty is ages is 9-15. While environment (social, cultural and ambient) is considered to play a huge role in the age onset of both genders, it is more and more widely accepted and believed that the determination of the onset of puberty is also controlled by interactions between the brain and the pituitary glands.

Environment has and continues to be considered an extremely important contributing factor in of all aspects of childhood and adolescent growth and development. Children that live in environments that include substance abuse tend to exhibit behavioral, emotional and social problems more readily than those that are not. Additionally, without adequate, healthy and appropriate social role models, children tend to have a difficult time forming positive social relationships with their peers. Without positive child-adult patterns, children's social growth and development is impaired. Research indicates without these, children have a much more difficult time acquiring skills needed later in life to carry out adult roles. Also, in adolescence, without proper social skill development through environmental influences, such as mentioned, healthy child-adult patterns, positive adult role models, students tend to have significant behavioral and development, negative consequences (i.e., sexual interactions at any early age, high risk behaviors, substance use/abuse, cigarette smoking, mental health problems). Other environment factors affecting growth and development of children and adolescents are adequate cleanliness, air quality, health care, neighborhood safety, parental involvement and family income.

Children's environments also need to provide or adequate sleep. Sufficient sleep for children is considered to be 7-8 hours a night and is critical for all areas of childhood growth and development. During sleep, the body performs many important cleansing and restoration tasks. Most importantly, the immune and excretory systems clear waste and repair cellular damage that accumulates in the body each day. Lack of sufficient amount of sleep leaves the body much more vulnerable and susceptible to infections and disease. Additionally, if children do not get a sufficient amount of sleep, their concentration levels, emotional control and equilibrium as well as their energy for activity will be negatively affected.

 Proper nutrition positively influences the quality of a child's physical activity level, their cognitive abilities, such as classroom concentration, as well as their emotional and mental growth. Adequate and proper nutrition is vital to encourage and support all aspects of children's development. Obesity, chronic diseases, high blood pressure, type 2 diabetes and even heart disease are just a few of the negative consequences that can result from poor nutrition in children. Additionally, obese children are at greater risk of becoming obese adults. Daily calorie intact is determined by children's age, size and their activity level. Meals should mainly include whole grains, low-fat or nonfat dairy products, vegetables, fruits and lean meats. It is also recommended introducing fish into children's diets along with reductions in the intake of beverages high in sugar and highly salted foods.

		Specific Nutritional Recommendations for Children				
		Nutrient Recommendations by Age				
Nutrient		2 - 3 years	4 - 8 years	9 - 13 years	14 - 18 yr girls	14 - 18 yr boys
Protein (grams)		13	19	34	46	52
Iron (mg)		7	10	8	15	11
Calcium (mg)		500	800	1300	1300	1300
Vitamin A (IU)		1000	1333	2000	2333	3000
Vitamin C (mg)		15	25	45	65	75
Fiber (g)		14 - 19	19 - 23	23- 28 (girls) 25- 31 (boys)	23	31-34
Sodium (mg)		1000- 1500	1200- 1900	1500-2200	1500-2300	1500-2300
Cholesterol (mg)		<300 for over age 2	<300	<300	<300	<300
Total Fat (g)**		33 - 54 (30 -35% of calories)	39 - 62 (25 - 35% of calories)	62 - 85 (25 - 35% calories)	55 - 78 (25 - 35% calories)	61 - 95 (25 - 35% of calories)
Saturated Fat (g)		12 - 16 (> age 2) (<10% calories)	16 to 18 (<10% calories)	girls: 18-22 boys: 20-24 (<10% calories)	22 (<10% calories)	24 - 27 (<10% calories)
Calories***		1000 - 1400 (2-3 years)	1400-1600	girls: 1600-2000 boys: 1800-2200	2000	2200- 2400

Source: American Heart Association

Heredity factors affecting children's growth and development include height, susceptibility to diseases and genetic predispositions to mental illnesses and developmental disabilities.

SKILL 1.3 Analyzing factors that affect maturation from childhood to adolescence and from adolescence to young adulthood and ways to address these transitions

A variety of influences affect a students' maturation from childhood to adolescence to adulthood. A variety of factors also influence student motor development and attitudes toward physical activity.

Societal – We cannot separate students from the societies in which they live. The general perceptions around them about the importance of fitness activities will have an effect on their own choice regarding physical activity. We should consider the "playground to PlayStation" phenomena and its negative affect on children's motor development and fitness.

Psychological – Psychological influences on motor development and fitness include a student's mental well-being, perceptions of fitness activities, and level of comfort in a fitness-training environment (both alone and within a group). Students experiencing psychological difficulties, such as depression, will tend to be apathetic and lack both the energy and inclination to participate in fitness activities. As a result, their motor development, overall attitude towards leading a healthy lifestyle and fitness levels will suffer. Factors like the student's confidence level and comfort within a group environment, related to both the student's level of popularity within the group and the student's own personal insecurities, are also significant. It is noteworthy, though, that in the case of psychological influences on attitudes, motor development and fitness levels, there is a more reciprocal relationship than with other influences. While a student's psychology may negatively affect their fitness levels, proper fitness training has the potential to positively affect the student psychologically, thereby reversing a negative cycle than can continue with them into adulthood.

Economic – Economic situation of student's families can affect their motor development, attitudes towards leading a healthy lifestyle and physical fitness levels. As a result of a lack of resources, parents may be unable to provide access to extra-curricular activities that promote physical fitness involvement, growth and development. Examples include, proper fitness training equipment, ranging from complex exercise machines to team sport uniforms, to something as simple as a basketball hoop. Additionally, inadequate transportation or lack thereof, to bring a student to an after school activity also is a result of a student's negative economic family situation. It must be noted, however, that low economic situations are becoming less and less an excuse or reason not to provide after school activity involvement for children. The vast majority of cities and counties now provide free recreation activities, as well as providing transportation for children.

Family – Student's family members attitude and "climate" towards health and physical activity also plays an enormous role in the maturation of the students own attitude concerning leading a healthy lifestyle and staying physically fit. A student's own attitude toward physical activity and a healthy lifestyle often reflect that of their caregivers and/or role models (like older siblings) . Specifically in regard to physical activity, it is not necessary for the parents to be athletically inclined, so much as it is important for them to encourage their child to explore fitness activities that they may enjoy.+

SKILL 1.4 Analyzing ways in which heredity, environment, and the complex interaction of both affect human growth and development

Genetic make-up (i.e. age, gender, and ethnicity) has a big influence on growth and development. Various genetic and environmental factors directly affect one's personal health and fitness. Poor health habits, living conditions and afflictions such as disease or disability can impact a person in a negative manner. A healthy lifestyle with adequate conditions and minimal physical or mental stresses will help to contribute in enabling a person to develop towards a positive, healthy existence. A highly agreed upon growth and development theory is the relationship between one's own heredity and environmental factors.

Children's developmental stages occur at different times for different individuals. Those student's that live in an environment that is considered healthy tend to develop and grow more rapidly than those who do not. However, if there is an inherited disability or genetic disorder, a student could be raised in the most ideal environment possible, yet still not develop and grow in the determined, normal, timely stages. Brain development is a physiological factor that is affected by both heredity and environment. Genetic programming as well as environmental factors, such as proper interactions with adults and other students and exposure to words at a young age, both interact to determine a student's human growth and development from one stage to another.

COMPETENCY 2.0   UNDERSTAND THE STRUCTURES AND FUNCTIONS OF THE MAJOR BODY SYSTEMS AND THE RELATIONSHIP OF PERSONAL HEALTH TO BODY SYSTEMS AND THEIR FUNCTIONING

SKILL 2.1   Identifying major components, functions, and actions of the endocrine, immune, skeletal, muscular, circulatory, respiratory, digestive, and reproductive systems

In this section, we will identify specific major body systems and the important role each plays in achieving and maintaining optimal personal health.

MUSCULAR SYSTEM

The function of the muscular system is to provide optimal movement for the parts of the human body. The specific functions of each muscle depend on its location. In all cases, however, muscle action is the result of the actions of individual muscle cells. Muscle cells are unique in that they are the only cells in the body that have the property of contractility. This gives muscle cells the ability to shorten and develop tension. This is extremely important for human movement.

Muscles are classified in three categories:

1. Skeletal: muscles that attach to the bone
2. Visceral: muscles that are associated with an internal body structure
3. Cardiac: muscles that form the wall of the heart

Skeletal muscles are the only voluntary muscles, meaning they contract as initiated by the will of a person.
Visceral and cardiac muscles are both involuntary muscles, meaning they are governed by nerve impulses found in the autonomic nervous system.

Skeletal and cardiac muscles are striated or band-like, whereas visceral muscles are smooth.

SKELETAL SYSTEM

The skeletal system has several functions:

1. Support: The skeleton acts as the framework of the body. It gives support to the soft tissues and provides points of attachment for the majority of the muscles.

2. Movement: The fact that the majority of the muscles attach to the skeleton and that many of the bones meet (or articulate) in moveable joints, the skeleton plays an important role in determining the extend and kind of movement that the body is capable of.
3. Protection: Clearly, the skeleton protects many of the vital, internal organs from injury. This includes the brain, spinal cord, thoracic, urinary bladder and reproductive organs.
4. Mineral Reservoir: Vital minerals are stored in the bones of the skeleton. Some examples are calcium, phosphorus, sodium and potassium.
5. Hemopoiesis or blood-cell formation: After a mother gives birth, the red marrow in specific bones produces the blood cells found in the circulatory system.

The human skeletal is composed of 206 individual bones that are held in position by strong fibrous ligaments. These bones can be grouped into two categories:
1. Axial skeleton: total 80 bones (skull, vertebral column, thorax)
2. Appendicular skeleton: total 126 bones (pectoral, upper limbs, pelvic, lower limbs)

The ENDOCRINE SYSTEM

The endocrine system is not a clearly defined anatomical system but rather is composed of various glands that are located throughout the body. The main function of this system is to aid in the regulation of body activities by producing chemical substances we know as hormones. Through a complicated regulation system, the bloodstream distributes hormones throughout the body with each hormone affecting only specific targeted organs.

The primary endocrine glands are the pituitary, thyroid, parathyroids, adrenals, pancreas and gonads. Additionally, the kidneys, gastrointestinal and placenta exhibit endocrine activity but to a lesser extent than the primary glands.

The hormones produced by the endocrine system do not fall into an easily defined class of chemical substances. Some are steroids (such as cortisol), others are proteins (such as insulin), and still others are polypeptides and amino acids (such as parathyroid hormone and epinephrine).

Irregardless of the specific chemical substance, the hormones produced by the endocrine system play a critical role in aiding in the regulation and integration of the body processes.

E SYSTEM

'ne system's function is to defend the human body against infectious
_ and other attacking forces, such as bacteria, microbes, viruses, toxins and
..,asites. Simply put, the immune system strives every day to keep human beings
healthy and free of disease and illness.

The immune system is made up of two main fluid systems, intertwined throughout the
body, that are responsible for transporting the agents of the immune system, the blood
stream and the lymph system. White blood cells are considered to be the most
important part of your immune system.

Different types/names of white blood cells are:
- Leukocytes – this is often used as the primary term for white blood cells
- Lymphocyte
- Monocytes
- Granulocytes
- B-cells
- Plasma cells
- T-cells
- Helper T-cells
- Killer T-cells
- Suppressor T-cells
- Natural killer cells
- Neutrophils
- Eosinophils
- Basophils
- Phagocytes
- Macrophages

A foreign substance that invades the body is referred to as an antigen. When an antigen
is detected, the immune system goes into action immediately through several types of
cells working together. These initial cells try to recognize and respond to the antigen,
thereby triggering white blood cells to release antibodies. Antigens and antibodies have
been referred to as fitting like a "key and a lock" throughout the scientific community.
Once these antigens have been produced in the body they stay in the body, meaning if
this same antigen enters the body again, the body is immune and protected.

Vaccines are antigens given in very small amounts. They stimulate both humoral and
cell mediated responses. After vaccination, memory cells recognize future exposure to
the antigen so the body can produce antibodies much faster.

There are three types of immunity:

1. Innate Immunity: the immunity (general protection) we are all born with
2. Adaptive Immunity: immunity that develops throughout our lives (antibodies) as we are exposed to diseases and illnesses
3. Passive Immunity: this is an immunity that comes from outside ourselves (outside antibiotics…)

There are two defense mechanisms in the immune system: non-specific and specific.

The **non-specific** immune mechanism has two lines of defense. The first line of defense is the physical barriers of the body. These include the skin and mucous membranes. The skin prevents the penetration of bacteria and viruses as long as there are no abrasions on the skin. Mucous membranes form a protective barrier around the digestive, respiratory, and genitourinary tracts. In addition, the pH of the skin and mucous membranes inhibit the growth of many microbes. Mucous secretions (tears and saliva) wash away many microbes and contain lysozyme that kills microbes.

The second line of defense includes white blood cells and the inflammatory response. **Phagocytosis** is the ingestion of foreign particles. Neutrophils make up about seventy percent of all white blood cells. Monocytes mature to become macrophages, which are the largest phagocytic cells. Eosinophils are also phagocytic. Natural killer cells destroy the body's own infected cells instead of the invading the microbe directly.

The other second line of defense is the inflammatory response. The blood supply to the injured area increases, causing redness and heat. Swelling also typically occurs with inflammation. Basophils and mast cells release histamine in response to cell injury. This triggers the inflammatory response.

The **specific** immune mechanism recognizes specific foreign material and responds by destroying the invader. These mechanisms are specific and diverse. They are able to recognize individual pathogens.

CIRCULATORY SYSTEM

The function of the closed circulatory system (**cardiovascular system**) is to carry oxygenated blood and nutrients to all cells of the body and return carbon dioxide waste to the lungs for expulsion. Or paraphrased simply, to transport blood leaving the heart to all parts of the body, permitting the exchange of certain substances between the blood and body fluids and ultimately returning the blood to the heart.

The circulatory system is composed of veins, arteries and capillaries. Arteries carry blood away from the heart, veins return blood to the heart and capillaries allow for the exchange of substances between the blood and the cells of the body. Capillaries are the most important vessels of the blood vascular system. Arteries must be able to withstand the greatest pressure and veins are the largest vessels of the system.

The heart, blood vessels, and blood make up the cardiovascular system, which clearly is closely related to the circulatory system.

The following diagram shows the structure of the heart, noting the specific arteries and veins:

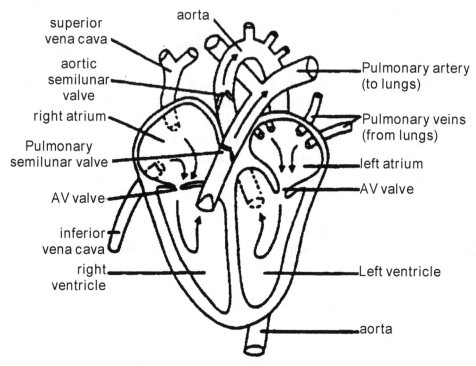

THE RESPIRATORY SYSTEM

The function of the respiratory system is, as oxygen is brought into the body through normal breathing or aerobic activity, carbon monoxide is removed, with the assistance of the circulatory system. The respiratory system also makes vocalization possible. We are able to speak, sing and laugh by varying the tension of the vocal cords as exhaled air passes over them.

The lungs are the respiratory surface of the human respiratory system. A dense net of capillaries contained just beneath the epithelium form the respiratory surface. The surface area of the epithelium is about $100m^2$ in humans. Based on the surface area, the volume of air inhaled and exhaled is the tidal volume. This is normally about 500mL in adults. Vital capacity is the maximum volume the lungs can inhale and exhale. This is usually around 3400mL.

To describe the respiratory more thoroughly, air enters the mouth and nose, where it is warmed, moistened and filtered of dust and particles. Cilia in the trachea trap and expel unwanted material in mucus. The trachea splits into two bronchial tubes and the bronchial tubes divide into smaller and smaller bronchioles in the lungs. The internal surface of the lung is composed of alveoli, which are thin walled air sacs. These allow for a large surface area for gas exchange. Capillaries line the alveoli. Oxygen diffuses into the bloodstream and carbon dioxide diffuses out of the capillaries and is exhaled from the lungs due to partial pressure. Hemoglobin, a protein containing iron, carries the oxygenated blood to the heart and all parts of the body.

The thoracic cavity holds the lungs. The diaphragm muscle below the lungs is an adaptation that makes inhalation possible. As the volume of the thoracic cavity increases, the diaphragm muscle flattens out and inhalation occurs. When the diaphragm relaxes, exhalation occurs.

THE DIGESTIVE SYSTEM

The function of the digestive system is to break food down into nutrients, absorb them into the blood stream, and deliver them to all cells of the body for use in cellular respiration. Every cell in the body requires a constant source of energy in order to perform its particular function(s). The digestive system breaks down or alters food ingested by mechanical and chemical processes so that it can ultimately cross the wall of the gastrointestinal tract and enter the blood vascular and lymphatic (circulatory) systems.

The digestive system consists of a tube called the gastrointestinal tract (alimentary canal) that extends from the mouth to the anus. As long as food remains in the gastrointestinal tract it is considered to still be outside of the body. To "enter" the body, it must cross the wall of the digestive tract. Emptying into the digestive tube are the secretions of the salivary glands, gastric glands, intestinal glands, liver and pancreas, all of which assist in the digestion of food. These regions include the mouth, esophagus, stomach, small and large intestines.

The digestive system activities can be divided into six parts:

1. ingestion of food into the mouth
2. movement of food along the digestive tract
3. mechanical preparation of food for digestion
4. chemical digestion of food
5. absorption of digested food into the circulatory and lymphatic systems (circulatory system)
6. elimination of undigestible substances and waste products from the body by defecation

REPRODUCTIVE SYSTEM

The reproductive system differs greatly from the other organ systems of the body in that it does not contribute to the survival or homeostasis of a human being. Instead, the organs of the reproductive system ensure the continuance of the species.

The reproductive system produces gametes (germ cells). Through sexual intercourse, the gametes (sperm) of the male joins with a gamete (ovum) of the female. This joining is called fertilization. The organs of the female reproductive system provide a suitable environment in which the fertilized ovum (zygote) can develop into a stage in which it is capable of surviving outside of the mother's body.

The organs that produce the gametes are referred to as the primary or essential sex organs. Specifically, these are the gonads (testes) in the male and the ovaries in the female. Additionally, the organs that produce the gametes also are responsible for producing hormones that influence the development of secondary sex characteristics and regulation of the reproductive system. In the male, specialized cells in the testes produce androgen hormones. The most active of these is testosterone. In the female, the ovaries produce estrogen and progesterone.

The structures that transport, protect and nourish the gamates in both the male and female are referred to as accessory sex organs. In the male, these include:

- the epididymis
- the ductus deferens
- the seminal vesicles
- the prostate gland
- the scrotum
- the penis

Female accessory sex organs include:

- the uterine tubes
- the uterus
- the vagina
- the vulva

PHYSICAL ACTIVITY AND FITNESS ADAPTATIONS

The structure and function of the human body adapts greatly to physical activity and exertion. When challenged with any physical task, the human body responds through a series of integrated changes in function that involve most, if not all, of its physiological systems. Movement requires activation and control of the musculoskeletal system. The cardiovascular and respiratory systems provide the ability to sustain this movement over extended periods. When the body engages in exercise training several times, each of these physiological systems undergoes specific adaptations that increase the body's efficiency and capacity.

When the body works, it makes great demand on every muscle of the body. Either the muscles have to 'shut down' or they have to do work. The heart beats faster during strenuous exercise so that it can pump more blood to the muscles, and the stomach shuts down during strenuous exercise so that it does not waste energy that the muscles need. Exercising makes the muscles work like motor that use up energy in order to generate force. Muscles, also known as 'biochemical motors', use the chemical adenosine triphosphate (ATP) as an energy source.

Physical activity affects the cardiovascular and musculoskeletal systems the most. However, it also helps in proper functioning of metabolic, endocrine, and immune systems.

For all the major organs to function properly, it is imperative that human beings apply a healthy lifestyle in the form of regular physical activity, proper nutrition, adequate rest and sleep, mental, social and emotional well-being and avoidance of substance abuse of any kind and cigarette smoking.

SKILL 2.2 Recognizing common health-related problems of childhood and adolescence and methods of preventing and treating childhood illnesses

Common health issues of children include allergies, asthma, conjunctivitis (pink eye), and pediculosis (lice). Physical and health educators should be able to recognize the signs and symptoms of these conditions, and should know how to treat and prevent them.

Allergies – Allergies result when the body identifies a generally innocuous substance (e.g., peanuts) as toxic, and responds the same way it would to an antigen introduced into the body. Excessive activation of mast cells and basophils results in a systematic inflammatory response. This can result in symptoms ranging from a runny nose, to life-threatening anaphylactic shock and death.

Many allergic reactions selectively affect particular organs or parts of the body. For example, the nasal passages and airways might swell up, eyes can become itchy and red, ears can feel stuffed and painful and skin can develop rashes. Occasionally, headaches also accompany allergic reactions.

There is limited mainstream medical treatment for allergies. The most important factor in rehabilitation is the removal of sources of allergens from the home and school environment. Once the individual has contracted an allergic reaction, though, they may require medical attention to keep them in stable condition.

Asthma – Asthma is a chronic disease of the respiratory system in which the airways will occasionally constrict, become inflamed, and become lined with excessive amounts of mucus. This happens in response to one or more triggers, which can include allergens, cold air, exercise or exertion, and emotional stress. In children, the most common triggers tend to be viral illnesses like the common cold. The narrowing of the airways causes symptoms such as wheezing, shortness of breath, chest tightness, and coughing.

The most effective treatment for asthma is identifying triggers (which can include, for example, pets or aspirin), and limiting/eliminating exposure to them. Smoking adversely affects asthmatics in several ways, and asthmatics should neither smoke nor expose themselves to second-hand smoke. For students who experience asthma attacks induced by exercise, higher levels of ventilation and cold, dry air will tend to exacerbate attacks. For these reasons, such students should avoid activities, like skiing and outdoor running, in which they will breathe large amounts of cold, dry air. Alternatively, activities such as swimming in an indoor, heated pool are a better option. There are various medical treatments available for asthmatics. Consult a physician for details specific to the case in question.

Conjunctivitis (pink eye) – Conjunctivitis is an inflammation of the outermost layer of the eye and the inner surface of the eyelid usually due to an allergic reaction or an infection. Other possible causes include overuse of contact lenses, foreign bodies in the eyes, vitamin deficiency and dryness of the eye. Symptoms include redness, irritation, and watering of the eyes, with a variable level of itchiness depending on the cause of conjunctivitis.

Treatment is usually a routine of antibiotics, though this may vary depending on the cause of the infection, prescribed by a physician. Soothing drops and cold compresses can provide relief. Conjunctivitis is highly contagious and it is important to isolate infected students and teachers who may have contracted it. Since conjunctivitis spreads by touch (infected students rub their eyes, touch their hands to other students, who then rub their own eyes), it is important to maintain good hygiene via frequent hand washings.

Diabetes – Most children with diabetes suffer from Type 1 (insulin-dependent or juvenile) diabetes. Type 1 diabetes limits the pancreas' ability to produce insulin, a hormone vital to life. Without insulin, the body cannot use the sugar found in blood. In order to stay alive, an individual suffering from Type 1 diabetes must take one or more injections of insulin daily.

Diabetics control their disease by keeping the level of sugar (glucose) in the blood as close to normal as possible. The means to achieve diabetes control include proper nutrition, exercise, and insulin. Most children with diabetes self-monitor blood glucose levels to track their condition and respond to changes.

Some rules of thumb to keep in mind when dealing with a diabetic child are:

- Food makes the glucose level rise
- Exercise and insulin make the glucose level fall
- Hypoglycemia occurs when the blood sugar level is low
- Hyperglycemia occurs when the blood sugar level is high

Pediculosis (lice) – Pediculosis is an infestation of lice (parasitic insects) on the bodies of humans. The condition is commonly known as head lice, body lice, or pubic lice (depending on where the lice happen to congregate). The most common form of pediculosis among children is head lice, which spread through direct head-to-head contact with an infested person. Body lice spread through direct contact with the skin, clothing, or other personal items of a person already carrying lice. Pubic lice generally spread by intimate contact with an infested person. Lice do not have wings, and cannot jump from one individual to another. Human lice are different from dog lice, and the two species are not interchangeable (so you can't get lice from your dog, or vice versa).

The most common symptom of lice infestation is itching. Excessive scratching of the invested area can cause sores, which may become infected. Treatment of lice infestation usually includes medicated shampoos or cream rinses. We can also use fine combs to remove lice and eggs from the hair. Laundering clothes at high temperatures can eliminate body lice. Treatment should focus on the hair, body, or clothes, not on the home environment.

It is important to remember, though, that despite having a solid base of knowledge from which to draw, health and physical education professionals are not qualified and actually put themselves at risk, if they provide students or parents with medical advice of any kind. If there is concern that a student may have a significant health risk, instructors should refer them to the school nurse immediately, and if not available sent them to the office to be sent home with the correct paperwork from the administrative office.

SKILL 2.3   Identifying ways in which various diseases affect the functioning of major body systems

MALFUNCTIONS OF THE BODY SYSTEMS

Malfunctions of the respiratory and excretory systems

Emphysema is a chronic obstructive pulmonary disease (COPD). This disease makes it difficult for a person to breathe. Additionally, partial obstruction of the bronchial tubes limits airflow, making breathing difficult. The primary cause of emphysema is smoking. People with a deficiency in $alpha_1$-antitrypsin protein production have a greater risk of developing emphysema and at an earlier age. This protein helps protect the lungs from damage done by inflammation. This genetic deficiency is rare and doctors can test for it in individuals with a family history of the deficiency. There is no cure for emphysema, but there are treatments available. The best prevention against emphysema is to refrain from smoking.

Nephritis usually occurs in children. Symptoms include hypertension, decreased renal function, hematuria, and edema. Glomerulonephritis (GN) is a more precise term to describe this disease. An antigen-antibody complex interaction causes inflammation and cell proliferation and produces nephritis. Nephritis damages normal kidney tissue and, if left untreated, nephritis can lead to kidney failure and death.

Malfunctions of the circulatory system

Cardiovascular diseases are the leading cause of death in the United States. Cardiac disease often results in a heart attack. A heart attack occurs when cardiac muscle tissue dies, usually from a coronary artery blockage. A stroke occurs when nervous tissue in the brain dies due to a blockage of arteries in the head or a broken blood vessel that leads to bleeding in the brain.

Atherosclerosis causes many heart attacks and strokes. Plaques form on the inner walls of arteries, narrowing the area in which blood can flow. Arteriosclerosis occurs when the arteries harden from the plaque accumulation. A healthy diet low in saturated fats and cholesterol and regular exercise can prevent atherosclerosis. High blood pressure (hypertension) also promotes atherosclerosis. Diet, medication, and exercise can reduce high blood pressure and prevent atherosclerosis.

Malfunctions of the immune system

The immune system attacks both microbes and cells that are foreign to the host or toxic antigen that has entered or surfaced in the body. This is the problem with skin grafts, organ transplantations, and blood transfusions. Antibodies to foreign blood and tissue types already exist in the body. Antibodies will destroy the new blood cells in transfused blood that is not compatible with the host. There is a similar reaction with tissue and organ transplants.

The major histocompatibility complex (MHC) is responsible for the rejection of tissue and organ transplants. This complex is unique to each person. Cytotoxic T-cells recognize the MHC on the transplanted tissue or organ as foreign and destroy these tissues. Suppression of the immune system with various drugs can prevent this reaction. The complication with immune suppression is that the patient is more susceptible to infection.

Autoimmune disease occurs when the body's own immune system destroys its own cells. Lupus, Grave's disease, and rheumatoid arthritis are examples of autoimmune diseases. There is no way to prevent autoimmune diseases. Immunodeficiency is a deficiency in either the humoral or cell mediated immune defenses. HIV is an example of an immunodeficiency disease.

Malfunctions of the digestive system

Gastric ulcers are lesions in the stomach lining. Bacteria are the main cause of ulcers, but pepsin and acid can exacerbate the problem if the ulcers do not heal quickly enough.

Appendicitis is the inflammation of the appendix. The appendix has no known function, but is open to the intestine and hardened stool or swollen tissue can block it. The blocked appendix can cause bacterial infections and inflammation leading to appendicitis. The swelling cuts the blood supply, killing the organ tissue. If left untreated, this leads to rupture of the appendix allowing the stool and the infection to spill out into the abdomen. This condition is life threatening and requires immediate surgery. Symptoms of appendicitis include lower abdominal pain, nausea, loss of appetite, and fever.

Malfunctions of the nervous and endocrine systems

Diabetes is the best-known endocrine disorder. A deficiency of insulin resulting in high blood glucose is the primary cause of diabetes. Type I diabetes is an autoimmune disorder. The immune system attacks the cells of the pancreas, ending the ability to produce insulin. Treatment for type I diabetes consists of daily insulin injections. Type II diabetes usually occurs with age and/or obesity. There is usually a reduced response in target cells due to changes in insulin receptors or a deficiency of insulin. Type II diabetics need to monitor their blood glucose levels. Treatment usually consists of dietary restrictions and exercise.

Hyperthyroidism is another disorder of the endocrine system. Excessive secretion of thyroid hormones is the cause. Symptoms are weight loss, high blood pressure, and high body temperature. The opposite condition, hypothyroidism, causes weight gain, lethargy, and intolerance to cold.

There are many nervous system disorders. The degeneration of the basal ganglia in the brain causes Parkinson's disease. This degeneration causes a decrease in the motor impulses sent to the muscles. Symptoms include tremors, slow movement, and muscle rigidity. Progression of Parkinson's disease occurs in five stages: early, mild, moderate, advanced, and severe. In the severe stage, the person is confined to a bed or chair. There is no cure for Parkinson's disease. Private research with stem cells is currently underway to find a cure for Parkinson's disease.

SKILL 2.4   Evaluating the impact of various factors (e.g., inactivity, disease, diet) on body systems

PHYSICAL ACTIVITY AND INACTIVITY

Physical activity and inactivity greatly affects many aspects of a person's life, including physical fitness abilities, general health, physical resilience, self-confidence, psychological well-being, and cognitive function. Regular physical activity can improve or increase these elements, while inactivity can damage or decrease these elements.

The most obvious and direct benefit of physical activity is the physical dimension, which includes fitness and general health. Regular physical activity leads to improved physical fitness, improved strength and endurance of the muscular and cardiorespiratory systems and improved function of the circulatory system. Improved function of all these systems means that the body expends far less energy is on day-to-day activities, significantly increasing overall energy levels and allowing the heart to not work as hard, by lowering blood pressure to a healthy state. Conversely, a lifestyle of physical inactivity will gradually lead to a deterioration of the muscular, cardiorespiratory, and circulatory systems, which leads to decreased energy levels and a negative encouragement for a host of other physical problems, such as hypertension (high blood pressure).

Regular physical activity also contributes to increased physical resilience. Regular physical activity coupled with sufficient rest and a healthy diet strengthens the musculoskeletal system, which makes the individual less susceptible to injury. Physical activity also tends to improve reflexes and balance, which also reduces the likelihood of injury. Conversely and as previously mentioned, a lifestyle of physical inactivity leads to a deterioration of the same physical systems that regular exercise strengthens and also contributes to a gradual "de-sharpening" of the reflexes and balance. In sum, these changes increase the likelihood and susceptibility of the individual to injury.

The bridge between physical and psychological benefits is the overall self-confidence derived from regular physical activity. The individual's increased ability to perform physical tasks leads to growth of their sense of ability to perform any physical activity (for example, you don't have to actually climb ten flights of stairs to know that you could if you wanted to – this is very liberating, as it creates options). Conversely, a lifestyle of physical inactivity, which implies a decreased fitness level, will eat away at the individual's overall self-confidence.

Regarding psychological well-being, physical activity causes the brain to release endorphins, which function to reduce stress levels (prolonged physical endurance activities can produce levels of endorphins that induce a pleasant and healthy "runner's high"). Most physical activities also mix a degree of repetitive motion and action that requires directed attention. In combination, this can function as a sort of meditative activity. For all of these reasons, regular physical activity contributes to psychological balance and well-being and reduced stress levels. Conversely, a lifestyle of physical inactivity allows physical confidence to deteriorate and removes alternatives of stress-relief, which can contribute negatively to the individual's psychological well-being.

Finally, regular physical activity benefits the circulatory system, which improves blood flow to the brain. This, in turn, leads to increased cognitive function and mental acuity. Those who are physically inactive do not experience these benefits.

NUTRITION AND EXERCISE

Exercise and diet maintain proper body weight by equalizing caloric intake to caloric output.

Nutrition and exercise are closely related concepts important to student health. An important responsibility of physical education instructors is to teach students about proper nutrition and exercise and how they relate to each other. The two key components of a healthy lifestyle are consumption of a balanced diet and regular physical activity. Nutrition can affect physical performance. Proper nutrition produces high energy levels and allows for peak performance. Inadequate or improper nutrition can impair physical performance and lead to short-term and long-term health problems (e.g. depressed immune system and heart disease, respectively). Regular exercise improves overall health. Benefits of regular exercise include a stronger immune system, stronger muscles, bones, and joints, reduced risk of premature death, reduced risk of heart disease, improved psychological well-being, and weight management.

DISEASE

- See Skill 2.4

SKILL 2.5   Analyzing the impact of body systems and their functioning on personal health

- See Skill 2.1

COMPETENCY 3.0   **UNDERSTAND NUTRITIONAL REQUIREMENTS AND THE IMPACT OF NUTRITION ON PERSONAL HEALTH**

SKILL 3.1   **Identifying functions and sources of nutrients (i.e., carbohydrates, proteins, fats, vitamins, minerals, and water) and the nutritional value of various foods**

NUTRITION AND WEIGHT CONTROL

Identify the components of nutrition

The components of nutrition are **carbohydrates, proteins, fats, vitamins, minerals, and water.**

Carbohydrates – the main source of energy (glucose) in the human diet. The two types of carbohydrates are simple and complex. Complex carbohydrates have greater nutritional value because they take longer to digest, contain dietary fiber, and do not excessively elevate blood sugar levels. Common sources of carbohydrates are fruits, vegetables, grains, dairy products, and legumes.

Proteins – are necessary for growth, development, and cellular function. The body breaks down consumed protein into component amino acids for future use. Major sources of protein are meat, poultry, fish, legumes, eggs, dairy products, grains, and legumes.

Fats – a concentrated energy source and important component of the human body. The different types of fats are saturated, monounsaturated, and polyunsaturated. Polyunsaturated fats are the healthiest because they may lower cholesterol levels, while saturated fats increase cholesterol levels. Common sources of saturated fats include dairy products, meat, coconut oil, and palm oil. Common sources of unsaturated fats include nuts, most vegetable oils, and fish.

Vitamins and minerals – organic substances that the body requires in small quantities for proper functioning. People acquire vitamins and minerals in their diets and in supplements. Important vitamins include A, B, C, D, E, and K. Important minerals include calcium, phosphorus, magnesium, potassium, sodium, chlorine, and sulfur.

Water – makes up 55 – 75% of the human body. Essential for most bodily functions. Attained through foods and liquids.

Determine the adequacy of diets in meeting the nutritional needs of students

Nutritional requirements *vary from person-to-person.* General guidelines for meeting adequate nutritional needs are: *no more than 30% total caloric intake from fats* (preferably 10% from saturated fats, 10% from monounsaturated fats, 10% from polyunsaturated fats), *no more than 15% total caloric intake from protein* (complete), *and at least 55% of caloric intake from carbohydrates* (mainly complex carbohydrates).

Exercise and diet help maintain proper body weight by equalizing caloric intake and caloric output.

Please refer to the chart on page 29 for more specific nutritional guidelines for children in regard to age and gender.

SKILL 3.2   Recognizing dietary disorders and health problems associated with nutritional deficiencies and excesses and the relationship between nutrition and disease prevention

EATING DISORDER RISK FACTORS

Gender – Females are much more likely to develop an eating disorder than males.

Socioeconomic Standing – Inhabitants of economically developed nations appear to have a higher risk for developing eating disorders.

Age – Eating disorders are most common between the ages of 12 and 25.

Athletics and Certain Professions – Dancers, jockeys, runners, gymnasts, etc. tend to be at higher risk for eating disorders since thinness in these activities is desirable. Models and entertainers also run a high risk of falling victim to eating disorders as many of them experience intense pressure to be thin.

SIGNS AND SYMPTOMS OF EATING DISORDERS

Anorexia
- Dramatic weight loss
- Basing self-worth on body weight and body image
- Frequent skipping of meals
- Eating only a few foods, especially those low in fat and calories
- Frequent weighing of oneself
- Wearing baggy clothes to cover up thinness
- Excessive focus on an exercise plan
- Loss of menstrual cycle
- Dizziness and headaches

Bulimia

- Secrecy surrounding eating
- Eating unusually large amounts of food, with no apparent weight gain
- Complex lifestyle schedules or rituals
- Discolored or callused finger joints or backs of the hands
- Tooth and mouth problems
- Stomach pain and intestinal irregularities

FALLACIES AND DANGERS UNDERLYING SELECTED DIET PLANS

High Carbohydrate diets (i.e. Pritikin, Bloomingdale's) can produce rapid or gradual weight loss, depending on caloric intake. Usually requires vitamin and mineral supplements because protein intake is low. These diets may or may not recommend exercising or permanent lifestyle changes, which are necessary to maintain one's weight.

High-Protein Diets promote the same myths, fallacies, and results as high carbohydrate diets. High-protein diets also require vitamin and mineral supplements. In addition, these diets are usually high in saturated fats and cholesterol because of the emphasis on meat products.

Liquid Formulas that are physician/hospital run (i.e. Medifast, Optifast) provide 800 or fewer calories a day consumed in liquid form. Dieters forgo food intake for 12 to 16 weeks in lieu of the protein supplement. Liquid diets require vitamin and mineral supplements and close medical supervision. Dieters should gradually reintroduce food after the initial fast. These diets can result in severe and/or dangerous metabolic problems in addition to an irregular heartbeat, kidney infections and failure, hair loss, and sensations of feeling cold and/or cold intolerance. These diets are very expensive and have a high rate of failure.

Over-The-Counter Liquid Diets (i.e. Slimfast) are liquid/food bar supplements taken in place of one or more meals per day. Such diets advocate an intake of 1,000 calories daily. Carbohydrate, protein, vitamin, and mineral intake may be so low that the diet can be as dangerous as the medically supervised liquid diets when relied on for the only source of nutrition. Because of the lack of medical supervision, the side effects can be even more dangerous.

Over-The-Counter Diet Pills/Aids and Prescription Diet Pills (appetite suppressants) have as their main ingredient phenyl propanolamine hydrochloride [PPA]. Keeping weight off by the use of these products is difficult. Dizziness, sleeplessness, high blood pressure, palpitation, headaches, and tachycardia are potential side effects of these products. Moreover, prescription diet pills can be addictive.

Low Calorie Diets (caloric restricted) are the most misunderstood method of weight loss. However, restricting the intake of calories is the way most people choose to lose weight. All the focus is on food, creating anxiety over the restriction of food - especially favorite foods. These diets are also difficult to maintain and have a high failure rate. Like the other diets, once the diet is over, dieters regain weight quickly because they fail to make permanent behavioral changes. Side effects of caloric restriction include diarrhea, constipation, Ketosis, a lower basal metabolic rate, blood-sugar imbalances, loss of lean body tissue, fatigue, weakness, and emotional problems. Low calorie diets require dietary supplements. Those who choose **fasting** (complete caloric restriction) to lose weight can deplete enough of the body's energy stores to cause death.

SKILL 3.3　Recognizing components and principles of the Food Guide Pyramid, the Dietary Guidelines for Americans, and regulations related to food labels and packaging

The Food Guide Pyramid illustrates the different components of a healthy diet and number of servings of each food group we should consume. Specifically, we should consume the greatest number of servings of carbohydrate-based products like cereals, breads, and pasta, a large number of vitamin- and mineral-rich carbohydrates like fruits and vegetables, protein-rich foods, and, finally, foods with higher fat content.

The Dietary Guidelines for Americans is a document published by the United States Department of Health and Human Services and the United States Department of Agriculture. It is a primary source of dietary health information for policymakers, nutrition educators, and health providers, so they can help direct the individuals that they represent, teach, and care for to make informed and healthy decisions regarding their diets.

Regulations related to food labels and packaging ensure that consumers receive accurate information about the products they buy. Food labels include the breakdown of ingredients, nonfood components, nutritional values, and accuracy of claims relating to the food product.

FOOD LABELS

Making informed choices based on particular dietary needs depends on the ability of consumers to recognize and interpret the relevant information on food labels. Some such considerations may include the need to limit fat or sodium intake, and the need to assemble an adequately nutritious diet on a limited budget.

Choosing items that are low in sodium is fairly straightforward. With fats, it is a little more complex, since there are different types of fats to consider. Consumers should avoid saturated fats (found primarily in food items derived from animal sources), as they will tend to increase LDL cholesterol. Consumers should consume unsaturated fats (monounsaturated and polyunsaturated, derived from vegetable sources and fish) in moderation because the body needs them to process fat-soluble vitamins like A, D, E and K.

When examining food labels, it is important to remember that the values are generally per serving, and not for the entire package. Thus, you must convert the amounts for proper comparison.

Ensuring adequate nutrition on a limited budget requires emphasizing nutritious staples instead of empty calories and more expensive alternatives (for example, brown or whole-wheat bread instead of white bread, tofu instead of meat products). A multi-vitamin supplement is also a good idea.

An additional skill that consumers should acquire is the ability to analyze claims relating to food, such as "organically grown" or "lower in fat". These claims are difficult to appraise because the concepts are ambiguous and not standardized. These claims are also comparative, often without providing the baseline for comparison (for example, "lower in fat" – lower than what?).

SKILL 3.4   Analyzing factors (e.g., psychological, economic, cultural) affecting food choices and eating habits and ways in which food choices and eating patterns affect growth and development, body composition, and health

RELATIONSHIP BETWEEN DIET AND THE PREVENTION OF DISEASE

Diet plays an important role in the prevention of disease. Consuming a healthy diet, rich in polyunsaturated fats, whole grains, fish, fruits, vegetables, and lean protein, and low in saturated fat and sugar, reduces the risk of many chronic diseases. Proper nutrition can help prevent heart disease, strokes, osteoporosis and many types of cancers. In addition, good nutrition helps boost the body's immune system, lowering the risk of infectious disease.

ISSUES RELATED TO IDEAL WEIGHT AND BODY COMPOSITION

Exercise and diet maintain proper body weight by equalizing caloric intake to caloric output.

Nutrition and exercise are closely related concepts important to student health. An important responsibility of health instructors is to teach students about proper nutrition and exercise and how they relate to each other. The two key components of a healthy lifestyle are consumption of a balanced diet and regular physical activity. Nutrition can affect physical performance. Proper nutrition produces high energy levels and allows for peak performance. Inadequate or improper nutrition can impair physical performance and lead to short-term and long-term health problems (e.g. depressed immune system and heart disease, respectively). Regular exercise improves overall health. Benefits of regular exercise include a stronger immune system, stronger muscles, bones, and joints, reduced risk of premature death, reduced risk of heart disease, improved psychological well-being, and weight management.

Exercise and diet help maintain proper body weight by equalizing caloric intake and caloric output.

Body composition management

It is vital to analyze procedures, activities, resources, and benefits involved in developing and maintaining healthy levels of body composition. Maintaining a healthy body composition allows an individual to move freely and to obtain a certain pattern that is necessary for a specific activity. Furthermore, maintaining a healthy body composition is positively related with long-term health and resistance to disease and sickness.

The total weight of an individual is a combination of bones, ligaments, tendons, organs, fluids, muscles and fat. Because muscle weighs three times more than fat per unit of volume, a person who exercises often gains muscle. This could cause an individual to be smaller physically, but weigh more than he/she appears to weigh.

The only proven method for maintaining a healthy body composition is following a healthy diet and engaging in regular exercise. A healthy diet emphasizes fruits, vegetables, whole grains, unsaturated fats, and lean protein, and minimizes saturated fat and sugar consumption. Such a program of nutrition and exercise helps balance caloric intake and output, thus preventing excessive body fat production.

DIFFERING NUTRITIONAL NEEDS FOR VARIOUS POPULATIONS AND PROBLEMS OF MALNUTRITION

Basic nutritional common sense tells us that people who use more energy need to eat more food to function at high levels of activity. It follows that this group includes the very young (infants up to age two), who are developing vital organs, muscles, and bones. Poor nutrition is most damaging in this age group, who suffer long-term effects of malnutrition. Youth, adolescents, athletes, and other very active people are also part of this group.

As we age, we need less food because we are fully-grown and often less active. Energy coming into the body as food must balance with that burned in activities in order to maintain a consistent body weight.

Also important is the type of food we eat. Our bodies need specific amounts of protein, minerals, and vitamins to grow and function properly. Bodies that aren't properly nourished for prolonged periods will suffer from malnutrition. Lack of food is not the only cause of malnutrition. A person may have plenty of food to eat, but he or she will suffer from malnutrition if the body doesn't receive enough protein and nutrients to support important functions. This can result from poor food choices and eating disorders. Endemic illness such as diarrhea also contributes to malnutrition, flushing nutrients out before the body can use them.

Compare the nutritional needs three different populations. Information is from the Recommended Dietary Allowance (RDA) determined by the National Academy of Sciences, 1997:

- A five-year old child needs 1850 kilo calories (Kcal) of food per day including at least 30 grams of protein. (A one-inch cube of cheese contains 6 grams of protein.)
- An 18-year old male needs 3000 Kcal per day including 59 grams of protein.
- A woman who is over 50 needs 1800 Kcal daily and 50 grams of protein. (http://www.jhhs.org/myjewishhospital/encyclopediaHTML/2935.html)

If all available food were evenly distributed, there would be no hunger. In reality, over 800 million people around the world do not have enough to eat.

Malnutrition causes an imbalance in the body's cells, which support functions like growth and health maintenance. Malnourishment in children stunts physical growth, slows thinking, and produces incomplete physiologic functions. Poorly nourished children are often irritable, anxious, and self-absorbed. Immune response diminishes, and imitates the responses seen in children with AIDS. Symptoms of edema are also common.

Undernourishment is the main reason for sickness and death in children throughout the world. Each year 300,000 children under five years old die due to malnutrition. Lack of protein in the diet, or protein-energy malnutrition (PEM), is most common in developing countries where poverty rates are high. Safe supplies of high protein foods and water are not available, and illness is wide spread. Malnourished bodies have a reduced ability to fight disease, trapping the poor in an uphill struggle to survive.

Although malnutrition has decreased worldwide, rates of under-nutrition and growth stunting have risen in Africa and Asia. Over 70% of children with PEM live in Asian countries, 26% live in eastern Africa, and the balance is in the Caribbean and Latin America (World Health Organization: Malnutrition - The Global Picture. 2000). Political unrest is responsible for most of the malnutrition in Africa, where refugees have lost their homes and land, and are without resources to feed their families.

South Asia (India and Bangladesh) produces surplus food, and yet has the highest percentage of malnourished in the population. The destructive cycle of malnutrition in India is due primarily to the subjugation of women. Indian girls are malnourished and underweight at birth. Parents favor male children, who receive nursing that is more comprehensive and more nutritious food. Female children often work as children and commonly do not receive proper care or education. Often married and pregnant while still a working teen, young women give birth to underweight and malnourished children, repeating the cycle.

Poorly nourished people get sick more often and cannot tolerate the physical stress of work. Improved sanitation may only benefit the wealthy, and costly irrigation water is often used on crops that are sold to other countries. Internal conflicts and wars also contribute to malnutrition by contaminating water supplies and destroying structures used to store and transport water and food.

Much of malnutrition in the past was due to famine, often resulting from drought and decreased agricultural yield. Today, governments and factions often use hunger as a political tool. Powerful countries enforce embargos as punishment to force developing countries to yield to their demands. Other impoverished countries attempt to gain world attention through sensationalizing hunger, as in Iraq and Korea.

Interventions that contribute to the prevention of malnutrition include:

- Clean and safe water supply, improved sanitation, and hygiene
- Teaching people the importance of a healthy diet
- Making healthy food available to the poor
- Helping developing countries to practice sustainable agriculture and industry

- Initiating programs to fortify foods with elements that are commonly missing from the diet such as Iodine, vitamin D, iron, and calcium.

SKILL 3.5   Evaluating the nutritional components of a balanced diet and nutritional requirements for individuals from different age groups and with special needs (e.g., young children, vegetarians, individuals with diabetes)

There are several key nutritional components that various fad-diets suggest you cut out (e.g., carbohydrates, proteins and fats) but they are all necessary to a healthy and balanced diet. The key is to ensure that the food items you purchase and consume are high quality and healthy, nutritionally justifying the corresponding caloric intake. Carbohydrates should be complex, low-calorie food items with low Glycemic Index scores, you should consume proteins in moderation, and fats should be unsaturated and consumed in moderation.

Specific demographic groups may have special dietary needs. For example, young children, vegetarians, and individuals with diabetes all have particular dietary needs that we must consider when constructing a healthy, balanced diet.

For young children whose bodies and brains are still developing, it is crucial that we cover all nutritional bases, especially vitamins and minerals that are crucial to healthy development. Children's diets should include sufficient quantities of fruits and vegetables and minimal quantities of "junk food".

Vegetarians are healthy individuals in normal stages of adult development and, as such, they have essentially the same dietary needs as everyone else. The act of cutting meat out of the diet, however, tends to result in a decrease in protein, which vegetarians must compensate and make up for through appropriate vegetarian sources such as tofu, soy products, nuts and dry beans.

Individuals suffering from diabetes have the same nutritional requirements as everyone else, but are not able to process sugar products properly. Thus, they have to avoid foods containing sugar, such as desserts, jams, and raw sugar. Diabetics can substitute artificial (aspartame-based) sweeteners.

SKILL 3.6   Demonstrating knowledge of how to evaluate weight management plans and dietary information in terms of sound nutritional practices and their lifelong effects on personal health

Health and physical education instructors should teach students to evaluate weight management plans and dietary information in terms of sound nutritional practices and their lifelong effects on personal health. Many weight management programs may achieve their effects at the expense of the health of the individual by cutting out key elements of a regular diet.

The key element to consider is that weight management programs operate based on a simple formula: calories consumed minus calories expended equals weight gained. In the event that the person expends more calories than he consumes, the difference equals weight lost. This equation is the basis of many weight management programs, but often such programs cut key nutritional elements out of the diet (e.g., no carbohydrates, no protein, or no fat). These diets may work (as cutting any of these nutritional elements out of a diet will tend to result in the consumption of fewer calories), but they are hazardous because the body needs all of these substances in order to function properly. Carbohydrates serve as the fuel for the muscles, the amino acids in proteins are necessary for the production of critical enzymes, and fats are necessary to dissolve fat-soluble vitamins (among other things).

Effective weight management programs that are beneficial in terms of sound nutritional practices and lifelong effects on personal health will moderate caloric intake and increase caloric expenditure by slightly decreasing meal size and increasing the quantity and/or intensity of physical activity. Effective programs do not rely on cutting any nutritional component completely out of the diet.

> **SKILL 3.7   Identifying principles, techniques, and methods for preparing, storing, and handling various types of food to preserve their nutritive value and to prevent food borne illnesses and other health risks**

PROPER FOOD PREPARATION AND HANDLING TECHNIQUES

Proper food preparation and handling are important for health and prevention of illness. Steps you can take to prevent contamination of food include:

- Wash hands thoroughly before handling food – Prevents spread of viruses and bacteria on hands to food.
- Monitor temperature – The optimal temperature for bacterial growth is 41° F to 140° F. Food can only remain in this temperature range for 4 hours. Thus, it is important to refrigerate perishable foods (e.g., dairy products, meat) and leftovers promptly.
- Keep kitchen surfaces clean – Cross-contamination of food is an ever-present concern. Using the same knife or cutting board when cutting raw meat and vegetables can contaminate the vegetables with bacteria from the meat. It is important to wash all utensils and surfaces after each use.
- Cook foods to proper temperature – To kill bacteria, it is important to cook all meats and foods containing raw eggs to a sufficiently high temperature. The safe temperature varies depending on the food, but approximately 160 °F is a safe target temperature for most foods.

COMPETENCY 4.0 **UNDERSTAND PRINCIPLES OF AND TECHNIQUES FOR PERSONAL CARE AND SAFETY**

SKILL 4.1 Identifying methods for promoting self-care, safe behaviors, and injury prevention techniques during childhood

Basic behavioral methods reduce the risk of injuries, illness, disease and other health problems.

Injuries are usually a result of unforeseen accidents, which many times can be a result of just not "paying attention" by an individual. Falls are the leading cause of death among home accidents. Falls occur most frequently for the elderly and young children. The most common location of falls is in bathtubs and showers. Examples of precautions that can help decrease the risk of falls include using rubber mats in bathtubs and showers, using safety gates to block young children from stairs, wearing appropriate safety equipment during physical activity, and promptly removing ice and snow from steps and sidewalks. Additionally, just practicing awareness in your day to day activities will help prevent accidents.

Positive health behaviors can help decrease the risk of illness and disease. Good nutrition and regular exercise can help prevent everyday illnesses such as colds and flu, and chronic diseases such as heart disease and cancer. Exercise and a healthy diet helps maintain a healthy body composition, reduces cholesterol levels, strengthens the heart, lungs, and musculoskeletal system and strengthens the body's immune system.

Avoiding substance abuse, sexual promiscuity and dangerous places and activities also helps promote self-care.

STRATEGIES FOR POSITIVE BEHAVIOR CHANGE

Strategies for positive behavior change in students will relate the teaching of new behaviors to the students' perceptions and frames of reference, and will focus on a series of small, incremental changes. Instructors should actively involve students in the process of change and instructors should positively reinforce steps in the right direction.

It is very important that when teaching the processes of behavioral change to the student (via discussion, classroom-type teaching, counseling, etc.) that the instructor present information in a way that corresponds with the student's perceptions, and works within the student's frame of reference.

It is better to encourage small, incremental changes, which the student can achieve on a regular basis and the instructor can reward, as opposed to larger, more major changes that are less likely to have a lasting impact because of the impracticality of application. Instructors should link new behaviors to existing behaviors, with the goal being to gradually modify the behavioral patterns and introduce new behaviors. Simply suppressing behaviors is a difficult process, and will often fail to work.

Instructors should actively involve students in the process of behavioral change by assisting them in understanding the importance of positive behaviors for themselves. This encourages the behavioral changes to be the goal of the student not the teacher. In this way, the process of change becomes intrinsically motivated, making it far more likely the student will seriously commit to the behaviors throughout their lifetimes. Obviously, the instructor should reinforce positive behaviors via reward, but not excessively – behavioral change should be (for the most part) intrinsically motivated.

SUPPORTING POSITIVE CHANGE

Proper health and fitness education is a necessary prerequisite for positive health choices. Obviously, without an understanding of the various choices available, and the ramifications of each choice, it is difficult to make a wise decision regarding personal and family health choices and behavior. This education should include an introduction to research skills, so that the individual has the freedom to inform themselves of pertinent information when new situations arise that call for them to make health decisions. Good venues for these personal research habits include the Internet, local libraries, and fitness and health-care professionals in the community.

Positive health choices and behavior will also require a layer of economic support, as healthy lifestyle choices will sometimes be more expensive than the less healthy alternative. It is also important for the environment to be conducive to positive choices and behavior regarding health. For example, the availability of resources (both educational and practical) and facilities (medical and fitness) in proximity to the individual can positively affect the decision-making process.

ASSESSING BEHAVIORAL RISK FACTORS

There are various resources available to assess the behavioral health risk factors of a community. The Centers for Disease Control and Prevention (CDC) annually publishes the Youth Risk Behavior Survey (YRBS). This survey explains national and state adolescent health risks. This information is available directly from the CDC. State education agencies compile and maintain statistics on youth health risks. Individual schools or school districts provide data regarding the types of problems seen in the school health room. Individual schools or school districts can also supply information regarding the number of referrals for pregnancy and substance abuse and data on absenteeism, dropouts, and disciplinary actions.

Other sources of information regarding community behavioral health risk factors include the state office of vital statistics, the state and local departments of health, and the medical examiners' office. The state police department can provide highway safety data. The poison control centers and local police departments can provide information regarding injuries, disease, and death. Additionally, emergency room and emergency medical services records and hospital discharge records can expose potential abuse.

Another source of information is social service agencies, as they have data on poverty, unemployment, and child abuse. Lastly, one could choose to assess the community's health behavior risk factors personally. When personally assessing a community's behavioral risk factors, utilize surveys, conduct health risk appraisals, and review healthcare utilization and cost data.

ACTIONS THAT PROMOTE SAFETY AND INJURY PREVENTION

The following is a list of practices that promote safety in all types of physical education and athletic activities.

1. Having an instructor who is properly trained and qualified.

2. Organizing the class by size, activity, and conditions of the class.

3. Inspecting buildings and other facilities regularly and immediately giving notice of any hazards.

4. Avoiding overcrowding.

5. Using adequate lighting.

6. Ensuring that students dress in appropriate clothing and shoes.

7. Presenting organized activities.

8. Inspecting all equipment regularly.

9. Adhering to building codes and fire regulations.

10. Using protective equipment.

11. Using spotters.

12. Eliminating hazards.

13. Teaching students correct ways of performing skills and activities.

14. Teaching students how to use the equipment properly and safely.

CRITICAL HEALTH RISK FACTORS

The Centers for Disease Control (CDC) has identified six critical health behaviors among youths and an additional six important health topics. The six critical health behaviors include Alcohol & Drug Use, Injury & Violence (including suicide), Tobacco Use, Nutrition, Physical Activity, and Sexual Risk Behaviors. Generally, people establish these behaviors during childhood, the behaviors are inter-related, and they are preventable. Besides causing serious health problems, they also contribute to educational and social problems, including failure to graduate from high school, unemployment, and criminal behavior.

Alcohol & Drug Use - Alcohol abuse is the third leading preventable cause of death in the United States (4% of the total deaths in 2000), and is a factor in approximately 41% of all deaths from motor vehicle crashes.

Injury & Violence - Injury and violence is the leading cause of death among youth aged 10-24 years: motor vehicle crashes (37% of all deaths), all other unintentional injuries (16%), homicide (18%), and suicide (13%).

Tobacco Use - Every day about 4,000 American youth aged 12–17 years try their first cigarette. The CDC estimates that smoking causes 435,000 deaths each year in the United States.

Nutrition - Almost 80% of young people do not eat the recommended servings of fruits and vegetables. Nearly 9 million youth in the United States aged 6–19 years are overweight.

Physical Activity - Participation in physical activity declines as children get older. Overall, in 2005, 36% of 9-12 graders had participated in at least 60 minutes per day of physical activity. Nearly 37% of 9th graders, but only 33% of 12th graders, participated in 60 minutes of physical activity on a regular basis.

Sexual Risk Behaviors - Each year, there are approximately 19 million new STD infections in the United States, and almost half of them are among youth aged 15 to 24. 34% of young women become pregnant at least once before they reach the age of 20.

SKILL 4.2 Recognizing the importance of developing personal hygiene habits required to maintain health and prevent illness or disease

Personal hygiene describes routine grooming and cleaning practices. Personal hygiene is important for health, general wellness, and pleasurable social interaction. A basic personal hygiene program should include regular washing of the body and hair, more frequent washing of the hands and face, brushing the teeth three times if possible, but at least twice a day, applying deodorant daily, and cleaning the clothes and place of residence. Such routine hygiene can help maintain health and prevent illness by killing disease-causing agents and preventing the transmission of disease from person to person.

SKILL 4.3 Recognizing safety principles and practices for use in the home, at school, on the playground, in and around motorized and nonmotorized vehicles, on the street, in or near water, and around animals

The environment surrounding children can be hazardous without appropriate safety principles and practices. Proper safety principles and practices clearly delineated by parents and educators can ensure that children enjoy and learn from their environments without taking unnecessary risks.

Safety principles and practices for use in the home include not touching potentially hazardous appliances (like the stove and oven), kitchen items (like knives), and electrical wiring and sockets. Parents and teachers should also teach children should guidelines for safe behavior, which include not opening the door to strangers, running up and down stairs, and so forth.

Safety principles and practices for use at school include prohibitions against running outside of designated areas and time periods (for example, recess and gym class), prohibitions against violence of any kind, and rules against other unsafe behavior such as standing on chairs and tables. Rules should also be in place limiting the noise levels, so that in the event that an educator has to give safety-related instruction, all children will be able to hear.

Safety principles and practices for use on the playground include prohibitions against playing on jungle-gym apparatus in ways that are potentially unsafe (these guidelines will vary relative to the age of the children in question). There should also be rules in place limiting appropriate behavior that will tend to grow rambunctious (for example, no pushing allowed). There should also be procedures in place by which students are required to line up so the instructor can count the students before returning to class to ensure that no children are left behind.

Safety principles and practices for use in and around motorized and non-motorized vehicles include crossing the street behind cars, and not in front, so that if the child is not seen they will not accidentally be run over. If children need to cross the street in front of a car, they should do it a safe distance, not directly beside it, where their short stature might prevent them from being seen. In regard to non-motorized vehicles (for example, bicycles), children should be taught to keep out of their way, as they are still dangerous, and not to play with the parts and gears, where their hands can get stuck.

Safety principles and practices for use on the street include establishing rules against playing in the street, or in the event of very quiet streets where parents allow their children to play, establishing clear procedures for vacating the street in the event of a passing car (playing in the street in general should be discouraged, as it is dangerous). Children should learn to look both ways before crossing the street, to ensure that it is safe. If they find themselves in the street when a car is approaching, they should either move forward or move back, but not freeze (which is a natural reaction that can prove hazardous).

Safety principles and practices for use in or near water include not running on areas that might be wet and slippery, keeping a certain prescribed distance from the water without appropriate life-preserving equipment (depending on the swimming abilities of the children), and prohibitions against getting within a certain distance of the swimming area when no supervising adult is present.

Safety principles and practices for use around animals include keeping a safe distance until it has been indicated to the child by the owner of the animal that it is safe, not petting or touching the animal without the owner's permission, and not approaching unfamiliar animals at all, and certainly not without the permission of their parents or supervising adult. Children should also learn not to feed animals.

SKILL 4.4   Recognizing the importance of adequate sleep, rest, exercise, and medical and dental checkups

Sleep gives the body a break from the normal tasks of daily living. During sleep, the body performs many important cleansing and restoration tasks. The immune and excretory systems clear waste and repair cellular damage that accumulates in the body each day. Similarly, the body requires adequate rest and sleep to build and repair muscles. Without adequate rest, even the most strenuous exercise program will not produce muscular development. Finally, lack of rest and sleep leaves the body vulnerable to infection and disease. The recommended amount of sleep is 7-8 hours per night.

Practicing healthy behaviors has many benefits. Regular physical activity and proper nutrition can help prevent diseases, illnesses, and injuries. In addition, regular exercise and a proper diet help maintain a healthy body composition, which is important physically and psychologically. Physically fit and healthy individuals are generally more productive at work. Finally, preventing disease and avoiding injury through healthy behaviors can reduce health-care costs.

Regular medical and dental checkups are important to identify and prevent medical problems and diseases. Early detection of potential health problems is essential for successful treatment and recovery. The recommendation by the American Dental Association is that individuals, particularly children and adolescents have their teeth cleaned by a professional dental hygienist every six months. Medically, females need to begin to have annual gynecology exam at the onset of their first menstrual cycle to aid in the prevention of diseases.

SKILL 4.5   Demonstrating knowledge of universal precautions, appropriate procedures for cardiopulmonary resuscitation (CPR), use of automated external defibrillator (AED), and first-aid and emergency care for shock, bleeding, broken bones, and other injuries

CPR BASICS

Cardiopulmonary resuscitation (CPR) is a first-aid technique used to keep victims of cardiac arrest alive. It is also prevents brain damage while the individual is unconscious and more advanced medical help is on the way. CPR keeps blood flowing through the body and in and out of the lungs.

CPR Steps
- Step 1 – Call 911
- Step 2 – Tilt head, lift chin, check breathing
- Step 3 – Give two breaths
- Step 4 – Position hands in the center of chest
- Step 5 – Firmly push down two inches on the chest 15 times

Continue with two breaths and 15 pumps until help arrives. The American Heart Association and the American Red Cross both offer classes to train individuals in CPR.

INJURY TREATMENT AND FIRST AID

Immediate treatment tips

When a student endures a physical injury, the first priority is to avoid further damage. Following an injury the teacher should look for the obvious cause of the accident (i.e., ill-fitting equipment, improper sliding technique, a missed step while running). The next step is to reduce swelling. The primary means of accomplishing this is a sequence of treatments (rest, ice, compression, elevation) known as **R.I.C.E.** It is vital to implement this procedure following an injury since swelling causes pain and a loss of motion. *Steps for the immediate treatment of an injury*

1. Stop the activity immediately
2. Wrap the injured part in a compression bandage (i.e., an ACE bandage).
3. Apply ice to the injured part (crushed ice or frozen vegetables are ideal) for no more than 15 minutes at a time. You should allow the area to warm periodically.
4. Elevate the injured part.
5. For a proper diagnosis, send the injured student to the school's nurse or, for more serious injuries, to a physician.

Treating specific illnesses

Low Blood Sugar (Hypoglycemia)
This is the diabetic emergency most likely to occur. Low blood sugar may result from eating too little, engaging in too much physical activity without eating, or by injecting too much insulin.

Symptoms:
- Headache
- Sweating
- Shakiness
- Pale, moist skin
- Fatigue/Weakness
- Loss of coordination

Treatment:

Provide sugar immediately. You may give the student ½ cup of fruit juice, non-diet soda, or two to four glucose tablets. The child should feel better within the next 10 minutes. If so, the child should eat some additional food (e.g. half a peanut butter, meat, or cheese sandwich). If the child's status does not improve, treat the reaction again.

High Blood Sugar (Hyperglycemia)

Hyperglycemia can result from eating too much, engaging in too little physical activity, not injecting enough insulin, or illness. You can confirm high blood sugar levels by testing with a glucose meter.

Symptoms:

- Increased thirst
- Weakness/Fatigue
- Blurred vision
- Frequent urination
- Loss of appetite

Treatment:

If hyperglycemia occurs, the instructor should contact the student's parent or guardian immediately.

Dehydration

Dehydration occurs when a person loses more fluids than he/she takes in. The amount of water present in the body subsequently drops below the level needed for normal body functions. The two main causes of dehydration are gastrointestinal illness (vomiting, diarrhea) and sports. It is essential to replace fluids lost by sweating to prevent dehydration, especially on a hot day.

Symptoms:

- Thirst
- Dizziness
- Dry mouth
- Producing less/darker urine

Prevention/Treatment:

- Drink lots of fluids. Water is usually the best choice.
- Dress appropriately (i.e., loose-fitting clothes and a hat).
- If you begin to feel thirsty/dizzy, take a break and sit in the shade.
- Drink fluids prior to physical activity and then in 20-minute intervals after activity commences.
- Play sports or train in the early morning or late afternoon. You will avoid the hottest part of the day.

EMERGENCY ACTION PLANS

The first step in establishing a safe physical education environment is creating an Emergency Action Plan (EAP). The formation of a well-planned EAP can make a significant difference in the outcome of an injury situation.

Components of an Emergency Action Plan
To ensure the safety of students during physical activity, an EAP should be easily comprehensible yet detailed enough to facilitate prompt, thorough action.

Communication
Instructors should communicate rules and expectations clearly to students. This information should include pre-participation guidelines, emergency procedures, and proper game etiquette. Instructors should collect emergency information sheets from students at the start of each school year. First-aid kits, facility maps, and incident report forms should also be readily available. Open communication between students and teachers is essential. Creating a positive environment within the classroom allows students to feel comfortable enough to approach an adult/teacher if she feels she has sustained a potential injury.

Teacher Education
At the start of each school year, every student should undergo a pre-participation physical examination. This allows a teacher to recognize the "high-risk" students before activity commences. The teacher should also take note of any student that requires any form of medication or special care. When a teacher is aware of his/her students' conditions, potential problems can be prevented. Teachers need to always understand, however, that they are never to give students any type of medication, including aspirin or Tylenol. If a student needs medication during the day, those arrangements must be made in conjunction with the administration office of the school and/or the school nurse.

Facilities and Equipment
It is the responsibility of the teacher and school district to provide a safe environment, playing area, and equipment for students. Instructors and maintenance staff should regularly inspect school facilities to confirm that the equipment and location is adequate and safe for student use.

First Aid Equipment
It is essential to have a properly stocked first aid kit in an easily reachable location for simple needs such band-aids, alcohol and fainting inhalers. Teachers must remember to always file an accident report whenever anything, however minor, occurs that requires first aid treatment.

Implementing the Emergency Plan

The main thing to keep in mind when implementing an EAP is to remain calm. Maintaining a sufficient level of control and activating appropriate medical assistance will facilitate the process and will leave less room for error.

STRATEGIES FOR INJURY PREVENTION

Participant screenings – evaluate injury history, anticipate and prevent potential injuries, watch for hidden injuries and reoccurrence of an injury, and maintain communication.

Standards and discipline – ensure that athletes obey rules of sportsmanship, supervision, and biomechanics.

Education and knowledge – stay current in knowledge of first aid, sports medicine, sport technique, and injury prevention through clinics, workshops, and communication with staff and trainers.

Conditioning – programs should be yearlong and participants should have access to conditioning facilities in and out of season to produce more fit and knowledgeable athletes that are less prone to injury.

Equipment – perform regular inspections; ensure proper fit and proper use.

Facilities – maintain standards and use safe equipment.

Field care – establish emergency procedures for serious injury.

Rehabilitation – use objective measures such as power output on an isokinetic dynamometer.

PREVENTION OF COMMON ATHLETIC INJURIES

Foot – start with good footwear, foot exercises.

Ankle – use high top shoes and tape support; strengthen plantar (calf), dorsiflexor (shin), and ankle eversion (ankle outward).

Shin splints – strengthen ankle dorsiflexors.

Achilles tendon – stretch dorsiflexion and strengthen plantar flexion (heel raises).

Knee – increase strength and flexibility of calf and thigh muscles.

Back – use proper body mechanics.

Tennis elbow – lateral epicondylitis caused by bent elbow, hitting late, not stepping into the ball, heavy rackets, and rackets with strings that are too tight.

Head and neck injuries – avoid dangerous techniques (i.e. grabbing facemask) and carefully supervise dangerous activities like the trampoline.

EQUIPMENT SELECTION

School officials and instructors should base equipment selection on quality and safety; goals of physical education and athletics; participants interests, age, sex, skills, and limitations; and trends in athletic equipment and uniforms. Knowledgeable personnel should select equipment; keeping in mind continuous service and replacement considerations, (i.e. what's best in year of selection may not be best the following year). One final consideration is the possibility of reconditioning versus the purchase new equipment.

INJURY FOLLOW UP AND REPORTING

Responding to accidents and injuries is an important responsibility of physical educators. After an injury occurs, instructors must fill out and file an accident report and turn it into the office. Such reports are important for recordkeeping, future evaluations, and protection against lawsuits. In addition, if the injured student requires immediate first aid, the instructor should send for the school nurse and/or an administrator, as not all schools have nurses in attendance at their school full-time.

Instructors should contact an injured student's parents or guardians as soon as possible after the injury. Such contact makes the parents aware of the injury and allows them to make necessary arrangements.

SKILL 4.6   Demonstrating knowledge of prevention strategies and first-aid care for sports- and activities-related injuries (e.g., sprains/strains, abrasions, concussions)

o   *See Skill 4.5*

SKILL 4.7 Identifying common causes and effects of accidents, factors that contribute to injuries (e.g., use of alcohol or drugs, fatigue), and methods of preventing various types of accidents

COMMON CAUSES AND EFFECTS OF ACCIDENTS

Injuries are usually a result of unforeseen accidents. Falls are the leading cause of death among home accidents. Falls occur most frequently for the elderly and young children. The most common location of falls is in bathtubs and showers. Examples of precautions that can help decrease the risk of falls include using rubber mats in bathtubs and showers, using safety gates to block young children from stairs, wearing appropriate safety equipment during physical activity, and promptly removing ice and snow from steps and sidewalks. The most common effects of minor accidents and falls are broken bones, injured joints, and cuts and bruises.

SAFETY AND ACCIDENT PREVENTION

Safety and accident prevention plays an important role in maintaining personal health. Physical education instructors must monitor and maintain a safe learning environment to prevent accidents and injuries. Accidental injuries are an inherent hazard in any physical activity. While physical activity is very beneficial to personal health, injuries can negatively affect both short- and long-term health.

IDENTIFYING EXERCISE EQUIPMENT AS EITHER SOUND OR UNSOUND USING PHYSIOLOGICAL PRINCIPLES

Rolling machines, vibrating belts, vibrating tables and pillows, massaging devices, electrical muscle stimulators, weighted belts, motor-driven cycles and rowing machines, saunas, and plastic or rubberized sweat and sauna suits **are all ineffective exercise equipment because they produce passive movement** (no voluntary muscle contractions).

Sound exercise equipment produces active movement resulting from the participant initiating the movement of the equipment or the participant voluntarily producing muscle contractions.

The more you analyze exercise equipment on the market the more you may wonder who is actually creating it. For example, equipment that has weight increments measured as light, medium, or difficult, is unsound. Such ambiguous labeling depends on who is using the equipment and their level of proficiency.

Some advertisements claim that their equipment uses all muscle groups at once. Just three minutes a day is as good as a total gym workout. Such claims are certainly false.

SAFETY AND INJURY PREVENTION

Instructors and participants should make safety and injury prevention top priority in exercise activities. There are a number of potential risks associated with physical activity, and instructors must be familiar with all the risks to prevent an emergency situation.

Equipment

Exercise equipment in poor condition has the potential for malfunction. Instructors should perform weekly checks to ensure all equipment is in proper working order. If it is not, the instructor or maintenance staff must repair the equipment before students use it. Placement of exercise equipment is also important. There should be adequate space between machines and benches to ensure a safe environment.

Technique

Instructors should stress proper exercise technique at all times, especially with beginners to prevent development of bad habits. Whether it's weightlifting, running, or stretching, participants should not force any body part beyond the normal range of motion. Pain is a good indicator of overextension. Living by the phrase, "No pain, no gain", is potentially dangerous. Participants should use slow and controlled movements. In addition, participants must engage in a proper warm-up and cool-down before and after exercise. When lifting weight, those who are doing the lifting should always have a spotter.. A spotter can help correct the lifter's technique and help lift the weight to safety if the lifter is unable to do so. A partner can also offer encouragement and motivation. Flexibility is an often overlooked, yet important, part of exercise that can play a key role in injury prevention. Participants should perform stretching exercises after each workout session.

STRATEGIES FOR IDENTIFYING AND AVOIDING DANGEROUS SITUATIONS

Actions that can avoid lawsuits

The following is a list of basic practices and actions that can prevent lawsuits related to physical education accidents.

1. Knowing the health status of each person in the program.

2. Considering the ability and skill level of participants when planning new   activities.

3. Grouping students to equalize competitive and ability levels.

4. Using safe equipment and facilities.

5. Properly organizing and supervising classes.

6. Never, ever leave a class unattended.

7. Know first aid (Do not diagnose or give any type of medication to a student)

8. Keeping copies of accident reports.

9. Giving instruction prior to difficult and potential hazardous activities or avoid.

10.. Being sure that injured students get medical attention and examination.

11. Getting exculpatory agreements (parental consent forms).

12. Having a planned, written disposition for students who suffer injuries or become ill.

13. Fill out detailed accident reports and file in main office.

But what is good equipment? Good equipment uses a safe range of motion, safe increments of weight progression, and is structurally sound. The components of good equipment are reliable and not likely to cause injury. Safe equipment can consist of a combination of pieces that, when used correctly, improve physiological processes by guiding range of motion.

SKILL 4.8 Demonstrating knowledge of dangers and safety precautions that individuals should take in special conditions

Environmental conditions can be very dangerous and potentially life threatening. Individuals must be cautious when exercising in extremely hot, cold, and/or humid conditions.

High humidity can slow the body's release of heat from the body, increasing the chances of heat related illnesses. Hydration in hot environments is very important. Drink two cups of water two hours before exercise and hydrate regularly during exercise at the same rate of the amount of sweat that is lost. In exercise lasting a long period, it is possible to drink too much water, resulting in a condition known as hyponutremia, or low sodium content in the body. Water cannot replace the sodium and other electrolytes lost through sweat. Drinking sports drinks can solve this problem.

Cold environments can also be a problem when exercising. The human body works more efficiently at its normal temperature. Wear many layers of clothing to prevent cold-related illnesses such as frostbite and hypothermia. In populations suffering from asthma, wearing a cloth over the mouth during exercise increases the moisture of the air breathed in and can help prevent an attack.

Weather concerns such as rapidly approaching thunderstorms and far off lightening create dangerous situations for outside activities. Anytime an instructor hears thunder and/or sees lightening, the students should immediately be brought into sheltered activity.

SUBAREA II.   **DISEASE AND HEALTH-RISK PREVENTION**

COMPETENCY 5.0   **UNDERSTAND TYPES OF DISEASE AND THE ROLE OF DISEASE PREVENTION AND CONTROL IN MAINTAINING HEALTH**

SKILL 5.1   Recognizing types, causes, and characteristics of diseases (e.g., chronic, degenerative, communicable, noncommunicable) and methods for detecting and preventing them

TYPES OF DISEASES THEIR CAUSES, THEIR CHARACTERISTICS, AND METHODS FOR DETECTING AND PREVENTING THEM

Pathogens that enter the body through direct or indirect contact cause communicable, or infectious, diseases. A pathogen is a disease-causing organism. Common communicable diseases include influenza, the common cold, chickenpox, pneumonia, measles, mumps, and mononucleosis. To minimize the circulation of pathogens that cause these illnesses, people can follow simple precautions. Individuals ill with these diseases should stay away from others during the contagious period of the infection. All people should avoid sharing items such as towels, toothbrushes, and silverware. At home, thorough clothes washing, dishwashing, and frequent hand washing can decrease pathogen transmission. Keeping immunizations up to date is also important in reducing the spread of communicable diseases.

Sexual activity is the source of transmission for other communicable diseases. The commonly used terms for these diseases are sexually transmitted diseases (STDs) or sexually transmitted infections (STIs). Common STIs include chlamydia, gonorrhea, syphilis, genital herpes, genital warts, bacterial vaginosis, human papillomavirus (HPV), pediculosis pubis (pubic lice), hepatitis B, and HIV. Certain STIs can result in infertility. HPV can result in a deadly form of cervical cancer. HIV may result in Acquired Immunodeficiency Syndrome (AIDS), which can be fatal. Some of these diseases, such as genital herpes, last for life.

A chronic disease is a disease that is long lasting. A chronic disease continues for more than three months. Examples of chronic conditions include diseases such as heart disease, cancer, and diabetes. These diseases are currently the leading causes of death and disability in America. Many forms of these widespread and expensive diseases are preventable. Choosing nutritious foods, participating in physical activity, and avoiding tobacco use can prevent or control these illnesses.

A degenerative disease is a condition where diseased tissues or organs steadily deteriorate. The deterioration may be due to ordinary wear and tear or lifestyle choices such as lack of exercise or poor nutritional choices. In addition, many degenerative diseases are of questionable origin, and may be linked to heredity and environmental factors. Some examples of degenerative diseases include: osteoporosis, Alzheimer's disease, ALS (Lou Gehrig's disease), osteoarthritis, inflammatory bowel disease (IBD), and Parkinson's disease.

HOW PRIMARY AND SECONDARY PREVENTION ACTIVITIES PROMOTE HEALTH AND THE ROLE OF THE BODY'S NATURAL DEFENSE MECHANISMS AND GENETIC FACTORS IN PREVENTING OR CAUSING DISEASE

Primary Prevention

Primary prevention activities are the most cost-effective in health care, as they help to avoid the suffering, cost, and burden associated with a particular disease or condition. These precautions promote health by targeting specific health care concerns.

Examples of primary prevention include both active and passive immunization against disease. Passive immunization is treatment that provides immunity through the transfer of antibodies obtained from an immune individual. Active immunization is treatment that provides immunity by challenging an individual's own immune system to produce an antibody against a particular organism. Recently developed vaccines include Hepatitis A and Chicken Pox.

Education to promote health protection is also a primary prevention strategy. Advising automobile drivers and passengers to use seat belts while in transit illustrates an action of primary prevention, as does advocating the use of helmets while riding a bicycle or motorcycle.

Secondary Prevention

Secondary prevention is early detection using accepted screening technologies. The intent is to identify patients with an increased risk since many conditions do not show symptoms until the disease is well established, significantly reducing chances of recovery. Finding problems early in the development of diseases such as hyperlipidemia, hypertension, and breast and prostate cancer can frequently curb or eliminate the damage and reduce pain and suffering.

Reference: U.S. Preventative Services Task Force (1996) Guide to Clinical Preventative Services (2d edition) Baltimore: Williams & Wilkins.

Children who are disruptive, inattentive, hyperactive, impulsive, and aggressive may be at heightened risk for the development of antisocial behavior, substance abuse, and school dropout in later years. (Barkley, Fischer, Edelbrock, & Smallish, 1990) Secondary prevention in such cases includes skill-building interventions such as teaching children problem-solving strategies and educating parents to use these techniques at home. Instructors can create environments that allow children to work together with their peers, their parents, and school personnel to channel their energy into positive outcomes (Weissberg, Caplan, & Sivo, 1989).

Natural Defense Mechanisms

The body fights disease through immunity, where special proteins called antibodies destroy infection. Lymphocytes or white blood cells and cells of the reticuloendothelial system are responsible for establishing active acquired immunity in the body. This is one of the body's defense mechanisms against disease.

Another defense mechanism the body uses to prevent the spread of infection is inflammation, which occurs in damaged tissues. Fluids surrounding the infection clot, preventing any flow from the damaged tissues to other areas.

SKILL 5.2 Recognizing how genetics and health-related choices contribute to disease and methods for reducing risks and delaying onset of disease

We do not inherit disease states the same way as eye color. Genetic factors will make a person more likely to develop a disease when exposed to specific environmental factors. What we actually inherit is a higher risk for certain diseases.

Type I diabetes is congenital, but poor eating habits induce the pancreas to secrete excess insulin, causing adult onset of the disease, known as type II diabetes. Many children are now developing this type of diabetes, which points to poor diet.

Examples of genetic disorders that parents pass to children are ADD/ADHD, bipolar disorder, and depression.

Asthma can be hereditary or exercise-induced. Obesity is another condition that may have environmental causes, although many overweight children often have overweight parents. Hyperlipidemia, poor lipid metabolism related to diet, often accompanies obesity.

This offers an explanation to the question of why the same environmental factors don't have the same effect on all exposed individuals. Take heart disease for example. A person who takes good care of their health and has "acceptable" cholesterol levels may suffer myocardial infarction at age 40. Another individual with poor eating habits who smokes and is overweight, has no heart disease. This difference in response is due partially to genetic variations.

SKILL 5.3 Demonstrating awareness of causes, symptoms, long-term effects, diagnostic tests, available treatments, and facts related to sexually transmitted diseases

o *See also Skill 5.1*

RESPONSIBLE SEXUAL BEHAVIOR AND CHOICES

There are many possible consequences for students who become sexually active. Possible consequences include HIV infection, infection with other sexually transmitted diseases, unintended pregnancies, and emotional difficulties.

The human immunodeficiency virus (HIV) is the virus that causes AIDS. Currently, there is no cure for AIDS. Many young adults currently infected with HIV acquired the infection during sexual activity in their adolescent years. In addition to HIV, there are also numerous other sexually transmitted diseases. Sexually transmitted diseases frequently reported in adolescents include gonorrhea, syphilis, pelvic inflammatory disease, bacterial vaginosis, genital herpes, chlamydia, genital warts, and human papillomavirus (HPV). Some of these diseases can result in infertility, and HPV can result in a deadly form of cervical cancer. Some of these diseases, such as genital herpes, are chronic. Additionally, condom use cannot prevent HPV and genital herpes.

Sexually transmitted disease infection can occur without having sexual intercourse. Oral or anal sex can cause infection with a sexually transmitted disease as easily as sexual intercourse. The only guaranteed method to prevent these diseases is abstinence.

In addition to possible infection with a sexually transmitted disease, adolescents that choose to become sexually active may also face the consequences of an unplanned pregnancy. Rates of child abuse and neglect are much higher in adolescent parents. Babies born to teenage parents are also more likely have a lower birth weight, which can affect the babies' overall wellbeing. The suicide rate among teen mothers is significantly higher than other teens.

There is no doubt that teachers must encourage students to choose abstinence and responsible sexual behavior. Abstinence is choosing not to engage in sexual activity. Choosing abstinence is often a difficult decision for a teenager. In order to stand firm against the pressures to become sexually active, adolescents can become involved in activities in their school and community, work to develop strong family relationships, socialize with other teens that have chosen abstinence, avoid situations that increase sexual feelings and temptation, avoid using alcohol and other drugs, and select wholesome entertainment.

SKILL 5.4 **Recognizing known ways in which HIV/AIDS is transmitted, behaviors that increase the risk of contracting HIV/AIDS, and the effects of HIV/AIDS infection**

o   *See also Skills 5.1 and 5.3*

HIV

The human immunodefiency virus (HIV) can devastate both individuals and society. Advances in treatment options, namely pharmaceuticals, have greatly improved the prospects of those who contract the disease. However, due to the expense of treatment, many people, especially those in underdeveloped countries, do not have access to treatment. Thus, prevention is still of utmost importance.

HIV is a retrovirus that attacks the human immune system and causes AIDS (acquired immunodefiency syndrome). AIDS is a failure of the immune system that allows normally benign viruses and bacteria to infect the body causing life-threatening conditions.

Humans acquire HIV through contact with bodily fluids of infected individuals. For example, transfer of blood, semen, vaginal fluid, and breast milk can cause HIV infection. The best means of prevention of HIV is sexual abstinence outside of marriage, practicing safe sex, and avoiding the use of injected drugs.

Because HIV is a sexually transmitted disease, it disproportionally affects people in the prime of their lives. Infected persons are often heads of households and families and key economic producers. Thus, the impact of HIV on society is particularly damaging. Not only are the costs of treatment great, but families often lose their mothers and fathers and communities lose their best producers and leaders. Society must find ways to fill these gaping voids.

SKILL 5.5 **Demonstrating knowledge of methods of preventing pregnancy and sexually transmitted diseases, including HIV/AIDS, and their effectiveness**

o   *See also Skills 5.1, 5.3, and 5.4*

PREVENTION OF PREGNANCY

There are many methods of contraception (birth control) that affect different stages of fertilization. Chemical contraception (birth control pills) prevents ovulation by synthetic estrogen and progesterone. Several barrier methods of contraception are available. Male and female condoms block semen from contacting the egg. Sterilization is another method of birth control. Tubil ligation in women prevents eggs from entering the uterus. A vasectomy in men involves the cutting of the vas deferens. This prevents the sperm from entering the urethra. The most effective method of birth control is abstinence. Programs exist worldwide that promote abstinence, especially amongst teenagers.

SKILL 5.6   Analyzing how public health policies and government regulations influence health promotion and disease prevention and how disease prevention and control are influenced by research, technology, and medical advances

PUBLIC HEALTH

Factors that influence public health include availability of health care in the community, pollution levels, community resources to promote and facilitate healthy living habits, and awareness of healthy living habits among adults in the community.

Availability of health care in the community that is both accessible and affordable has a critical influence on public health. When health care is not readily available to the community, relatively minor problems will tend to go untreated, and develop into bigger problems.

Pollution levels in the community can affect public health by exposing the community as a whole to toxic and carcinogenic chemicals that negatively affect systems including (but not limited to) the circulatory and respiratory systems.

Community resources are an important influence on public health. When financing is available to support health education and programs that encourage the development of healthy living habits, the health of the community will benefit. Conversely, if the community does not dedicate resources to this cause, the health of the community will suffer. Related to this is the issue of awareness of healthy living habits among adults in the community. A strong personal commitment among responsible community members sets an important example for others to follow.

HEALTH CARE PROVIDERS

There is a variety of health care providers, agencies, and organizations involved with the maintenance of student health. On site, the school nurse assists ill or injured students, maintains health records, and performs health screenings. School nurses also assist students who have long-term illnesses such as diabetes, asthma, epilepsy, or heart conditions. School nurses usually serve more than one school, however they are still responsible for all the record keeping and serving of students at each school they are assigned. Most schools maintain relationships with other outside health care agencies in order to offer more extensive health care services to students. These community partnerships offer students services such as vaccinations, physical examinations and screenings, eye care, treatment of minor injuries and ailments, dental treatment, and psychological therapy. These community partnerships may include relationships with the following types of health care professionals: physicians, psychiatrists, optometrists, dentists, nurses, audiologists, occupational therapists, physical therapists, dieticians, respiratory therapists, and speech pathologists.

Physicians are health care professionals licensed to practice medicine. A physician may choose to specialize in a specific area of medicine or to work in primary care. A psychiatrist is a physician who specializes in the care of psychological disorders. Optometrists are health care practitioners who conduct eye examinations and prescribe corrective lenses. Dentists are health care professionals who provide care of the teeth. They may either work in general practice or specialize in areas such as orthodontics (correction of abnormalities of the teeth). Nurses are allied health care professionals who provide medical care under the supervision of a medical doctor. Audiologists conduct screenings to detect hearing problems. An occupational therapist helps people with disabilities to learn skills needed for activities of daily living. They also help people who have sustained injuries regain their fine motor skills. Physical therapists are allied health care professionals who help people with disabilities and injuries regain their gross motor skills. Dieticians provide counseling regarding nutrition and perform meal planning. Respiratory therapists specialize in identification and treatment of breathing disorders. Speech pathologists help people with speech problems.

There are also various agencies and organizations involved in maintaining the well-being of students. The state and local health departments provide a wide range of services such as services for children with disabilities, chronic disease control, communicable disease control, mental health programs, consumer safety, and health education. The state department of human services investigates reports of child abuse or neglect. The police department prevents crime and captures offenders. Police also work with schools to provide violence and substance abuse prevention programs. Firefighters extinguish fires, check for fire hazards, install smoke detectors, check fire alarms, and give presentations on fire safety. The National Health Information Center is a federal agency that provides references for trustworthy health information.

TECHNOLOGY

The technology market is rapidly changing. Consumers are progressively turning to technology for a healthier life. Consumer-focused healthcare information technology helps patients handle the significant demands of healthcare management.

Healthcare information technology is a term describing the broad digital resources that are available to promote community health and proper health care for consumers. Healthcare information technology empowers patients to direct their healthcare and to advocate for themselves and their families as they use health care services. Healthcare information technology enables consumers, patients, and informal caregivers to gather facts, make choices, communicate with healthcare providers, control chronic disease, and participate in other health-related activities. Consumers should take caution when reviewing healthcare information on the internet, as much information is invalid. Consumers need to be educated in regards to website evaluation before using information from the internet in making healthcare decisions.

Healthcare information technology functions in numerous ways. The functions include providing general health information, supporting behavior change, providing tools to self-manage health, providing access to online groups, providing decision-making assistance, aiding in disease control, and providing access to healthcare tools. Information technology has the power to bring patients into full partnership with their healthcare providers. Specifically, instead of waiting for a return phone call, patients can simply e-mail the physician regarding his or her non-urgent condition. Healthcare providers can then respond to patient e-mails.

Many healthcare facilities are also moving towards complying with the executive order mandating electronic personal healthcare records. At some point in the near future, all healthcare facilities will link personal healthcare records. Consumers can also utilize computerized re-ordering systems for prescription refills. Many pharmacies and physicians are also moving towards electronic prescriptions. The increasingly widespread use of electronic personal healthcare records and computerized prescriptions will decrease the number of medical errors.

COMPETENCY 6.0   UNDERSTAND THE ROLE OF PREVENTION OF TOBACCO, ALCOHOL, AND DRUG USE IN THE PROMOTION OF PERSONAL HEALTH

SKILL 6.1   Recognizing safe and appropriate use of medicine, benefits of drugs for medical purposes, and concepts and terms associated with medicines and drugs

CLASSES OF DRUGS

Autonomic and cardiovascular drugs – These drugs imitate, augment, or block activities of the sympathetic and parasympathetic autonomic nervous system (ANS). Examples include vasodilators and constrictors, diuretics, anticoagulants, and antihistamines.

Central nervous system drugs – General anesthetics render a patient unconscious and are commonly used in surgical procedures. Regional anesthetics such as Novocain and others in the "cain" family of drugs, block sensation locally. This group of drugs also includes central nervous system stimulants, depressants, and narcotics.

Systemic drugs – Gastrointestinal and respiratory drugs include antacids for treatment of ulcers, laxatives, oxygen, expectorants, and non-narcotic cough remedies.

Endocrine drugs – Hormones and agents work as biologically active medications of a single organ system. Examples are birth control pills, steroids, insulin, and thyroid and pituitary (growth) hormones.

Drugs used for nutritional and metabolic derangements – These include medications for gout, vitamins, minerals such as iron and fluoride, and electrolytes, mainly sodium and potassium. These agents provide essential elements for enzyme and other necessary metabolic reactions.

Chemotherapeutic agents – Drugs that fight infection and reduce the viability of bacteria and viruses. These include antimicrobials as well as agents used for the treatment and control of cancer.

USES AND BENEFITS OF DRUGS MOST OFTEN USED IN SCHOOL-AGED CHILDREN FOR MEDICAL PURPOSES

Analgesics are used for reduction of pain and inflammation. Drugs such as Ibuprofen, Aleve, Motrin, Naprosyn, and Advil are non-steroidal anti-inflammatory agents (NSAID) in this category. Tylenol is another common analgesic used for aches and pains.

Antihistamines block the effects of histamine, which produces allergic reactions. The older agents have more side effects like drowsiness, dry mouth, blurred vision, and irritability. There are cautions against using machinery and driving with these medications. Examples are Benadryl and Chlor-Trimeton. Newer drugs in this class like Claritin, Zyrtec and Alegra have less sedative effects. All antihistamines work by blocking the action of histamine to avert allergic symptoms. Severe allergies can require steroids such as Prednisone. There are no serious side effects for short duration, low dose treatments of steroids if patients decrease dosage gradually when completing the course of treatment.

Inhalers are the method of delivery for most asthma drugs. Asthmatics use inhalers and asthma drugs to treat chronic, acute, and exercise-induced asthma. The two main categories are bronchodilators that open the airways and steroids that prevent the airways from constricting. It is important to rinse the mouth after using steroid inhalers to prevent thrush (a fungal infection of the mouth).

Doctors often prescribe stimulant drugs to treat children afflicted with ADD and ADHD. These agents stimulate an inhibitory center of the brain, which calms children. Ritalin is a common stimulant used in young children, and is similar to amphetamine or speed. Other medications in this class are Adderall, Concerta, and Strattera. These medications can cause loss of appetite, sleep disturbances (especially when beginning treatment), stomach upset, headache, and sadness.

Antibiotics fight infections. For best results, patients should adhere to the strict rules of administration. Some antibiotics work best when taken with food, while others work best on an empty stomach. A major national heath care issue is antibiotic resistance. Antibiotic resistance occurs when doctors and patients misuse antibiotics or discontinue use before completion of the full course of treatment. This is why it is important to take all doses dispensed. Antibiotics are not effective for viral infections like the common cold. The misuse of antibiotics for viral infections is another cause of antibiotic resistance. Broad-spectrum antibiotics can kill good bacteria in the body as well as the target bacteria. Killing the bacteria native to the intestinal tract can cause diarrhea.

Another important health problem is diabetes. There are two types of diabetes, type I (previously call juvenile) and type II (previously called adult onset). In type I, the pancreas fails to produce insulin. Insulin is a hormone that decreases blood sugar. Adequate food intake is important to balance insulin injections and keep blood sugar at an optimum level. The best method of keeping blood sugar levels up is with small, frequent, high-protein snacks throughout the day. When blood sugar drops, the patient may become nauseous and may lose consciousness. Serious metabolic consequences include prolonged coma and death.

Type II diabetes usually develops later in life and may result from poor eating habits, being overweight, and having a large waist measurement. High cholesterol, triglycerides, and hypertension are also associated with this type of diabetes. Oral hypoglycemic agents are effective in controlling type II diabetes.

Obese children may have trouble with lipid metabolism. Doctors often prescribe statin drugs to treat this disorder. These drugs may cause muscle soreness or weakness, and parents should report any such symptoms to the healthcare provider.

Doctors are increasingly prescribing antidepressants to young people. The FDA has a "Black Box Warning" for these agents cautioning the potential for suicide in children. Some antidepressants have stimulant effects, making children agitated and excitable. Others make children more lethargic. All work on controlling the action of neurotransmitters in the brain and have different effects.

Quick Reference

Classes of drugs	Physiological effects
Analgesics	pain relief
Stimulants	calming in children with ADD/ADHD
Steroids	reduce inflammation
Antibiotics	kill bacteria; non-specific, so eliminates pathogens as well as good flora
Anti-depressants suicides	moderates mood swings; some have been linked to teen

It is imperative that children are taught as soon as they are old enough to read and understand the concept of medicine (usually around the age of 11-12) that they are to follow the directions of whatever medicine has been prescribed for them. Parents or guardians can assist them with this and help them grow into this learning by reading and showing them how to understand medicine prescriptions.
Additionally, children must be taught that they are never to give their medicine to anyone. The understanding that medicines are only to be given to those they are prescribed to is an important and safe measure necessary for children to learn.

SKILL 6.2   Demonstrating knowledge of the dangers of taking medicines or drugs for nonmedical purposes and the effects of drug interactions that occur with using medicines in combination

There are serious dangers involved in taking medical and non-medical drugs for non-medical purposes. Drugs are chemicals that alter body chemistry to achieve a particular desired effect, but they often work by "treating the symptom". This tends to have other effects on the body's system that are either acceptable (i.e., side effects of medicines that are deemed within safe limits) or not sufficiently understood. For both of these reasons, taking any drug when not absolutely necessary is a very dangerous course of action. The chemicals in question will affect body and brain chemistry in ways that are probably not understood by the individual taking the substance, and may have long-lasting effects.

There are many unsafe effects of drug interactions that can occur when using medicines in combination. Given the complex nature of the interactions between different drug substances and our own physiology, it is sometimes hard to predict what effect is likely to occur. Different individuals may also react differently to the same drug combinations. For these reasons, we should attempt to avoid combining drugs.

SKILL 6.3   Demonstrating knowledge of the classification and characteristics of alcohol, tobacco, and other drugs and the body's reactions to various classes of drugs

Substance abuse can lead to adverse behaviors and increased risk of injury and disease. Any substance affecting the normal functions of the body, illegal or not, is potentially dangerous and students and athletes should avoid them completely.

Anabolic steroids – The alleged benefit is an increase in muscle mass and strength. However, this substance is illegal and produces harmful side effects. Premature closure of growth plates in bones can occur if abused by a teenager, limiting adult height. Other effects include bloody cysts in the liver, increased risk of cardiovascular disease, increased blood pressure, and dysfunction of the reproductive system.

Alcohol – This is a legal substance for adults but is very commonly abused. Moderate to excessive consumption can lead to an increased risk of cardiovascular disease, nutritional deficiencies, and dehydration. Alcohol also causes ill effects on various aspects of performance such as reaction time, coordination, accuracy, balance, and strength.

Nicotine – Another legal but often abused substance that can increase the risk of cardiovascular disease, pulmonary disease, and cancers of the mouth. Nicotine consumption through smoking severely hinders athletic performance by compromising lung function. Smoking especially affects performance in endurance activities.

Marijuana – This is the most commonly abused illegal substance. Adverse effects include a loss of focus and motivation, decreased coordination, and lack of concentration.

Cocaine – Another illegal and somewhat commonly abused substance. Effects include increased alertness and excitability. This drug can give the user a sense of over confidence and invincibility, leading to a false sense of one's ability to perform certain activities. A high heart rate is associated with the use of cocaine, leading to an increased risk of heart attack, stroke, potentially deadly arrhythmias, and seizures.

Narcotics (analgesics) - These are extremely addictive drugs. Most narcotics are in some way or another related to opium. Examples of narcotics, which are frequently prescribed for pain are: morphine, codeine, papaverine, Demerol, dilaudid, numorphan, nisentil and methadone.

Narcotics do reduce pain, however they also, alter moods and behavior, induce sleep and/or stupor and if used in excessive, more than prescribed amounts, can lead to death. Heroin is a highly addictive narcotic and is so dangerous that it has been banned by both federal and state laws under all circumstances.

SKILL 6.4   Recognizing factors (e.g., media messages, peer pressure) that contribute to the use of tobacco, alcohol, and other drugs and the health risks and social costs of self-medication, alcohol and chemical dependency, and substance abuse

FACTORS THAT CONTRIBUTE TO THE MISUSE AND ABUSE OF TOBACCO, ALCOHOL, AND OTHER DRUGS

Factors that contribute to misuse and abuse of tobacco, alcohol, and other drugs include mental health problems, stress, difficult life circumstances, and peer pressure. Additionally, the media, by way of television ads, celebrity endorsements and magazine ads certainly market tobacco and alcohol and play incredibly strong factors in contributing to the misuse of these substances. Identifying alternatives to substance abuse is an important prevention and coping strategy.

Alternatives to substance use and abuse include regular participation in stress-relieving activities like meditation, exercise, and therapy, all of which can have a relaxing effect (a healthy habit is, for example, to train oneself to substitute exercise for a substance abuse problem). More importantly, the acquisition of longer-term coping strategies (for example, self-empowerment via practice of problem-solving techniques) is key to maintaining a commitment to alternatives to substance use and abuse.

Aspects of substance abuse treatment that we must consider include the processes of physical and psychological withdrawal from the addictive substance, acquisition of coping strategies and replacement techniques to fill the void left by the addictive substance, limiting access to the addictive substance, and acquiring self-control strategies.

Withdrawal from an addictive substance has both psychological and physical symptoms. The psychological symptoms include depression, anxiety, and strong cravings for the substance. Physical withdrawal symptoms stem from the body, adapted to a steady intake of the addictive substance, adapting to accommodate the no-longer available substance. Depending on the substance, medical intervention may be necessary.

Coping strategies and replacement techniques, as discussed earlier, center around providing the individual with an effective alternative to the addictive substance as a solution to the situations that they would feel necessitate the substance.

Limiting access to the addictive substance (opportunities for use) is important, because the symptoms of withdrawal and the experiences associated with the substance can provide a strong impetus to return to using it. Finally, recovering addicts should learn strategies of self-control and self-discipline to help them stay off the addictive substance.

IMPLICATIONS OF SUBSTANCE ABUSE

Disease and substance abuse issues have significant implications for both individuals and for society as a whole. Specific implications, though, will depend greatly on the perception of the disease or substance abuse problem (defined by the Surgeon General as a disease) in the society. Education that gives the individuals in a society a clear understanding of the nature of diseases – what they are and are not linked to, how they can and cannot be transmitted, and what effects they will and will not exert on the afflicted individuals – will positively impact the both the afflicted individual and society as a whole.

This same education is often the deciding factor dictating the willingness of the community to allocate resources to programs for treatment and prevention of both diseases and substance abuse problems. It is this willingness to "get involved" on a societal level that plays a central role in the likelihood of improved treatment and prevention.

On the individual level, a very important implication of disease and substance abuse problems relate to responsible behavior. This is not a simple matter, as both disease and especially substance abuse problems (as with any addiction) will often lead to highly impaired judgment. There remains, however, the choice to act responsibly and seek out help. On the flip side, individuals in a society must act responsibly to help those around them, through intervention techniques, who are diseased or in the throes of a substance abuse problem seek help and treatment.

SKILL 6.5   Analyzing how alcohol, tobacco, and the nonmedical use of drugs affect personal goals, educational opportunities, and occupational choices

   o   See Skill 6.4

SKILL 6.6   Recognizing how adolescent and teen use of alcohol and drugs contributes to accidents, crime, suicide, and mortality

Adolescent and teen use of alcohol and drugs contributes to accidents, crime, suicide, and mortality by removing inhibitions and exacerbating existing tendencies, and by creating negative, descending spirals of behavior that create crises for adolescents.

Part of the contributing factors of adolescent and teen use of alcohol and drugs, stems from the fact that adolescents are at a period in their lives where they are relatively uninhibited, eagerly taking risks without properly appraising the real dangers involved. Drugs and alcohol further remove inhibitions, highly increasing the chances of making unwise decisions.

Further, alcohol and drugs create a spiraling pattern of behavior involving dependency, impaired mental function, and deception (parents and guardians are generally kept in the dark regarding this particular sort of developing habit). This makes it increasingly likely that situations will arise where adolescents feel the need to make "difficult" decisions that can have very negative consequences.

SKILL 6.7   Demonstrating awareness of alcohol, tobacco, and other drug dependencies as treatable diseases or conditions and of appropriate community resources for treatment

   o   *See Skill 6.4*

COMPETENCY 7.0   **UNDERSTAND THE IMPORTANCE OF VIOLENCE PREVENTION AND CONFLICT RESOLUTION IN THE PROMOTION OF PERSONAL HEALTH**

SKILL 7.1   **Identifying potentially risky, threatening, and violent situations (e.g., abusive relationships, gang involvement) and appropriate strategies for minimizing risk factors and avoiding or reducing exposure to such situations**

THE NATURE AND EFFECTS OF VIOLENCE AND METHODS OF AVOIDING VIOLENCE

Violence is a primary concern of educators. Assault, rape, suicide, gang violence, and weapons in school are major issues confronting educators in today's schools. Violence is no longer an issue confined to secondary schools in large urban areas. Violence involving younger students at the elementary level and in rural areas is also on the rise. Additionally, more adolescents are regularly witnessing violence in their schools and communities. Clearly, violence poses a serious threat to students' personal safety; however, violence also creates another challenge for schools. The fear of possible violence negatively affects students' growth, development, and ability to learn. In order to promote learning and healthy growth and development, schools must be violence-free. In order to accomplish this, schools must enact policies and procedures that promote an environment free from crime, drugs, and weapons. For some schools, this may include locker searches, full-time school security officers, and metal detectors. Some school systems may choose to utilize separate alternative schools for students proven to be violent or abusive.

In addition to experiencing violence at school, students may also be involved in various forms of harmful relationships in their homes or communities. Harmful relationships may include abuse, violence, and co-dependence. Students can use self-protection strategies to decrease the risk of becoming a victim of violence in their school, home, and community. Students should learn to have faith in their feelings about people and situations. If their instincts indicate that a person or situation is potentially dangerous, they should trust their feeling and remove themselves from the situation. They should always be attentive and aware of the actions of the people near them. They should avoid situations that increase the chance that something harmful will happen. Lastly, adult mentors can play a vital role in helping young people to stay safe. Educators are in a unique position to mentor young people and to act as a resource to help students avoid violence.

TYPES OF HURTFUL INTERPERSONAL AND WAYS OF AVOIDING OR CONFRONTING THESE BEHAVIORS IN A PROACTIVE MANNER

There is a wide range of hurtful interpersonal behaviors that students may experience from peers or adults in their lives. These include ridicule, sexual abuse, exploitation, dating violence, unwanted sexual contact, discrimination, and harassment.

Health instructors can teach students ways of avoiding or confronting these behaviors in a pro-active manner. For example, students should learn to refuse to accept the hurtful behavior, negotiate to prevent it, or collaborate to change the behavioral patterns in question.

Refusing to accept hurtful behavior from others is a fundamental step that students should learn (i.e. "just say no"). Every student (and individual) has the right to decide that certain types of behavior directed at him or her are unacceptable.

Negotiating works similarly to refusal, but takes it a step further. While showing the negatively behaving individual that their behavior is unacceptable, a mediator guides him or her towards alternate forms of behavior. Collaboration works similarly, except that the targeted student becomes an active partner in encouraging the alternate (more positive) behavioral patterns.

It is important to note that while it is our responsibility, as instructors, to teach students these techniques, we also have a legal obligation to take action when we suspect students are in danger.

SKILL 7.2 Identifying the consequences associated with unsafe behavior and the use of alcohol and drugs (e.g., violence, date rape, driving under the influence) and methods for countering aggressive behavior and intimidation

There are several consequences associated with unsafe behavior and the use of alcohol and drugs, such as violence, date rape, and driving under the influence of alcohol. Violence can result from alcohol and drug use because both substances suppress inhibitions and better judgment, making it more likely both that a situation will occur that could escalate to violence, and that an escalating situation will in fact turn to violence. Similar factors can lead to date rape, but perpetrators can also use drugs and/or alcohol assist in making potential victims more vulnerable. Driving under the influence, similarly, is dangerous because judgment and reflexes are impaired. This makes it more likely that an individual will drive poorly and that an individual will make the unwise decision to drive while in such a state.

There are several viable strategies for countering this sort of aggressive behavior and intimidation. Partially, it is a matter of conflict handling (verbal assertiveness and conversational techniques), avoidance (leaving the premises of individuals in an intoxicated state and avoiding places where individuals are likely to become intoxicated) and physical confrontation (physically defending oneself from date rape and forcibly taking car-keys from an inebriated individual).

SKILL 7.3   Demonstrating knowledge of effective communication and conflict-resolution skills for managing interpersonal conflicts (e.g., identifying nature of conflict, restating, collaborating, expressing feelings, active listening, using empathy)

CONFLICT MANAGEMENT

Interpersonal conflict is a major source of stress and worry. Common sources of interpersonal conflict include problems with family relationships, peers, classmates, other students, teachers and authority figures. Teaching students to manage conflict will help them reduce stress levels throughout their lives, thereby limiting the adverse health effects of stress. The following is a list of conflict resolution principles and techniques.

1. Think before reacting – In a conflict situation, it is important to resist the temptation to react immediately. You should step back, consider the situation, and plan an appropriate response. In addition, do not react to petty situations with anger. Stop and Think.

2. Listen – Be sure to listen carefully to the opposing party. Try to understand the other person's point of view.

3. Find common ground – Try to find some common ground as soon as possible. Early compromise can help ease the tension.

4. Accept responsibility – In every conflict there is plenty of blame to go around. Admitting when you are wrong shows you are committed to resolving the conflict.

5. Attack the problem, not the person – Personal attacks are never beneficial and usually lead to greater conflict and hard feelings.

6. Focus on the future – Instead of trying to assign blame for past events, focus on what we need to do differently to avoid future conflict.

SKILL 7.4   Demonstrating knowledge of appropriate strategies for preventing and managing negative social situations (e.g., refusal, resistance, negotiation, seeking help)

o   *See Skills 7.1 and 7.3*

SKILL 7.5   Analyzing causes of conflict among youth (e.g., bullying, sexual harassment, gangs) and appropriate strategies for handling such conflicts

There are several types of conflict common among young people including bullying, sexual harassment, and gang behavior. Generally, these conflicts grow out of struggles over power dynamics and attempts by students to assert themselves and force certain behaviors (submissive and/or sexual, in the aforementioned examples) from their peers. These behaviors tend to grow out of a very egocentric world-view. If one only considers himself, and not the needs or feelings of others, there is less compunction about harassing and bullying others.

Appropriate strategies for handling such conflicts include techniques for conflict-resolution, avoidance, and physical confrontation (as a last resort). Conflict-resolution techniques include verbal assertiveness ("just say no"), as well as conversational techniques to change the focus of the encounter. Avoidance is straightforward, a matter of staying out of situations where these dynamics tend to develop, and leaving the scene when they do. Physical confrontation is a last resort, but is sometimes necessary. Children who find themselves on the receiving end of negative confrontations may want to enroll in a self-defense class of some kind.

SKILL 7.6   Recognizing threats to children's safety (e.g., neglect, abuse), procedures for addressing these threats (e.g., identifying, reporting), and local support systems related to children's safety

Child abuse can come in physical and psychological forms, and ranges from neglectful parenting to directed assaults (physical or psychological) against the child. Child abuse often stems from poor parenting by inexperienced parents, who do not know how to care for a child properly. Stressful home conditions can also cause abuse. These stressors, including poverty, divorce, sickness, and disability (either of the parent or the child), can bring out the worst in parents. Another major cause of child abuse and neglect is a parent's substance abuse problem. Substance abuse can cause both neglect and directed physical and psychological assault on a child.

Child abuse and neglect is a crime, and educators in all 50 states are now legally obligated to report even reasonable suspicions of child abuse to the police or local child protective services.

SKILL 7.7 Recognizing signs, symptoms, and causes of self-destructive behavior (e.g., poor schoolwork, health problems) and identifying appropriate sources of help for individuals exhibiting these behaviors

Educators need to be on the lookout for the signs and symptoms of self-destructive behavior, which can include poor school work, health problems, behavior issues, isolation, not eating lunch and obvious emotional problems such as unexplained crying. Self-destructive behavior (for example, alcohol and drug use) can lead to poor schoolwork due to impaired mental function caused by the actual substance and frustration and general lack of focus that is involved in developing and sustaining this sort of illicit habit.

Self-destructive behavior of this kind can result from personal crisis (e.g., loss of a family member, marital difficulties at home, economic difficulties, or situations where a parent or guardian is exhibiting similar self-destructive behavior patterns), psychological difficulties like depression, and negative social influences (in which case the self-destructive behavioral patterns can begin fairly "innocently", but quickly spiral out of control).

There are several appropriate sources of help available for individuals exhibiting these sorts of destructive behaviors. School nurses, guidance counselors, school psychologists, family therapists, and other organizations can provide assistance. The first step that educators should always take when they suspect a student is engaging of in self-destructive behaviors is to consult with other school faculty (e.g., the school principal), as they will be most equipped to arrange for the student to receive the proper interventions.

COMPETENCY 8.0   UNDERSTAND THE ROLE OF CRITICAL THINKING AND DECISION-MAKING SKILLS IN REDUCING RISKS TO PERSONAL AND COMMUNITY HEALTH

SKILL 8.1   Demonstrating knowledge of the personal and social consequences of risk-taking behaviors (e.g., injury, legal difficulties) and how personal decisions about health-related behaviors can affect self and others

ASSESSING BEHAVIORAL RISK FACTORS

There are various resources available to assess the behavioral health risk factors of a community. The Centers for Disease Control and Prevention (CDC) annually publishes the Youth Risk Behavior Survey (YRBS). This survey explains national and state adolescent health risks. This information is available directly from the CDC. State education agencies compile and maintain statistics on youth health risks. Individual schools or school districts provide data regarding the types of problems seen in the school health room. Individual schools or school districts can also supply information regarding the number of referrals for pregnancy and substance abuse and data on absenteeism, dropouts, and disciplinary actions.

Other sources of information regarding community behavioral health risk factors include the state office of vital statistics, the state and local departments of health, and the medical examiners' office. The state police department can provide highway safety data. The poison control centers and local police departments can provide information regarding injuries, disease, and death. Additionally, emergency room and emergency medical services records and hospital discharge records can expose potential abuse.

Another source of information is social service agencies, as they have data on poverty, unemployment, and child abuse. Lastly, one could choose to assess the community's health behavior risk factors personally. When personally assessing a community's behavioral risk factors, utilize surveys, conduct health risk appraisals, and review healthcare utilization and cost data.

RISK TAKING

Healthy risk taking is a positive tool in an adolescent's life for discovering, developing, and consolidating his or her identity. It is important to remember that learning how to assess risks is a process that we work on throughout our lives. Children and adolescents need support, tools, and practice in order to do this. Teachers can help support students by encouraging a student to participate in something that may stretch their abilities, but not to the point where their limitations place them in a dangerous situation. For example, participation in an unfamiliar sport where the other students welcome and support the student which in turn will provide a degree of satisfaction and accomplishment for the student. A bad example would be putting a student on a team of large football players when he is either small-framed, inexperienced, or both.

You can observe the styles of risk taking by the way a student handles a new social situation. Although there are many styles, we can observe certain patterns, such as the cautious risk taker, the middle-of-the-roader, the adventurer or high-end risk taker, and the social risk taker whose boldness increases when he or she is with friends. It is also important to note that some children may be risk takers in one area – social, physical, intellectual, artistic – and not in others.

From a legal standpoint, students need to be aware that though the are considered juveniles, that there are offenses and situations in which they can be tried as adults as well as their juvenile records do now follow them. States and the Federal Government no longer "turn away" crimes committed by those underage as just "kids getting into trouble." If a student has a goal to attend college, a felony on his record will, in the vast majority of cases, prevent this at all state universities and most private higher education institutions. Additionally, students risk being judge ordered into juvenile detention centers as well as jail. Students must understand the long term ramifications of risk behaviors, particularly in regard to their future goals.

SKILL 8.2   Identifying the relationship between particular behaviors and health (e.g., the link between smoking and cancer) and the short-term and long-term benefits of a healthful lifestyle

Physical activity and inactivity greatly affects many aspects of a person's life, including physical fitness abilities, general health, physical resilience, physical self-confidence, psychological well-being, and cognitive function. Regular physical activity can improve or increase these elements, while inactivity can damage or decrease these elements.

The most obvious and direct benefit of physical activity is the physical dimension, which includes fitness and general health. Regular physical activity leads to improved physical fitness, improved strength and endurance of the muscular and cardiorespiratory systems and improved function of the circulatory system. Improved function of all these systems means that the body expends far less energy is on day-to-day activities, significantly increasing overall energy levels. Conversely, a lifestyle of physical inactivity will gradually lead to a deterioration of the muscular, cardiorespiratory, and circulatory systems, which leads to decreased energy levels.

Regular physical activity also contributes to increased physical resilience. Regular physical activity coupled with sufficient rest and a healthy diet strengthens the musculoskeletal system, which makes the individual less susceptible to injury. Physical activity also tends to improve reflexes and balance, which also reduces the likelihood of injury. Conversely, and as previously mentioned, a lifestyle of physical inactivity leads to a deterioration of the same physical systems that regular exercise strengthens and also contributes to a gradual "de-sharpening" of the reflexes and balance. In sum, these changes increase the likelihood and susceptibility of the individual to injury.

The bridge between physical and psychological benefits is the physical self-confidence derived from regular physical activity. The individual's increased ability to perform physical tasks leads to growth of their sense of ability to perform any physical activity (for example, you don't have to actually climb ten flights of stairs to know that you could if you wanted to – this is very liberating, as it creates options). Conversely, a lifestyle of physical inactivity, which implies a decreased fitness level, will eat away at the individual's physical self-confidence.

Regarding psychological well-being, physical activity causes the brain to release endorphins, which function to reduce stress levels (prolonged physical endurance activities can produce levels of endorphins that induce a pleasant and healthy "runner's high"). Most physical activities also mix a degree of repetitive motion and action that requires directed attention. In combination, this can function as a sort of meditative activity. For all of these reasons, regular physical activity contributes to psychological balance and well-being and reduced stress levels. Conversely, a lifestyle of physical inactivity allows physical confidence to deteriorate and removes alternatives of stress-relief, which can contribute negatively to the individual's psychological well-being.

Finally, regular physical activity benefits the circulatory system, which improves blood flow to the brain. This, in turn, leads to increased cognitive function and mental acuity. Those who are physically inactive do not experience these benefits.

WELLNESS

Wellness has two major components: understanding the basic human body functions and how to care for and maintain personal fitness, and developing an awareness and knowledge of how certain everyday factors, stresses, and personal decisions can affect one's health. Teaching fitness needs to go along with skill and activity instruction. Life-long fitness and the benefits of a healthy lifestyle need to be part of every Health and physical education teacher's curriculum as required and in direct proportion to the States standards. Cross-discipline teaching and teaching thematically with other subject matter in classrooms would be the ideal method to teach health to adolescents.

Incorporating wellness into the P.E. teacher's lesson plan doesn't need to take that much time or effort. For example, have students understand the idea that if you put more calories in your body than what you burn, you will gain weight. Teaching nutrition and the caloric content of foods in P.E. can be as simple as learning the amount of calories burned when participating in different sports for a set amount of time. To teach a more sophisticated lesson on nutrition that can have students understand the relationship between caloric intake and caloric expenditure, students could keep a food diary, tabulating the caloric content of their own diets while comparing it to an exercise diary that keeps track of the calories they've burned.

Another example of incorporating wellness into the health and physical education curriculum would be when participating in endurance running activities. Having students run a set distance and then giving them a finish time rewards the faster students and defeats the slower students. In addition to a final time, teach students a more beneficial way of measuring one's cardiovascular fitness by understanding pulse rate.

Teach students how to take their own pulse, how pulse rates vary at different stages of exercise (i.e. resting pulse, target pulse, recovery pulse, etc.), how pulse rates can differ between boys and girls, and encourage them to keep track of their own figures. As students gather their data, teacher-led discussions amongst classmates about similarities, differences and patterns that are developing would teach students how to monitor effectively and easily their own vital signs.

BENEFITS OF PHYSICAL ACTIVITY AND FITNESS

Practicing healthy behaviors has many benefits. Regular physical activity and proper nutrition can help prevent diseases, illnesses, and injuries. In addition, regular exercise and a proper diet help maintain a healthy body composition, which is important physically and psychologically. Physically fit and healthy individuals are generally more productive at work. Finally, preventing disease and avoiding injury through healthy behaviors can reduce health-care costs.

Physically educated individuals are better able to care for their own health and use nutrition and exercise to prevent long-term health problems. The following is a list of benefits of a physically active lifestyle.

Physiological benefits of physical activity include:

- improved cardio-respiratory fitness

- improved muscle strength

- improved muscle endurance

- improved flexibility

- more lean muscle mass and less body fat

- quicker rate of recovery

- improved ability of the body to utilize oxygen

- lower resting heart rate

- increased cardiac output

- improved venous return and peripheral circulation

- reduced risk of musculoskeletal injuries

- lower cholesterol levels

- increased bone mass

- cardiac hypertrophy and size and strength of blood vessels

- increased number of red cells

- improved blood-sugar regulation

- improved efficiency of thyroid gland

- improved energy regulation

- increased life expectancy

Psychological benefits of physical activity include:

- relief of stress

- improved mental health via better physical health

- reduced mental tension (relieves depression, improves sleeping patterns)

- better resistance to fatigue

- better quality of life

- more enjoyment of leisure

- better capability to handle some stressors

- opportunity for successful experiences

- better self-concept

- better ability to recognize and accept limitations

- improved appearance and sense of well-being

- better ability to meet challenges

- better sense of accomplishments

Sociological benefits of physical activity include:

- the opportunity to spend time with family and friends and make new friends

- the opportunity to be part of a team

- the opportunity to participate in competitive experiences

- the opportunity to experience the thrill of victory

ROLE OF EXERCISE IN HEALTH MAINTENANCE

The health risk factors improved by physical activity include cholesterol levels, blood pressure, stress related disorders, heart diseases, weight and obesity disorders, early death, certain types of cancer, musculoskeletal problems, mental health, and susceptibility to infectious diseases.

CRITICAL HEALTH RISK FACTORS

The Centers for Disease Control (CDC) has identified six critical health behaviors among youths and an additional six important health topics. The six critical health behaviors include Alcohol & Drug Use, Injury & Violence (including suicide), Tobacco Use, Nutrition, Physical Activity, and Sexual Risk Behaviors. Generally, people establish these behaviors during childhood, the behaviors are inter-related, and they are preventable. Besides causing serious health problems, they also contribute to educational and social problems, including failure to graduate from high school, unemployment, and criminal behavior.

Alcohol & Drug Use - Alcohol abuse is the third leading preventable cause of death in the United States (4% of the total deaths in 2000), and is a factor in approximately 41% of all deaths from motor vehicle crashes.

Injury & Violence - Injury and violence is the leading cause of death among youth aged 10-24 years: motor vehicle crashes (37% of all deaths), all other unintentional injuries (16%), homicide (18%), and suicide (13%).

Tobacco Use - Every day about 4,000 American youth aged 12–17 years try their first cigarette. The CDC estimates that smoking causes 435,000 deaths each year in the United States.

Nutrition - Almost 80% of young people do not eat the recommended servings of fruits and vegetables. Nearly 9 million youth in the United States aged 6–19 years are overweight.

Physical Activity - Participation in physical activity declines as children get older. Overall, in 2005, 36% of 9-12 graders had participated in at least 60 minutes per day of physical activity. Nearly 37% of 9th graders, but only 33% of 12th graders, participated in 60 minutes of physical activity on a regular basis.

Sexual Risk Behaviors - Each year, there are approximately 19 million new STD infections in the United States, and almost half of them are among youth aged 15 to 24. 34% of young women become pregnant at least once before they reach the age of 20.

SKILL 8.3   Demonstrating knowledge of goal-setting and decision-making skills and procedures that enhance health

Goal setting and decision making skills and procedures that enhance health involve many different types of strategies. One strategy that will be of great value to students involves a three-step process through which students make decisions, set goals, identify strategies to use to meet those goals and determine a timeline and schedule needed to implement the strategies. This is a process that can be used repeatedly as students set new goals for new projects or concerns and as they establish new goals to replace those not achieved.

As a teacher leads students through the process of decision making, setting health enhancing goals, strategies and timelines, it is essential that students experience success in achieving initial goals so they will be reinforced to continue setting new goals for future growth and development. It is also important to continually emphasize to students that they must think about what is important to them and their well-being and thus what new goals they may want to or need to set. Finally, school personnel must act as resources to give students needed assistance in doing whatever is necessary to establish and reach goals.

In goal setting, it is important to emphasis to the students that goals are to be realistic, achievable and measurable and affect the student positively in their growth and development. Some definitions that students need to demonstrate knowledge of:

- Goal: a target for which to aim
- Achievable: what can be reached
- Schedule: timetable
- Strategy: a plan or series of maneuvers for reaching a specific goal or result
- Measurable: able to determine the degree to which the goal has been achieved

Example decision making and goal setting questions for students to consider and have knowledge of are:

- Where are you going with your life?
- Do you want to graduate form high school (middle school) ?
- Do you desire to go to college?
- Do you need to complete your assigned tasks and complete them on time?
- Do you desire to be a healthy and productive student?

SKILL 8.4   Recognizing how sexual decisions are influenced by external factors (e.g., environment, media, peers) and identifying techniques for resisting persuasive tactics regarding sexual involvement

FACTORS THAT AFFECT DECISIONS ABOUT SEXUAL BEHAVIOR

Cultural norms

Sexual matters are taboo in many cultures, and parents may not be willing to accept the fact that either their child has a certain sexual health condition, or that they might have performed the actions that can lead to the development of the condition (i.e. parents may be unwilling to accept the fact that their child is sexually active). This can make it very difficult to help a student receive necessary treatment.

Peer pressure

Peer pressure can greatly affect many aspects of adolescent behavior, including sexual behavior. Hormonal changes, sexual development, and the prevalence of sex in movies, television, and the media, make sexual behavior a topic of great importance to adolescents. Just like with other risky behaviors (e.g. drug use, alcohol use), adolescents will often feel pressure from friends and peers to become sexually active to comply with group norms. In addition, adolescents may experience intense pressure from their boyfriends or girlfriends.

Influence of alcohol and drugs

Alcohol and drug use impairs judgment. People under the influence of drugs and alcohol are more likely to engage in risky or dangerous behaviors. This includes engaging in unprotected sex. When under the influence of drugs and alcohol, adolescents are not able to make sound decisions. Research indicates that teens that use alcohol and drugs are more likely to be sexually active. In addition, when under the influence of alcohol and drugs, teens are more likely to engage in dangerous, unprotected sexual activity.

HOW PEERS AND PEER RELATIONSHIPS AFFECT PERSONAL HEALTH

Adolescents spend most of their spare time with peers. Adolescence is a time characterized by friendly relationships that mature and become deeper. At this stage, teenagers tend to distance themselves from their parents in a quest for more independence. This is a very crucial stage for teenagers as they have a tendency to acquire the attitudes and behaviors of their peers unconsciously. Parents must understand the critical stage their child is going through while still acting as a guiding force. For example, parents should encourage their child to be selective in choosing her friends. If she happens to spend time in the company of peers who spend most of their time studying, chances are they too will become studious. However, if her group of friends frequents bars and clubs and stays out late, she will be more likely to do the same. This can have a domino effect on the child and cause a lack of sleep and related physical and psychological ailments. If this behavior becomes habitual, she will later be prone to absenteeism and may develop a negative reputation.

In order to prevent this negative situation, an appropriate inquiry for a parent, guardian, or teacher is to ask what kind of company the child is keeping. It is also beneficial for a parent to become familiar and friendly with their child's friends.

EFFECTS OF PEER PRESSURE AND STRATEGIES FOR RESPONDING TO PEER PRESSURE IN A POSITIVE MANNER

Peer pressure can cause children to make decisions, both positive and negative. For example, a child that interacts with other children that practice dangerous behaviors such as drug use and sex are more likely to mimic such behaviors. On the other hand, interacting with children that are committed to exercise may encourage a previously inactive child to become physically active.

Standing up to negative peer pressure requires self-confidence and a healthy level of self-esteem. When pressured by peers to engage in unhealthy or dangerous activities, students should respond firmly and concisely. Offering a simple, "No thanks," and walking away from the situation is often the best strategy. While students should try to help their friends and peers, they must avoid being judgmental or overbearing. Maintaining a low-key presence is often the best way to avoid conflict, protect one's self, and help others.

SKILL 8.5 Critically analyzing alcohol, tobacco, and drug advertisements and promotional tactics for developing counterarguments and resisting persuasive marketing techniques

The common themes of advertisements for alcohol, tobacco, and drugs is the portrayal of the users of the drug in question as a happy, well-rounded and successful individual, respected by others and lacking neither resources nor popularity. Further, the function of the drug itself is either to augment (or create) this personal magnetism or to compensate for a condition that would prevent this sort of happy, positive lifestyle. This is especially effective because most people crave this sort of lifestyle.

Responding effectively with sound counter-arguments that will help children resist these persuasive marketing techniques center on education about the drug in question. Teachers should teach students that alcohol impairs judgment, damages the liver, and can lead to obesity. Tobacco damages the respiratory and circulatory systems, is carcinogenic, can cause loss of calcium (and decrease in bone-density), and contains many toxins. The situation is slightly more complex with medical drugs. Children should learn that medical drugs are also dangerous, can have many side effects, and should not be taken without a doctor's prescription.

SKILL 8.6 Recognizing the use of positive behavior alternatives and sound decision making in preventing the transmission of disease

Children should learn the importance of preventing transmission of disease by recognizing positive behavior alternatives (personal hygiene issues) and employing sound and informed decision-making (practice safe sex or abstinence).

Positive behavior alternatives include hygiene considerations for prevention of communicable diseases. For example, hand washing on a regular basis and particularly before meals and avoiding blood-to-blood contact (as that is an easy way for diseases to infect new hosts). Children should also learn to avoid dangerous situations that can result in injury, as injury increase susceptibility to disease, both by creating opportunities for infection, and by generally weakening the immune system.

Informed decision-making includes the practice of safe sex or abstinence to avoid the spread of sexually transmitted diseases such as Auto Immune Deficiency Syndrome (AIDS), Syphilis, Gonorrhea, certain forms of Herpes, and other diseases. Children should also learn that needles are a potential means of disease transmission (in addition to stressing the other dangers of intravenous drug use).

SUBAREA III.   FAMILY AND SOCIAL RELATIONSHIPS

COMPETENCY 9.0   UNDERSTAND INTERPERSONAL
                      RELATIONSHIPS

SKILL 9.1   Recognizing the importance of the components of character
             education (e.g., respect, honesty)

Instructors can foster sensitive interactions with and among learners primarily by way of
communication and respect. An encouraging learning environment has open and
unhindered lines of communication and a clear sense of respect between learners and
between learners and their teacher.

Instructors can foster open communication in the classroom by reminding students that
they can and should approach the teacher with issues and concerns. Of course,
instructors must follow-through on their promises by making themselves available to
students and maintaining a patient attitude that accounts for the students' worldviews
concerning the issues that they raise. Teachers should also devote classroom time to
open (but moderated) discussions in which students can air their concerns relating to
issues between classmates. The instructor can serve as a mediator.

Similarly, respect is fundamental; otherwise, students will not bring issues to the
attention of their teacher more than once. The teacher must be genuinely respectful of
the concerns and backgrounds of their students, and demand respect in turn.
Instructors must also stress that they will not tolerate disrespectful behavior between
students.

SKILL 9.2   Recognizing the importance of positive self-concept and
             psychological well-being as the basis for healthy interpersonal
             relationships

THE STAGES OF SOCIAL DEVELOPMENT

Social development – Small children (ages 3-5) are socially flexible. Different children
will prefer solitary play, parallel play, or cooperative play. Frequent minor quarrels will
occur between children, and boys will tend to be more aggressive (children at these
ages are already aware of gender roles).

Early elementary school children (ages 6-8) are increasingly selective of friends (usually
of the same sex). Children at this age enjoy playing games, but are excessively
preoccupied by the rules. Verbal aggression becomes more common than physical
aggression, and adults should encourage children of this age to solve their own
conflicts.

Pre-adolescent children (ages 9-11) place great importance on the (perceived) opinions of their peers and of their social stature, and will go to great lengths to 'fit in'. Friendships at this age are very selective, and usually of the same sex.

Young adolescents (ages 12-14) develop greater understanding of the emotions of others, which results in increased emotional sensitivity and impacts peer relationships. Children at this age develop an increased need to perform.

In the later stages of adolescence (ages 15-17), peers are still the primary influence on day-to-day decisions, but parents will have increasing influence on long-term goals. Girls' friendships tend to be close and intimate, whereas boys' friendships are based on competition and similar interests. Many children this age will work part-time, and educators should be alert to signs of potential school dropouts.

BODY IMAGE

Expectations relating to body image influence the development of self-concept by creating a benchmark of assumed correlations between body image and other traits. For example, a slight and skinny (ectomorphic) student may see himself as unathletic, even though students with ectomorphic body types often excel at endurance sports. Students are also likely to generalize from body image to perceived ability to master new physical skills (for example, an athletic child might expect to be better at a new sport than less athletic children, even if the sport is new to both of them).

PHYSICAL APPEARANCE

Expectations relating to physical appearance influence the development of self-concept by virtue of assumptions correlating physical appearance with likeability. In fact, the relationship is reciprocal, and stronger in the opposite direction (students that are popular will tend to develop a more positive self-concept about their physical appearance).

SKILL LEVEL

Expectations relating to skill level influence the development of self-concept by setting the baseline for the performance that students will expect to deliver, both when attempting tasks that they are familiar with and new tasks (students with a high skill level will expect to do well, and students who are good at several things will expect to be good at other, new things).

MEDIA

Media-based expectations influence the development of self-concept by setting media-based role models as the benchmarks against which students will measure their traits. Self-concept is a set of statements describing the child's own cognitive, physical, emotional, and social self-assessment. These statements will usually tend to be fairly objective ("good at baseball" or "has red hair"), media-based expectations can change the statements to be measurements against role models ("athletic like this actor" or "tall like that pop star").

CULTURE

Cultural expectations influence the development of self-concept by suggesting to the child traits they should include in their personal self-assessment. For example, students from a very warm and energetic cultural background, where there is a strong emphasis on family life, may develop self-concepts that incorporate those traits into their personal self-description. Cultural gender roles may also express themselves in this way.

SKILL 9.3   Recognizing the functions and expectations of various types of interpersonal relationships (e.g., positive, negative, dependent)

There are several broad types of interpersonal relationships: positive and negative interpersonal relationships and dependant relationships, which fall into a slightly different category. Each type of relationship comes with a unique set of functions and expectations.

Positive interpersonal relationships tend to be constructive and mutually supportive. This sort of relationship will generally include overlapping layers of emotional sharing, common interests (which are functionally important, as they serve as the glue or "excuse" to maintain the relationship), and a well-developed sense of respect and trust.

Negative interpersonal relationships tend to involve a destructive power dynamic, where either one or both sides of the relationship tend to affect the other negatively. These relationships are often more controlling than trusting and lack respect. Though in this case (as with positive relationships), there will still be elements of common interest.

Dependant interpersonal relationships fall between the positive and negative categories. They will often have elements of both sides, but they are further complicated by a sense that not only does one side depend on the other, but one side actually needs the other. Need creates a sense of being beholden and prevents proper exploration of relevant interpersonal issues that arise. This sort of relationship is not necessarily destructive, but dependencies tend to complicate situations.

SKILL 9.4   Identifying ways in which various skills (e.g., social interaction skills, listening skills) affect interpersonal relationships

There are several communication skills, for example social interaction skills and listening skills, which can have a powerful and positive effect on interpersonal relationships.

Social interaction skills involve developing an understanding of the behavioral norms that govern social interactions (which, of course, differ across groups of people and different situations for social interaction). Since we all abide by certain "unwritten rules" governing how to behave with other people, following these conventions puts everyone at ease. On the other hand, breaking these social norms tends to make others feel uncomfortable, as it suggests that the general behavioral patterns of the individual in question may be harder to predict.

Listening skills are fundamental to positive social interactions and the development of interpersonal relationships because they involve shifting one's focus away from personal egocentrism and towards a genuine interest in others. Developing listening skills (for example, by practicing active listening) will tend to increase consideration of others, which is a critical element of interpersonal relationships.

SKILL 9.5   Analyzing social and cultural influences on interpersonal communication and ways in which verbal and nonverbal communication skills help build and maintain positive relationships

There are many personal differences among students that can affect communication. Instructors should consider cultural, economic, and environmental differences when addressing their students.

Cultural differences that can affect communication may include varying perceptions of what falls into the category of acceptable behavior. For example, a child may or may not believe it is appropriate to speak without having been directly spoken to, look an educator in the eye, or speak out in a classroom setting (some cultures view all of these actions as aggressive behavior). There is also the issue of cultural-linguistic norms, which students may not understand. For example, "John, would you like to do your homework?" really means "John, do your homework!"

Economic differences may also affect communication. Children from different socio-economic backgrounds are likely to have very different frames of reference for many commonly used elements in communication. This can include references to "normal" after school activities (whether the child spends it in front of the television or computer will obviously depend on whether the family is able to afford the equipment – this can be a significant classroom communication issue when homework requires a computer) and benchmarks of value (what is seen as valuable, both in dollar amounts and in commodities).

Environmental differences are similar to the previously described categories, to the point of blending into them. The differences between an urban and rural environment is a major cultural difference (depending on context), and often corresponds to major relative differences in economic means.

SKILL 9.6   Applying knowledge of techniques for developing and maintaining friendships, the characteristics and benefits of healthy peer relationships, the effects of harmful friendships, the effects of peer pressure, and strategies for responding to peer pressure in a positive manner

- o   See also Skill 8.4

Mutual respect, shared values and interests, and a mutually felt ability to trust and depend on each other characterize responsible friendship. Genuine respect for one's friends is vital for the creation of a positive and responsible friendship. It is much easier to dismiss commitments towards and the needs of those who we do not respect. Shared values are a foundation for mutual respect, and shared interests are necessary for the exploration and development of a friendship. Trust and dependability are the cement that holds responsible friendships together.

We can develop positive interpersonal relationships by devoting time to character-building activities to strengthen the traits listed above. Individuals can work to become people who espouse the values that they would like to see in their friends, and can make efforts toward becoming trustworthy and dependable individuals. Specific techniques that we can apply to develop positive interpersonal relationships with others include active listening and considerate respect for the things others value.

Active listening is the process of repeating back what was said in the form of a question (e.g. if someone tells you, "I'm thinking of taking a vacation, maybe to Florida", you might repeat back, "You're saying that you want to take a vacation to Florida?"). We should not perform this exercises mechanically (i.e. parroting), but rather we should use active listening as a personal reminder to listen to the concerns and interests of the person before us.

We can develop considerate respect by actively asking ourselves what about the current scenario that we are facing would others see as significant. It is an exercise aimed at placing value and emphasis on the priorities of others.

Social support systems are the networks that students develop with their peers that provide support when students experience challenges and difficulties. The support offered by these systems is often emotional and sometimes logistical. Financial support in these relationships is generally inappropriate. Social support systems are vital to students (and individuals in general), especially students who don't have other support mechanisms in place.

The benefits of maintaining healthy peer relationships include having a social support system to assist in difficult times and having the knowledge of the existence of that system. This means that students can feel confident to take greater risks (within reason) and achieve more because they know the support system is there if they need it.

HARMFUL RELATIONSHIPS

There is a wide range of hurtful interpersonal behaviors that students may experience from peers or adults in their lives. These include ridicule, sexual abuse, exploitation, dating violence, unwanted sexual contact, discrimination, and harassment.

Health instructors can teach students ways of avoiding or confronting these behaviors in a pro-active manner. For example, students should learn to refuse to accept the hurtful behavior, negotiate to prevent it, or collaborate to change the behavioral patterns in question.

Refusing to accept hurtful behavior from others is a fundamental step that students should learn (i.e. "just say no"). Every student (and individual) has the right to decide that certain types of behavior directed at him or her are unacceptable.

Negotiating works similarly to refusal, but takes it a step further. While showing the negatively behaving individual that their behavior is unacceptable, a mediator guides him or her towards alternate forms of behavior. Collaboration works similarly, except that the targeted student becomes an active partner in encouraging the alternate (more positive) behavioral patterns.

It is important to note that while it is our responsibility, as instructors, to teach students these techniques, we also have a legal obligation to take action when we suspect students are in danger.

SKILL 9.7 Recognizing factors that affect decisions about dating (e.g., cultural norms, peer pressure) and the social, emotional, intellectual, and economic aspects of dating

Several factors affect decisions about dating among youths in addition to normally developing drives to pursue a connection with a member of the opposite sex. Other important factors include cultural norms and peer pressure.

Cultural norms have changed over the past decades, significantly lowering the ages at which all stages of dating behavior (first date, first kiss, sexual activity, etc.) are acceptable or appropriate. It is not uncommon for children to be dating and involved in sexual activity in their early teenage years. This is very problematic, for several reasons. Children at this age are not yet developmentally ready or necessarily interested in this sort of interaction and are squandering potentially valuable experiences. Their lack of maturity and awareness also leads to very poor decision-making, which can have long-lasting consequences (for example, sexually transmitted diseases and teen pregnancy). These same cultural norms will often push children to make decisions that they are socially, emotionally, and intellectually unprepared to make.

Peer pressure enforces these cultural norms. Many children would be satisfied to sit out the "culturally normal" premature dating activities, but feel forced by peers who are pressuring them to comply. This too can cause students to make unwise decisions regarding all aspects of dating (social, emotional, intellectual and economic). The best intervention for an adult is not to "preach" to children (as this is generally ineffective with children at this age), but work to instill in them the confidence to make their own decisions.

COMPETENCY 10.0 **UNDERSTAND FAMILY RELATIONSHIPS AND THEIR IMPACT ON THE WELL-BEING OF INDIVIDUALS AND SOCIETY**

SKILL 10.1 **Identifying types of families, the roles of family members, the role of the family in the community, and the benefits of family participation in community activities**

THE VARIETY OF FAMILIES AND FAMILY STRUCTURES AND STRATEGIES AND BEHAVIORS THAT PROMOTE HEALTHY FAMILY RELATIONSHIPS

Today's family is often quite different from the traditional mom, dad, and biological children. Divorce, stepfamilies, and adoption have changed the typical American family. Children suffer the most with divorce, remarriage, and stepfamily situations. They are particularly at-risk if their biological parents are in conflict. Divorce takes a long time, and unhappy parents, who are focused on severing ties with the ex-spouse and starting over, often overlook their children. Relationships with the absent parent change as well. (*Family Relations* (Vol. 52, No. 4, pages 352–362) by Emery of UVA and Joan B. Kelly, PhD)

Adjustment of children of divorce is more dependent on the child's resiliency than anything else. Contributing factors include the child's age during the divorce, the amount of time elapsed, parenting style, financial security, and parental conflict. In addition, fifty percent of adjustment problems for children of divorce are due to economic problems faced by divorced households.

Adoptions of international children and those of races different from the parents are creating multicultural families and communities. Attachment disorder is often a problem in these types of adoptions due to lack of nurturing early in a child's life. More same-sex couples and single parents adopt, and grandparents often adopt their grandchildren following parental abuse or neglect. The 21st century American family is very different from what was common 30 years ago. (Adam Pertman, "Adoption Nation: How the Adoption Revolution is Transforming America", Basic Books, 2001.

The demographics of stepfamilies are complex, with nearly 25% of the parents unmarried. Both heterosexual parents and gay, lesbian, or bisexual partners may head families. Stepfamilies are a blend of parents, their respective children, the nonresidential parents of those children, grandparents and other members of the extended family, and children born to remarried ex-spouses.

The blended family's challenges include parenting, disciplining, developing new relationships between the stepparent and other spouse's children, strengthening the marital relationship, and working to include nonresidential family – divorced spouses and children not living with the stepfamily.

One in three Americans is part of a stepfamily, each with its own character. The stepchildren rarely see a new stepparent as a "real parent", and years may pass before they gain acceptance. It is also difficult for parents in second marriages to treat their biological children the same as their stepchildren. Children are often given too much power in the new family, and may try to create conflict between their biological parent and the stepparent in an attempt to make the stepparent leave.

Creating family stability requires the same steps whether the situation is a first-marriage, stepfamily, or a single-parent family. What really matters is that parents maintain a routine that fosters security. How families resolve conflicts is also important. Children need an anchor when it seems that everything in their lives is changing. This could be a special friend, neighbor, or relative outside the immediate family. Consistency in school settings helps predict positive adjustment in children, especially when their home lives are chaotic.

Strategies recommended for parents of second marriages include:

- Discuss and decide on finances before getting married.
- Build a strong marital bond because it will benefit everybody.
- Develop a parenting plan, which likely will involve having the stepparent play a secondary, non-disciplinary role for the first year or two. Letting the children adjust slowly prepares for a successful transition.
- Take time to process each change.
- Make sure that big changes are communicated adult-to-adult, not via the children.
- Work with therapists who are specially trained in stepfamily dynamics.

Key factors that contribute to healthy adjustment post-divorce include appropriate parenting, access to the non-residential parent, custody arrangements, and low parental conflict. Appropriate parenting includes providing emotional support, monitoring children's activities, disciplining authoritatively, and maintaining age-appropriate expectations. Finally, the research demonstrates that the best predictor of child adjustment following divorce is the parents' psychological health and the quality of the parent-child relationship.

FAMILY HEALTH

The primary factors that affect family health include environmental conditions such as pollution and proximity to industrial areas, smoking and drinking habits of family members, economic conditions that affect nutritional factors, and general levels of education among family members as related to an understanding of healthy living habits.

The relative levels of pollution in the family's area can significantly contribute to family health. For example, proximity to industrial areas, which may be releasing carcinogenic emissions, can be dangerous. Similarly, a smoking habit within the home environment is highly detrimental, as it will negatively affect the respiratory and circulatory systems of all members of the household. A drinking habit can also pose a risk both to the individual and to those in proximity to him or her.

Economic conditions can affect family health in that lower economic means can lead to neglect of some nutritional factors (which are critical to healthy living and proper physical and cognitive development). Similarly, families with two working parents may not have as much time to spend with children to monitor their eating habits. Education levels among family members as related to an understanding of healthy living habits are also significant. Even with all of the required financial means, parents/caregivers may not have the requisite knowledge to direct them to habits for healthy living.

SKILL 10.2 Recognizing the family as a social system and the influence of families on individuals and society

o   See Skills 10.1 and 10.3

SKILL 10.3 Analyzing the nature of healthy family relationships and strategies and behaviors that promote caring and respectful family relationships

THE NATURE OF HEALTHY RELATIONSHIPS WITHIN FAMILIES

There are several types of peer and family dynamics whose benefits and challenges we will explore: dependencies, power dynamics, and social roles (including family roles, gender roles and group dynamics).

Dynamics of dependencies refers to the relationships of who is dependant on whom in a family or social circle. Children are dependant on their parents for affection and emotional and financial support. Parents are dependant on their children and each other for affection and on each other for emotional and logistical support. One parent may be dependant on the other financially (i.e. families with one "breadwinner" and one stay-at-home parent). The sorts of dependencies that may develop in a social circle include emotional, logistical (i.e. help with homework), social (i.e. a child depending on another for acceptance within a social group), and material (i.e. children dependant on each other for access to toys and games). On the face of it, many of these dependant relationships seem very opportunistic and self-serving, but this is generally not the case. Relationships between individuals (both children and adults) are reciprocal in nature. It is normal for people to offer to others the things that they have in abundance, and accept from others the things that they lack (for example, an insecure child may depend on a peer for encouragement).

Power dynamics refers to the hierarchies that develop in most circles involving more than one individual. Most peer groups will have a hierarchy of authority and, of course, hierarchies exist within a family (there may be a more dominant parent, and then there is the authority of parents over their children). The benefits of these dynamics are that they can enforce and strengthen positive examples set by those towards the top of the hierarchies. The challenges of these dynamics is that, especially with regards to social circles, the hierarchies are not necessarily topped by the best examples, but the leader of a peer group will nonetheless exert a great deal of influence (which may be hard for a parent or educator to counteract). This is less of a problem in families, where the parents are generally appropriate role models for their children.

Social roles refer to the set of connected behaviors, rights, and obligations based on their hierarchical position and relationships with others in the group setting. Individuals (adults and children) adopt family roles (e.g., I am the authoritative father, indulging mother, well-behaved child), gender roles (e.g., as a man, woman, boy, or girl, I am expected and I expect myself to do certain things in certain ways), and group dynamics (my role within this group is to be the funny one, the leader, or the one who looks out for others). The benefit of social roles is that they can create a framework for individuals to adopt very positive behavior traits. The challenge of social roles is when individuals feel their social role is destructive to themselves or others (for example, when children see themselves cast as the social misfit or academic failure), it creates a self-fulfilling prophecy.

SKILL 10.4　Applying knowledge of effective communication and coping techniques within families and ways of expressing appreciation of the diverse perspectives, needs, and characteristics of individuals and families

- ○　*See Skills 10.1 and 10.3*

SKILL 10.5 Recognizing the social, cultural, and economic conditions that affect the family; community, private, and government resources and services available to assist families with a variety of disadvantaging conditions; and factors related to providing family services (e.g., sensitivity to cultural differences, confidentiality)

Social, cultural, and economic conditions that affect modern-day families include racial tensions and unhealthy group dynamics within a community, culture-based divisions, economic inequalities and educational opportunities. Racial tensions within a community can lead to families feeling unwelcome or even ostracized in their communities. Unhealthy, destructive group dynamics can have a similar effect. Culture-based divisions (stemming either from the culture itself or the perception that the rest of the community has of that culture) are similarly destructive. Finally, economic inequalities can be a very alienating influence, causing families to feel that they do not "measure up" to the standards of others around them.

Community, private, and government resources and services available to assist families with a variety of disadvantaging conditions include community centers, twelve-step programs, and employment and health services. Community centers will often run a range of programs and activities geared at helping individuals acquire skills and network successfully in their communities. Twelve-step programs are a good resource available to individuals who are trying to break out of a destructive pattern of behavior. Private and government employment services can help individuals find proper employment to support their families. Finally, private and government health services can assist disadvantaged individuals and families (especially children) with health care.

Factors that we must consider in relation to providing family services include sensitivity to cultural differences and matters of confidentiality. An awareness of cultural differences should guide the way in which service providers approach families and individuals. Cultural differences will sometimes dictate (or at least influence) both the services offered and the method of delivery. Confidentiality is also a crucial issue. Issues relating to family services are generally quite sensitive and, for individuals to feel comfortable interacting with these service providers, it is important that they understand and believe that everything relating to these interactions is strictly confidential.

SKILL 10.6 Demonstrating knowledge of factors and considerations related to preparation for parenthood, the responsibilities of parents, and the role of parents in guiding and directing children's behavior

PARENTING RESPONSIBILITIES AND SKILLS

When a couple decides to have children, they consciously or unconsciously commit to providing a loving and safe environment for their offspring. The obligation of parents encompasses physical care, social development, and emotional and financial support.

This environment should include constant and reliable shelter, education, medical care, physical safety, and nourishment. The family offers guidance and nurturing necessary for children to mature as healthy, well-adjusted adults.

The most important job you will have in life is parenting your children. Parenting skills are the most powerful influences in a child's life. Lacking formal training, most parents follow the model of their own parents, for better or for worse.

Parenting skills address behavior management, communication, and conflict resolution. A young child acts to fulfill basic needs. A parent's duty is to teach the child how to meet these needs in a socially acceptable manner, thus guiding him or her toward developing into a well balanced, healthy, and happy individual.

Successful parents use numerous skills including:

- Active listening
- Consultation
- Joint problem solving

All of these skills show that the parent has an interest in the child's point of view and facilitate effective communication without emotionally charged power struggles. They also promote responsibility, independence, and sound decision making in children.

(http://psychologyinfo.com/treatment/parenting_skills.html)
Dr. Thomas Gordon, *Parent Effectiveness Training*, Three Rivers Press, CA, October, 2000.

SKILL 10.7 Recognizing considerations and procedures in family planning; stages of and physical changes that occur during pregnancy and childbirth; effects of drugs, diseases, lifestyle, and environmental conditions on prenatal health; and nutritional requirements during pregnancy

o *See also Skill 2.1 – "Human Reproductive System"*

FAMILY PLANNING

Family Planning has come a long way since public health nurse Margaret Sanger was arrested in 1916 for opening the first birth control clinic in Brooklyn, New York. Nearly 50 years later in 1965, a Supreme Court decision made birth control legal for married couples. Today, families are able to control family size as well as birth spacing of their children.

Trends among couples in the 20th century were to have smaller families, which improved the health of infants and women. Family size decreased from an average of 7 children to 2.2. Family planning services are now publicly supported, and prevent over one million unplanned pregnancies each year.

Unintended pregnancy is still a problem in the U.S., which is ranked highest in the industrialized world in unintended pregnancy. Abortion rates in the U.S. are second highest among western countries. Nearly half of all pregnancies are unplanned and over 50% end in abortion.

The most common methods of modern birth control are female sterilization, oral contraceptives, and inter-uterine devices (IUDs). New methods include the female condom, vaginal microbicides, and the controversial morning-after pill. Among the many benefits of family planning is reduction of sexually transmitted diseases and cervical cancer.

Although family planning has made significant progress, population growth is a major concern throughout the world. Population figures have more than doubled since 1900, and the world population in 1999 exceeded six billion.

(http://www.cdc.gov/mmwr/preview/mmwrhtml/mm4847a1.htm)

COMPETENCY 11.0 UNDERSTAND COMMUNITY RELATIONSHIPS, COMMUNITY HEALTH ISSUES, AND COMMUNITY HEALTH-CARE RESOURCES

SKILL 11.1 Recognizing the dynamics of different types of community groups (e.g., clubs, organizations, teams, gangs), positive and negative influences of community groups, and the nature and importance of social support systems

Different types of community groups (e.g., clubs, organizations, teams, and gangs) will tend to have different dynamics associated with them. Clubs will tend to have a fairly informal group dynamic – since the organization of clubs is often less formal, club members will develop a dynamic that is friendly and informal, but not excessively fraternal or committed. Organizations tend to be more formal and hierarchical in their structure, and so will often have dynamics that are somewhat more regimented and committed than clubs. Teams generally involve a flatter hierarchy and will often develop very strong fraternal bonds between members. Gangs, unfortunately, are community groups characterized by very strong ties between individuals due to the shared risk involved in the sometimes-questionable activities they pursue.

Social support systems are the networks that students develop with their peers that provide support when students experience challenges and difficulties and serve as a sounding board for emotions and ideas. The support offered by these systems is most often in the realm of emotional and sometimes logistical support. Financial support in these relationships is generally inappropriate. Social support systems are vital to students (and individuals in general), especially students who do not have other support mechanisms in place.

SKILL 11.2 Identifying types, sources, and characteristics of community health-care information (e.g., libraries, health agencies, health practitioners) and appropriate local health resources, clinics, or services for various health needs and problems

CONSUMER EDUCATION

We can find information relating to physical activity at local public and university libraries and online. Educators should regularly inform themselves about updates in the field, and should periodically search for resources that they can use with their students. Instructors should encourage students should to make use of free resources like libraries, and especially the Internet, to expand their own knowledge and understanding of the subject matter.

We can find products relating to physical activity at sporting goods stores, gym boutiques, nutritional supplement stores, and wholesalers. Local community centers may also sell or rent equipment, and prices may be more favorable.

We can find services for promoting consumer awareness skills in relation to physical activity, recreation, fitness, and wellness online and at local community centers. Many community centers have outreach programs to increase public participation in physical activities. Health food stores may also offer seminars on fitness and wellness. Physical education professionals can work to build ties between these publicly offered services and their own curriculums.

There is generally a wide array of information available related to health, fitness and recreational activities, products, facilities, and services. It can be difficult for the untrained consumer to sort through it all to find information that is pertinent and accurate.

When evaluating information relating to fitness and sports equipment, consumers (for example, parents of students who are seeking to equip their home with training facilities for themselves and their children) should ask the sales staff about the differences between their choices; not just in terms of prices, but also in terms of potential fitness benefits and especially safety (Is the equipment in question safe to use? Is it safe for all ages? Is a spotter required for its use?).

When evaluating weight control products and programs, consumers should ask sales staff to explain the mechanism by which the program functions, (e.g. does it limit caloric intake, maximize caloric expenditure, or function by means of some other process?). The word of the sales staff is not sufficient, however, and consumers should investigate further using the tools at their disposal, which include public and university libraries, the internet, and physical education professionals at their children's schools.

When evaluating fitness-training facilities, consumers should consider several factors. These factors are quality and availability of training equipment, hygiene of the facility, and overall atmosphere. You can determine the general quality of the equipment by its age and you can glean further information from a discussion with the training staff on-site. You can investigate the availability of the equipment by visiting the facility at peak training times (which vary depending on the demographics of the facility – again, you should ask the training staff for the appropriate times). If it takes too long for equipment to become available and lines seem to form, this may not be the best facility for your needs (unless you're not interested in visiting the facility during those hours). Most important, though, is the atmosphere at the facility. The best way to get a feel for this is to have some short conversations with some customers about their experiences there.

THE ROLES OF VARIOUS TYPES OF HEALTH AGENCIES IN PROVIDING HEALTH INFORMATION

Various types of health agencies have an important role in providing health information to the public. The nature of the information may be very specific or very general, depending on the organization.

American Cancer Society (www.cancer.org) – Provides the public with accurate, up-to-date information on cancer. The Society provides information on all aspects of cancer through a toll-free information line, web site, and a variety of published materials.

American Medical Association (www.ama-assn.org) – The American Medical Association's (AMA) mission is "to promote the art and science of medicine and the betterment of public health." They strive to accomplish this mission by working to become an essential part of the professional lives of physicians. As such, they are an important source of information for medical professionals.

Centers for Disease Control and Prevention (www.cdc.gov) – The Centers for Disease Control and Prevention (CDC) is one of the 13 major operating components of the Department of Health and Human Services (HHS – a United States government agency). They direct a range of health marketing activities aimed at promoting awareness of health issues and healthy habit-forming actions.

In addition to national organizations, local clinics and prevention centers are excellent sources of information that are often very pro-active in their approaches, running community campaigns to raise awareness of relevant health issues and best practices. Local clinics and prevention centers are often the best starting point in a search for information, as they tend to be well connected within the health community, and will be able to refer the individual to a qualified information source if they are not able to provide the information themselves.

SKILL 11.3　Analyzing cost, accessibility, and availability issues related to health-care services (e.g., immunizations, family planning)

HEALTH CARE

There is a variety of health care providers, agencies, and organizations involved with the maintenance of student health. On site, the school nurse assists ill or injured students, maintains health records, and performs health screenings. School nurses also assist students who have long-term illnesses such as diabetes, asthma, epilepsy, or heart conditions. Most schools maintain relationships with other outside health care agencies in order to offer more extensive health care services to students. These community partnerships offer students services such as vaccinations, physical examinations and screenings, eye care, treatment of minor injuries and ailments, dental treatment, and psychological therapy. These community partnerships may include relationships with the following types of health care professionals: physicians, psychiatrists, optometrists, dentists, nurses, audiologists, occupational therapists, physical therapists, dieticians, respiratory therapists, and speech pathologists.

Physicians are health care professionals licensed to practice medicine. A physician may choose to specialize in a specific area of medicine or to work in primary care. A psychiatrist is a physician who specializes in the care of psychological disorders. Optometrists are health care practitioners who conduct eye examinations and prescribe corrective lenses. Dentists are health care professionals who provide care of the teeth. They may either work in general practice or specialize in areas such as orthodontics (correction of abnormalities of the teeth). Nurses are allied health care professionals who provide medical care under the supervision of a medical doctor. Audiologists conduct screenings to detect hearing problems. An occupational therapist helps people with disabilities to learn skills needed for activities of daily living. They also help people who have sustained injuries regain their fine motor skills. Physical therapists are allied health care professionals who help people with disabilities and injuries regain their gross motor skills. Dieticians provide counseling regarding nutrition and perform meal planning. Respiratory therapists specialize in identification and treatment of breathing disorders. Speech pathologists help people with speech problems.

There are also various agencies and organizations involved in maintaining the well-being of students. The state and local health departments provide a wide range of services such as services for children with disabilities, chronic disease control, communicable disease control, mental health programs, consumer safety, and health education. The state department of human services investigates reports of child abuse or neglect. The police department prevents crime and captures offenders. Police also work with schools to provide violence and substance abuse prevention programs. Firefighters extinguish fires, check for fire hazards, install smoke detectors, check fire alarms, and give presentations on fire safety. The National Health Information Center is a federal agency that provides references for trustworthy health information.

SKILL 11.4 Recognizing issues related to abuse, eating disorders, sexually transmitted diseases, teen pregnancy, violence, and suicide and their effects on community health

o   *See also Skills 3.2, 7.1, 5.1, and 5.3 (Suicide, Violence, STD's, and Teen Pregnancy, respectively)*

DEPRESSION AND SUICIDE RISK FACTORS

Depression – The most common mental health problem among adults also affects up to 5% of American children. Symptoms of depression in children include withdrawal from friends or activities, loss of interest in activities, frequent sadness and crying, low energy, increased irritability, poor concentration, and frequent complaints of physical illnesses such as stomachaches and headaches. Possible treatments include counseling and antidepressant medication.

Depression (clinical depression or major depressive disorder) is a state of intense sadness, melancholia, or despair that disrupts the social and/or professional function of the individual. While we often refer to a regular feeling of sadness as "feeling depressed", it is not the same thing as clinical depression. Depression is a clinically diagnosed condition, and is much more severe than normal depressed feelings.

Suicide is particularly troubling problem. Adolescent suicide is always devastating to families and communities. The main cause of adolescent suicide is mental disease, such as depression or anxiety. When untreated, such disorders can cause intense feelings of hopelessness and despair that can lead to suicide attempts. Suicides can tear families apart, often leaving behind feelings of guilt among friends and family members. The best means of suicide prevention is close monitoring of changing behaviors in adolescents. Parents, friends, and family members should watch for and never ignore signs of depression, withdrawal from friends and activities, talk of suicide, and signs of despair and hopelessness. Proper counseling, medication, and care from mental health professionals can often prevent suicide.

Risk factors relating to suicide include previous suicide attempts or a family history of suicide, history of mental disorders (particularly depression), a personal history of alcohol or substance abuse, a family history of child abuse, feelings of hopelessness, impulsive or aggressive tendencies, barriers to accessing mental health treatment, loss (can include relational, social, professional or financial), physical illness, easy access to means for suicide, unwillingness to seek help because of the stigma attached to mental health disorders, local epidemics of suicide (which can serve as a mental trigger to see suicide as a possible course of action), and feelings of isolation or being cut off from other people.

Suicide prevention strategies should help teachers and counselors identify the broad spectrum of at-risk students, and ensure that qualified school staff (e.g. counselors) is available to help identified students. Teachers and counselors should seek to diminish predisposing conditions (e.g., attempt to make the school social environment more inclusive, intervene with students displaying risk factors in a timely fashion). Good suicide prevention strategies will also focus on developing coping skills among students. Schools can do this, for example, by offering drama classes focusing on common teen problems, or providing cards students can carry that list coping skills and peer support hotlines.

SKILL 11.5 Demonstrating knowledge of the influence of culture, media, environment, technology, and other factors on community health

THE SOURCES AND POTENTIAL HEALTH EFFECTS OF VARIOUS ENVIRONMENTAL FACTORS AND METHODS FOR MINIMIZING OR COPING WITH HEALTH RISKS IN THE ENVIRONMENT

Environmental health demonstrates concern about environmental issues. Examples of environmental issues include outdoor air pollution, indoor air pollution, noise pollution, food-borne bacteria and viruses, water contamination, radiation exposure, disposal of hazardous wastes, and recycling.

Air pollution is a primary environmental health hazard. Various air pollutants are highly dangerous. Examples of air pollutants include motor vehicle emissions such as carbon monoxide, sulfur oxide, nitrogen oxide, hydrocarbons, and airborne lead. The Clean Air Act of 1979 reduced some motor vehicle emissions; however, the levels remain dangerously high due to large numbers of vehicles on the road, long commutes, and oversized vehicles. Carpooling and the use of smaller vehicles could significantly decrease the amount of motor vehicle emissions.

Another type of pollution is indoor air pollution. The most dangerous types of indoor pollution are tobacco smoke, carbon monoxide, asbestos, radon, and lead. To prevent indoor air pollution, avoid tobacco smoking indoors and ensure that indoor areas have adequate ventilation with fresh outdoor air. Remove the sources of any pollutants. Keep appliances and heating systems in good condition and follow the regular maintenance schedule. Homes should have at least one carbon monoxide detector located near the sleeping area. Check homes for asbestos, lead, and radon. When detected, safely remove them.

Noise is an additional environmental concern. To protect the ears, keep headphones at a low level, sit at a safe distance from the speakers at concerts, and wear earplugs when exposed to loud sounds.

Another major environmental hazard is water pollution. Water pollution can cause dysentery (a severe intestinal infection), increases in hypertension (due to increased sodium content), and chemical poisoning (such as mercury poisoning). The Safe Water Drinking Act passed in 1974 requires water treatment facilities to notify consumers when they violate safe drinking water requirements; however, this regulation is not strictly enforced. To ensure safe drinking water, consumers should not assume that their facility is following the regulations. They should contact their individual facility to determine the contaminant levels in their drinking water. Additionally, consumers should avoid dumping garbage or chemicals in lakes, rivers, on the ground, or down the drain. Instead, take chemicals to a hazardous waste disposal center. Finally, everyone should practice water conservation. Methods of water conservation include installing a low-flow showerhead, running the dishwasher and washing machine only when completely full, turning off the water while brushing teeth and washing hands, taking quick showers, and watering the lawn at the coolest time of the day.

Radiation exposure is also an environmental concern. Application of a 30 SPF sunscreen every hour and the use of ultraviolet-ray-blocking sunglasses can minimize the effects of ultraviolet radiation exposure.

One final environmental concern is the proper disposal of hazardous wastes. Consumers should always read and follow label information regarding the proper disposal of household products. Recycling is the process of breaking down products to their fundamental elements for use in another product. Recycling can help reduce air, water, and soil contaminants. Consumers should buy recycled products and recycle their own household materials. Additionally, consumers should avoid one-use products, especially disposable products made of plastic, paper, and foam.

TRENDS IN ADVERTISING AND MARKETING

Current trends in media advertising and marketing practices related to fitness, recreational, and sports products and programs will typically display happy and fit individuals participating in the activity or making use of the advertised product. This trend has positive and negative ramifications for the work of physical educators.

On the positive side, the media advertising and marketing trend paints physical activity in a very positive light (as it should). The exposure that students have to the media today makes this a very helpful reinforcement of the messages that physical education professionals work to promote in the classroom and school gymnasium. On the negative side, these trends ignore the reality that the current national level of fitness is poor, and obesity and heart disease are on the rise.

Students and the public often have commonly held misconceptions about exercise and diet. To promote better understanding of health concepts and eliminate misconceptions and faulty practices, physical education instructors must teach the fundamentals of exercise and diet. Instructors must also encourage students to rely on their own knowledge and learning in evaluating health claims, rather than relying on advertising or the media. We will consider common misconceptions related to two important areas of health, diet plans and exercise.

IDENTIFY EXERCISE MYTHS AND GIMMICKS

Exercise myths and gimmicks include:

- drinking beer/alcoholic beverages is a good way to replenish loss of body fluids after exercising,

- women should not exercise while menstruating or pregnant,

- physically fit people will not die from heart disease,

- you cannot be too flexible,

- spot reduction is effective,

- children are naturally active and do not need to exercise,

- muscle will turn into fat with the cessation of exercising,

- fat can turn into muscle,

- women will develop large muscles by weight training, you should exercise while sick regardless how ill you are,

- cardiac hypertrophy developed by exercising is harmful to health,

- exercise increases the appetite,

- exercise gets rid of sagging skin and wrinkles,

- yoga is a good way to develop fitness;

EFFECTS OF MEDIA AND ADVERTISING ON SELF-CONCEPT

Media-based expectations influence the development of self-concept by setting media-based role models as the benchmarks against which students will measure their traits. Self-concept is a set of statements describing the child's own cognitive, physical, emotional, and social self-assessment. These statements will usually tend to be fairly objective ("good at baseball" or "has red hair"), media-based expectations can change the statements to be measurements against role models ("athletic like this actor" or "tall like that pop star"). The media historically has had a stronger effect on female adolescents than male, particularly in regard to body weight. This is reflected in the increasing rates of bulimia and anorexia in the United States among our youth.

TECHNOLOGY AND HEALTH INFORMATION

The technology market is rapidly changing. Consumers are progressively turning to technology for a healthier life. Consumer-focused healthcare information technology helps patients handle the significant demands of healthcare management.

Healthcare information technology is a term describing the broad digital resources that are available to promote community health and proper health care for consumers. Healthcare information technology empowers patients to direct their healthcare and to advocate for themselves and their families as they use health care services. Healthcare information technology enables consumers, patients, and informal caregivers to gather facts, make choices, communicate with healthcare providers, control chronic disease, and participate in other health-related activities. Consumers should take caution when reviewing healthcare information on the internet, as much information is invalid. Consumers need to be educated in regards to website evaluation before using information from the internet in making healthcare decisions.

Healthcare information technology functions in numerous ways. The functions include providing general health information, supporting behavior change, providing tools to self-manage health, providing access to online groups, providing decision-making assistance, aiding in disease control, and providing access to healthcare tools. Information technology has the power to bring patients into full partnership with their healthcare providers. Specifically, instead of waiting for a return phone call, patients can simply e-mail the physician regarding his or her non-urgent condition. Healthcare providers can then respond to patient e-mails.

Many healthcare facilities are also moving towards complying with the executive order mandating electronic personal healthcare records. At some point in the near future, all healthcare facilities will link personal healthcare records. Consumers can also utilize computerized re-ordering systems for prescription refills. Many pharmacies and physicians are also moving towards electronic prescriptions. The increasingly widespread use of electronic personal healthcare records and computerized prescriptions will decrease the number of medical errors.

SKILL 11.6 Identifying legislation, agencies, and policies (e.g., those related to smoking in public places, seat belts, helmets) that support the community, protect the public, and promote health-related practices

Part of the role of government is to support the community, protect the public, and promote health-related practices. Government accomplishes these tasks by way of legislation, agencies, and policies. Examples include, legislation forbidding smoking in public places, policies requiring individuals to wear seat belts while riding in a motorized vehicle, and policies requiring individuals to wear helmets while operating motorcycles and bicycles. The helmet policy however has within the last few years been eliminated in many of the states throughout the country. For example Florida and California do not require helmet use when riding a motorcycle. Unfortunately since the passing of this law, the death rate has increased dramatically in motorcycle accidents in the majority of states without the requirement law. These legislations on the pro safety and prevention side, are all meant to prevent individuals from indulging in self-destructive behavior, which may be hazardous to others as well. Riding without a helmet is potentially harmful to oneself, and smoking and riding in cars without seat belts is harmful both to the individual and those nearby (second-hand smoke is a proven danger and individuals not wearing a seat belt may be flung at others in or out of the vehicle during a collision).

TEST II.   PHYSICAL EDUCATION

SUBAREA IV.   MOTOR LEARNING, MOTOR DEVELOPMENT AND MOVEMENT CONCEPTS

COMPETENCY 12.0   UNDERSTAND PRINCIPLES OF MOTOR DEVELOPMENT AND MOTOR LEARNING

SKILL 12.1 Recognizing principles, stages, sequences, and characteristics of motor development and motor learning

Motor development is defined as how spontaneous actions within the structured central nervous system, environmental and social fields assemble temporary linkings of muscle groups to do different and sequential kinds of work. Although the sequence of motor development is fairly uniform across children, differences still may exist individually. A baby may develop slowly in one stage but then "catch up" in the next. Concern arises if a child motor development is delayed in many motor skill areas, not just one.

Listed below are the stages, sequences and characteristics of motor development and motor learning and the general ages each stage occurs:

1. Newborn to 2 months: while laying on the stomach, an infant pushes up on arms and lifts and holds head up
2. 2 to 6 months: Uses hands to support self in sitting, roles from back to tummy, while standing with support, accepts entire weight with legs
3. 7 to 8 months: Sits and reaches for toys without falling, moves from tummy or back into sitting position, creeps on hands and knees with alternate arm and leg movement (crawling)
4. 9 to 11 months: Pulls to stand and cruises along furniture, stands alone and takes several independent steps
5. 12 months on: Walks independently and seldom falls, squats to pick up toy(s)

Age appropriate specific motor skills development:

- By age 3, walking is automatic
- By age 4, the child has mostly achieved an adult style of walking
- By age 4-5, a child can run, stop and turn
- By age 5-6, a child's running is in the style of an adult running
- Between ages 3 and 6, a child should be able to climb using ladders
- By age 6, children can hop and jump longer than before distances

After age six, it becomes increasingly more difficult to describe changes and differences in motor skills among children. Changes are usually to fine motor skills only and are more subtle. By age nine, eye-hand coordination normally has developed to a good point and growth continues on, but slowly from this point. The motor skills that have been achieved are stabilized and perfected.

At the onset of puberty, motor skills of faster running, jumping higher, throwing further and balancing and coordination increase. Of course all of these skills are dependent on body size, weight, age and strength.

SKILL 12.2 Demonstrating knowledge of the impact of cognitive, social, emotional, environmental, and health factors on motor development and learning and of how physical and developmental changes affect motor performance

O   *See also Skill 1.3*

RELATIONSHIP OF MOTOR DEVELOPMENT TO PHYSICAL, COGNITIVE, PSYCHOSOCIAL, AND EMOTIONAL DEVELOPMENT

Instructors should place students in rich learning situations, regardless of previous experience or personal factors, which provide plenty of positive opportunities to participate in physical activity. For example, prior to playing a game of softball, have students practice throwing by tossing the ball to themselves, progress to the underhand toss, and later to the overhand toss.

Studies show that physical activity leads to improved motor development in children. Physical activity also enables various other progressions that shape the mind and personality of an individual. Such developments, which are the result of physical activity, include cognitive, psychosocial, and emotional growth.

Very often, we ignore the close relationship shared by motor development and the other aspects of development. Motor development, which starts with the proper nutrition, deeply affects the other aspects of development in an individual. Children acquire a vast range of motor development skills such as grasping, crawling, walking, running, and even speaking during the early stages of their lives. Gradually, such motor skills further develop leading to participation in sport and play activities that promote confidence in children and allow them to develop responsibility, deep emotions, and social etiquette. Through participation in sports, children learn to cooperate and develop competitive skills that will aid them in adulthood.

Studies reveal that the different types of play in childhood link motor development with the other aspects of development. Different kinds of play or physical activity such as cognitive play, social play, physical play, and emotional play, help in the overall development of a child.

Simple motor skills such as repeatedly hitting the ground with a shovel or building sand castles help in developing thinking and cognitive skills. Social play helps children to play with their peers cooperatively, to develop their motor skills, and to develop a sense of social togetherness. Motor activities greatly influence physical development as well. They help in providing the foundation for a normal and healthy physical education program suitable for all children. Research also shows that free play among peers leads to significant cognitive developments (such as improvement of reasoning abilities).

The manner in which children hop, jump, skip, run, climb, and play greatly facilitates their motor and physical development and helps to build other aspects of their personality. Children accomplish this development through their constant interaction with surrounding elements, environments, and persons.

Thus, motor skill development, which encompasses all motor movements by children, is strongly related to the physical, social, and emotional development of children.

SKILL 12.3   Recognizing motor-learning concepts, such as practice, feedback, retention, transfer of learning, observational learning, and motor skill analysis

In addition to a thorough knowledge of the motor development process, physical education instructors must understand the principles of learning and information transfer to facilitate student progress. Important concepts include practice, feedback, observational learning, and self-assessment.

PRACTICE

Frequent, structured practice of motor skills enhances skill development in children. Without practice and instruction, natural ability and talent dictates the extent of motor skill development.

FEEDBACK

Physical education instructors generally use two types of feedback, descriptive (general) and prescriptive (specific). Descriptive or general feedback is broad and comprehensive when given to students in regard to a motor skills performance. Examples of this type of feedback would be phrases such as "good job", "well done", "way to go" or "nice try." This type of instructor feedback is socially reinforcing and offers the student encouragement, however it does not give the student any information that might help them improve whatever skill they may be attempting nor does it relay to the student exactly what is good or not good.

Prescriptive or specific feedback is considered to be more helpful in addressing and improving student's motor skills. Examples of this type of feedback are phrases such as "bend your knees" (to a tennis player), "keep your left arm straight" (to a golfer hitting a drive) or "don't look at the ball while dribbling it".

This type of feedback gives the student exact, tangible information for them to work on in the next go round of this motor skill activity. As far as the quickest and most effective type of feedback to give to students for motor skills improvement, definitely prescriptive feedback is the better choice for instructors.

There are several important feedback tools with which physical education instructors should be familiar. First, videotape is an invaluable feedback tool. Videotaping a student performing a motor skill allows the student to view, first-hand his or her own performance and recognize errors that are not visible from the performer's perspective. Second, kinesthetic feedback is the physical guidance of a student through a motor skill by an instructor. For example, an instructor might guide a student's arms through the process of swinging a baseball bat. Kinesthetic feedback is particularly effective when teaching young children. Finally, instructors can use verbal and nonverbal cues in teaching sport skills and strategy. For example, "follow through" is a common phrase used by tennis coaches in instructing students. Conversely, if the instructor swings the racket the correct way to demonstrate a proper follow through, he uses a nonverbal cue.

SELF-ASSESSMENT

Self-assessment is a powerful tool in motor skill development. Requiring students to assess their own skills and abilities encourages students to reflect upon their current skill level and take control of the development process.

OBSERVATIONAL LEARNING

Many physical education instructors believe that observational learning is the most effective method of learning motor skills. Visual observation of proper skill performance by an instructor or peer is generally more effective in promoting skill development than verbal instructions.

ERRORS IN SKILL PERFORMANCE

Because performing a skill has several components, determining why a participant is performing poorly may be difficult. Instructors may have to assess several components of a skill to determine the root cause of poor performance and appropriately correct errors. **An instructor should have the ability to identify performance errors by observing a student's mechanical principles of motion during the performance of a skill. Process assessment** is a subjective, observational approach to identifying errors in the form, style, or mechanics of a skill.

APPROPRIATE OBJECTIVE MEASUREMENTS OF FUNDAMENTAL SKILLS

Instructors should use **product assessments**, quantitative measures of a movement's end result, to evaluate objectively fundamental skills. Quantitative measures of product assessments refers to how far, how fast, how high or how man in reference to a skill.

A **criterion-referenced test** (superior to a standardized test) or a **standardized norm-referenced test** can provide valid and reliable data for objectively measuring fundamental skills.

SKILL ASSESSMENT INFORMATION USED TO CORRECT ERRORS IN SKILL PERFORMANCE

Instructors can use criterion-referenced standards to diagnose weaknesses and correct errors in skill performance because such performance standards define appropriate levels of achievement. However, instructors can also use biomechanical instructional objectives. The following list describes the skill assessment criteria in several representative activities:

- Archery - measuring accuracy in shooting a standardized target from a specified place.

- Bowling - calculating the bowling average attained under standardized conditions.

- Golf - the score after several rounds.

- Swimming - counting the number of breaststrokes needed to swim 25 yards.

After assessing student skill performance, the instructor should design drills or tasks that will develop the weakest component of the student's performance. For example, an instructor notices that a group of students attempting to shoot basketball free throw shots cannot get the ball to the basket because they do not use their legs to add power to the shot. The instructor should use this observation to construct drills that encourage leg use and develop strength.

SKILL 12.4 Applying knowledge of developmentally appropriate practice opportunities that promote acquisition of motor skills

Motor-development learning theories that pertain to a general skill, activity, or age level are important and necessary teacher background information for effective lesson planning. Motor-skill learning is unique to each individual but does follow a general sequential skill pattern, starting with general gross motor movements and ending with specific or fine motor skills. Teachers must begin instruction at a level where all children are successful and proceed through the activity to the point where frustration for the majority is hindering performance.

Students must learn the fundamentals of a skill, or subsequent learning of more advanced skills becomes extremely difficult. Instructors must spend enough time on beginning skills so they become second nature. Teaching in small groups with enough equipment for everyone is essential. Practice sessions that are too long or too demanding can cause physical and/or mental burnout. Teaching skills over a longer period of time, but with slightly different approaches, helps keep students' attentive and involved as they internalize the skill. The instructor can then teach more difficult skills while continuing to review the basics. If the skill is challenging for most students, allow plenty of practice time so they retain it due to learning in depth before having to use it in a game situation.

Visualizing and breaking the skill down mentally is another way to enhance the learning of motor movements. Instructors can teach students to "picture" the steps involved and see themselves executing the skill. An example is teaching dribbling in basketball. Start teaching the skill with a demonstration of the steps involved in dribbling. Starting with the first skill, introduce key language terms and have students visualize themselves performing the skill. A sample-progression lesson plan to teach dribbling could begin with students practicing while standing still. Next, add movement while dribbling. Finally, introduce how to control dribbling while being guarded by another student.

KNOWLEDGE OF ACTIVITIES FOR BODY MANAGEMENT SKILL DEVELOPMENT

Sequential development and activities for locomotor skills acquisition

Sequential Development = crawl, creep, walk, run, jump, hop, gallop, slide, leap, skip, step-hop.

- **Activities to develop walking skills** include walking slower and faster in place; walking forward, backward, and sideways with slower and faster paces in straight, curving, and zigzag pathways with various lengths of steps; pausing between steps; and changing the height of the body.

- **Activities to develop running skills** include having students pretend they are playing basketball, trying to score a touchdown, trying to catch a bus, finishing a lengthy race, or running on a hot surface.

- **Activities to develop jumping skills** include alternating jumping with feet together and feet apart, taking off and landing on the balls of the feet, clicking the heels together while airborne, and landing with a foot forward and a foot backward.

- **Activities to develop galloping skills** include having students play a game of Fox and Hound, with the lead foot representing the fox and the back foot the hound trying to catch the fox (alternate the lead foot).

- **Activities to develop sliding skills** include having students hold hands in a circle and sliding in one direction, then sliding in the other direction.

- **Activities to develop hopping skills** include having students hop all the way around a hoop and hopping in and out of a hoop reversing direction. Students can also place ropes in straight lines and hop side-to-side over the rope from one end to the other and change (reverse) the direction.

- **Activities to develop skipping skills** include having students combine walking and hopping activities leading up to skipping.

- **Activities to develop step-hopping skills** include having students practice stepping and hopping activities while clapping hands to an uneven beat.

Sequential development and activities for nonlocomotor skill acquisition

Sequential Development = stretch, bend, sit, shake, turn, rock and sway, swing, twist, dodge, and fall.

- **Activities to develop stretching** include lying on the back and stomach and stretching as far as possible; stretching as though one is reaching for a star, picking fruit off a tree, climbing a ladder, shooting a basketball, or placing an item on a high self; waking and yawning.

- **Activities to develop bending** include touching knees and toes then straightening the entire body and straightening the body halfway; bending as though picking up a coin, tying shoes, picking flowers/vegetables, and petting animals of different sizes.

- **Activities to develop sitting** include practicing sitting from standing, kneeling, and lying positions without the use of hands.

- **Activities to develop falling skills** include first collapsing in one's own space and then pretending to fall like bowling pins, raindrops, snowflakes, a rag doll, or Humpty Dumpty.

MANIPULATIVE SKILL DEVELOPMENT

Sequential Development = striking, throwing, kicking, ball rolling, volleying, bouncing, catching, and trapping.

- **Activities to develop striking** begin with the striking of stationary objects by a participant in a stationary position. Next, the person remains still while trying to strike a moving object. Then, both the object and the participant are in motion as the participant attempts to strike the moving object.

- **Activities to develop throwing** include throwing yarn/foam balls against a wall, then at a big target, and finally at targets decreasing in size.

- **Activities to develop kicking** include alternating feet to kick balloons/beach balls, then kicking them under and over ropes. Change the type of ball as proficiency develops.

- **Activities to develop ball rolling** include rolling different size balls to a wall, then to targets decreasing in size.

- **Activities to develop volleying** include using a large balloon and, first, hitting it with both hands, then one hand (alternating hands), and then using different parts of the body. Change the object as students progress (balloon, to beach ball, to foam ball, etc.)

- **Activities to develop bouncing** include starting with large balls and, first, using both hands to bounce and then using one hand (alternate hands).

- **Activities to develop catching** include using various objects (balloons, beanbags, balls, etc.) to catch and, first, catching the object the participant has thrown him/herself, then catching objects someone else threw, and finally increasing the distance between the catcher and the thrower.

- **Activities to develop trapping** include trapping slow and fast rolling balls; trapping balls (or other objects such as beanbags) that are lightly thrown at waist, chest, and stomach levels; trapping different size balls.

RHYTHMIC SKILL DEVELOPMENT

Dancing is an excellent activity for the development of rhythmic skills. In addition, any activity that involves moving the body to music can promote rhythmic skill development.

Through continued experience, he or she will become a skillful, seasoned dancer whose technique and ability will transcend any form of dance.

COMBINATION AND INTEGRATION OF MOTOR SKILLS

Locomotor skills are movements that take an individual from one place to another. Walking and running are the simplest examples of locomotor skills. Skipping, jumping, leaping, hopping, and sliding are other locomotor skills that physical educators teach their students.

Trainers adopt various strategies to incorporate the locomotor, nonlocomotor, and object control skills into their workout schedule. These skills are very effective in making students stronger and healthier.

Initially, instructors try to combine those locomotor skills into their training schedule in an easy-to-follow manner. Combining running and sliding or running and jumping will play a huge part in making children understand the fundamentals of locomotor skills.

Once they become familiar with the procedure, physical educators can show students how to balance and transfer weight through the use various locomotor skills. However, the teacher should demonstrate how to control locomotor movements at proper speeds and forces. Shot put, tumbling, and give-and-go are some examples of how to teach students the nuances of locomotor skills.

We can apply the same strategies to nonlocomotor skill instruction. First, the students should learn the basics of every skill from simple nonlocomotive movements such as 360-degree turns and lifting weights, to complex movements like tug-of-war and scissors kicks. It is important for the instructor to maintain a smooth transition. This makes comprehension as unproblematic as possible.
Locomotor and nonlocomotor skills make children agile and physically fit. It is the job of a physical educator to make learning and practicing the skills more enjoyable and entertaining.

Combinations of Object Control Skills

Object control skills help students remain fit and agile. These skills also help students to become better performers. Physical educators will often combine a number of object control skills to enhance a child's reflexes.

Catch and throw is an ideal example of integrating such skills. This type of skill requires a high level of concentration and nimbleness. A combination of object control skills is always at the heart of any physical activity.

Object control skills make all the difference in successful athletic performance. An ideal combination of these skills keeps students healthy and satisfied.

Integration Strategies

Physical education instructors should develop innovative strategies to help students learn the nuances of locomotor, nonlocomotor, and object control skills. Physical education instructors should also present these skills in an entertaining manner for students.

If a teacher starts a training schedule with simple activities, they are more likely to keep the students interested. Once students develop interest, teachers should introduce complex activities such as running and catching, pivoting and throwing, and running and jumping.

Finally, traditional sports activities are a perfect venue for the application of combined skills.

Sports and Games

All sports require the application of motor skills in complex forms. For example, the motor skills required to play tennis include running, jumping, turning and many different types of fine motor skills. Successful tennis players are able to combine motor skills. For example, a player often has to strike the ball while running and jumping at the same time. To play any sport at a high level, athletes must master many motor skills and develop the ability to combine those skills to master sport-specific movements.

SPORT SPECIFIC SKILL DEVELOPMENT

It is sometimes important for a physical educator to select, adapt and/or modify sports activities with the express aim of improving students' performance in the activity. This can include promoting the use of combinations of motor skills or providing practice in specific sports skills in game like situations. There are several factors that instructors should consider when modifying activities.

Activities should emphasize discrete elements of the sports skill without detaching the movement from the rest of the activity. Properly educating students about the activities they are performing is important and, of course, the activities themselves should be rewarding and fun.

Emphasizing discrete elements of the sports skill means that if a student needs to improve in a specific aspect of the activity (e.g., they specifically need to improve their throwing ability in baseball), then they should practice that specific element (throwing) rather than the entire sport skill (playing baseball).

That said, students should perform techniques within the context of the activity, and as part of a kinetic chain. For this reason, it is important that students practice the skill in situations that are as close to the main activity as possible. To continue with the baseball example, rather than having two students toss a tennis ball back and forth to improve throwing, they should practice with a baseball and glove.

Cognitive education should always accompany the physical practice of the activity. Students should understand not only what they should and shouldn't be doing (in terms of technique execution), but also why the correct way is biomechanically correct and why the incorrect way is biomechanically incorrect.

This will make it possible for the students to focus better on their weaknesses and to self-monitor their own progress.

Finally, students should understand the connection between their current training activity and the sports skills they are developing. Also of great importance is that the activities are fun. A more fun and rewarding training experience increases student motivation, which leads to better training results.

ADAPTING SELECTED ACTIVITIES

Physical education instructors must be able to adapt and modify activities to meet the needs of students of varying developmental levels, student characteristics and skill levels, and instructional goals. The following is a list of common motor skill activities and adaptations for different purposes.

Walking: adapt distance, distance over time, and number of steps in specified distance; provide handrails for support; change slope for incline walking; and change width of walking pathway.

Stair climbing: change pathway, pace of climbing, and number and height of steps.

Running: change distance over time, use an incline-changing slope (distance over time), and form a maze (distance over time).

Jumping: change distance and height of jump, change distance in a series and from a platform, change participants' arm positions.

Hopping: change distance for one and two hops (using preferred and non-preferred leg) and distance through obstacle course.

Galloping: change number of gallops over distance, change distance covered in number of gallops, and widen pathway.

Skipping: change number of errorless skips, change distance covered in number of skips, change number of skips in distance, and add music for skipping in rhythm.

Leaping: change distance and height of leaps.

Bouncing balls: change size of ball (larger), have participant use two hands, reduce number of dribbles, bounce ball higher, have participant stand stationary and perform bounces one at a time.

Catching: use larger balls and have participant catch balls thrown at chest level from a lower height of release, shorten catching distance, have participant stop and then catch ball (easier than moving and catching).

APPROPRIATE ACTIVITIES AND ADAPTATIONS FOR STUDENTS WITH LIMITATIONS

Appropriate activities are those activities in which handicapped students can successfully participate.

Adaptations include individualized instruction and modified rules, modified environments, and modified tasks. As needs warrant, instructors can move participants to less restrictive environments. Instructors can also initiate periodic assessments to advance a student's placement, review progress, and determine what the least restrictive environment is for each participant (including changing services to produce future optimum progress). However, the most appropriate placement depends on meeting the physical education needs, both educational and social, of the handicapped student.

FUNCTIONAL ADAPTATIONS

Instructors can provide blind students with auditory or tactile clues to help them find objects or to position their bodies in the activity area. Blind students also can learn the patterns of movement by manually mimicking the correct patterns or by verbal instructions.

Deaf students can read lips or learn signing to communicate and understand instructions.

Physically challenged students may have to use crutches to enable them to move.

Asthmatics can play goalie or similar positions requiring less cardio-respiratory demands.

Simplifying rules can accommodate a retarded participant's limited comprehension.

ADAPTING FOR PROBLEMS WITH STRENGTH, ENDURANCE, AND POWER ACTIVITIES

1. Lower basketball goals or nets; increase size of target.

2. Decrease throwing distance between partners, serving distance, and distance between bases.

3. Reduce size or weight of projectiles.

4. Shorten length and/or reduce weight of bat or other striking apparatus.

5. Play games in lying or sitting positions to lower center of gravity.

6. Select a "slow ball" (one that will not get away too fast), deflate ball in case it gets away, or attach a string to the ball for recovery.

7. Reduce playing time and lower number of points to win.

8. Use more frequent rest periods.

9. Rotate often or use frequent substitution when needed.

10. Use mobilization alternatives, such as using scooter boards one inning/period and feet for one inning/period.

ADAPTING FOR BALANCE AND AGILITY PROBLEMS

1. Verify if balance problem is due to medication (you may have to consult physician).

2. Use chairs, tables, or bars to help with stability.

3. Have participants learn to utilize eyes optimally for balance skills.

4. Teach various ways to fall and incorporate dramatics into fall activities.

5. Use carpeted surfaces.

6. Lower center of gravity.

7. Have participant extend arms or provide a lightweight pole.

8. Have participant keep as much of his/her body in contact with the surface.

9. Widen base of support (distance between feet).

10. Increase width of walking parameters.

ADAPTING FOR COORDINATION AND ACCURACY

Throwing Activities: use beanbags, yarn or nerf balls, and/or smaller-sized balls.

Catching and Striking Activities: use larger, softer, and lighter balls; throw balls to mid-line; shorten distance; and reduce speed of balls.

Striking/Kicking Activities: enlarge striking surface, choke up on bats, begin with participant successfully striking stationary objects and then progress to striking with movement, and increase target size.

EXERCISE PHYSIOLOGY ADAPTATIONS

Decrease the amount of weight, amount of reps/sets, pace, and/or distance of exercise; increase the amount of intervals; and combine together any of the previous modifications.

SKILL 12.5 Demonstrating knowledge of appropriate instructional prompts and cues for providing feedback to students about their motor performance

> o   *See also Skill 12.3*

Physical education instructors need to have knowledge of all motor skills involved in the subject areas of their curriculum provided by the state standards. Students need to be given practice opportunities as well as specific feedback in regard to their motor performance in these subject areas.

One of the goals of physical education instructors is to enable the students to understand how a motor skill needs to be performed to be optimal and most effective. The student may not be able to produce or perform the skill to this degree yet, however if they have the knowledge to know what they need to do to get to this goal, then they can evaluate themselves. At this point, instructors can provide opportunities, prompts and cues to assist the students in developing their motor skills. For example the instructors can:

- Team or pair students up and have them evaluate and point out specifics to one another
- Provide a type of checklist that provides photo's or descriptions of how a motor skill should be executed to be optimal
- Videotape the students and then allow them to critique their own performance along with their classmates

COMPETENCY 13.0   **UNDERSTAND MOVEMENT CONCEPTS AND THEIR ROLE IN IMPROVING MOTOR SKILLS**

SKILL 13.1   **Recognizing skill themes (e.g., locomotor, nonlocomotor, manipulative) and ways to promote application of these themes through exploration of movement concepts (e.g., spatial awareness, effort, relationships)**

LOCOMOTOR SKILLS

Locomotor skills move an individual from one point to another.

1. **Crawling** - A form of locomotion where the person moves in a prone position with the body resting on or close to the ground or on the hands and knees.

2. **Creeping** - A slightly more advanced form of locomotion in which the person moves on the hands and knees.

3. **Walking** - with one foot contacting the surface at all times, walking shifts one's weight from one foot to the other while legs swing alternately in front of the body.

4. **Running** - an extension of walking that has a phase where the body is propelled with no base of support (speed is faster, stride is longer, and arms add power).

5. **Jumping** - projectile movements that momentarily suspend the body in midair.

6. **Vaulting** - coordinated movements that allow one to spring over an obstacle.

7. **Leaping** - similar to running, but leaping has greater height, flight, and distance.

8. **Hopping** - using the same foot to take off from a surface and land.

9. **Galloping** - forward or backward advanced elongation of walking combined and coordinated with a leap.

10. **Sliding** - sideward stepping pattern that is uneven, long, or short.

11. **Body Rolling** - moving across a surface by rocking back and forth, by turning over and over, or by shaping the body into a revolving mass.

12. **Climbing** - ascending or descending using the hands and feet with the upper body exerting the most control.

NONLOCOMOTOR SKILLS

Nonlocomotor skills are stability skills where the movement requires little or no movement of one's base of support and does not result in change of position.

1. **Bending** - movement around a joint where two body parts meet.

2. **Dodging** - sharp change of direction from original line of movement such as away from a person or object.

3. **Stretching** - extending/hyper-extending joints to make body parts as straight or as long as possible.

4. **Twisting** - rotating body/body parts around an axis with a stationary base.

5. **Turning** - circular moving the body through space releasing the base of support.

6. **Swinging** - circular/pendular movements of the body/body parts below an axis.

7. **Swaying** - same as swinging but movement is above an axis.

8. **Pushing** - applying force against an object or person to move it away from one's body or to move one's body away from the object or person.

9. **Pulling** - executing force to cause objects/people to move toward one's body.

MANIPULATIVE SKILLS

Manipulative skills use body parts to propel or receive an object, controlling objects primarily with the hands and feet. Two types of manipulative skills are receptive (catch + trap) and propulsive (throw, strike, kick).

1. **Bouncing/Dribbling** - projecting a ball downwards.

2. **Catching** - stopping momentum of an object (for control) using the hands.

3. **Kicking** - striking an object with the foot.

4. **Rolling** - initiating force to an object to instill contact with a surface.

5. **Striking** - giving impetus to an object with the use of the hands or an object.

6. **Throwing** - using one or both arms to project an object into midair away from   the body.

7. **Trapping** - without the use of the hands, receiving and controlling a ball.

RHYTHMIC SKILLS

Rhythmic skills include responding and moving the body in time with the beat, tempo, or pitch of music. To develop rhythmic skills, instructors can ask students to clap their hands or stomp their feet to the beat of the music. Dancing and gymnastics requires high levels of rhythmic competency. As with all physical skills, development of rhythmic skills is a sequential process.

CONCEPT OF BODY AWARENESS APPLIED TO PHYSICAL EDUCATION ACTIVITIES

Body awareness is an individuals understanding of his or her own body parts and their capability of movement.

Instructors can assess body awareness by playing and watching a game of "Simon Says" and asking the students to touch different body parts. You can also instruct students to make their bodies into various shapes, from straight to round, and varying sizes, to fit into different sized spaces.

In addition, you can instruct children to touch one part of their body to another and to use various body parts to stamp their feet, twist their neck, clap their hands, nod their heads, wiggle their noses, snap their fingers, open their mouths, shrug their shoulders, bend their knees, close their eyes, bend their elbows, or wiggle their toes.

CONCEPT OF SPATIAL AWARENESS APPLIED TO PHYSICAL EDUCATION ACTIVITIES

Spatial awareness is the ability to make decisions about an object's positional changes in space (i.e. awareness of three-dimensional space position changes).
Developing spatial awareness requires two sequential phases: 1) identifying the location of objects in relation to one's own body in space, and 2) locating more than one object in relation to each object and independent of one's own body.
Plan activities using different size balls, boxes, or hoops and have children move towards and away; under and over; in front of and behind; and inside, outside, and beside the objects.

CONCEPTS OF SPACE, DIRECTION, AND SPEED RELATED TO MOVEMENT CONCEPTS

Research shows that the concepts of space, direction, and speed are interrelated with movement concepts. Such concepts and their understanding are extremely important for students, as they need to relate movement skills to direction in order to move with confidence and avoid collisions.

A student or player in motion must take the elements of space, direction, speed, and vision into consideration in order to perform and understand a sport. A player must decide how to handle their space as well as numerous other factors that arise on the field.

For a player, the concepts are all interlinked. He has to understand how to maintain or change pathways with speed. This ability allows him to change motion and perform well in space (or the area that the players occupy on the field).

SKILL 13.2   Demonstrating knowledge of how movement concepts are applied in the learning and development of new skills (e.g., using spatial awareness and body relationships in dance, throwing objects using opposition)

- o   See also Skill 13.1

Perceptual-motor development refers to one's ability to receive, interpret, and respond successfully to sensory signals coming from the environment. Because many of the skills acquired in school rely on the child's knowledge of his body and its relationship to the surroundings, good motor development leads directly to perceptual skill development. Development of gross motor skills leads to successful development of fine motor skills, which in turn help with learning, reading, and writing. Adolescents with perceptual-motor coordination problems are at risk for poor school performance, low self-esteem, and inadequate physical activity participation. Without a successful intervention, these adolescents are likely to continue avoiding physical activity and experience frustration and teasing from their peers.

Children with weak perceptual-motor skills may be easily distracted or have difficulty with tasks requiring coordination. They spend much of their energy trying to control their bodies, exhausting them so much that they physically cannot concentrate on a teacher-led lesson. Unfortunately, perceptual-motor coordination problems do not just go away and they don't self-repair.

Practice and maturity are necessary for children to develop greater coordination and spatial awareness. Physical education lessons should emphasize activities that children enjoy doing, are sequential, and require seeing, hearing, and/or touching. Discussing with students the actual steps involved in performing a fundamental skill is a great benefit. Activities and skills that can be broken down and taught in incremental steps include running, dribbling, catching or hitting a ball, making a basket in basketball, and setting a volleyball. Recommended strategies include introducing the skill, practicing in a variety of settings with an assortment of equipment, implementing lead-up games modified to ensure practice of the necessary skills, and incorporating students into an actual game situation.

RHYTHMIC SKILL IMPROVEMENT TECHNIQUES

Instructors can accommodate different learning styles and characteristics by applying techniques like body percussion and the creation of charts and song mappings. These techniques merge different learning styles and senses to help students better grasp the rhythmic-skills content.

Body percussion (i.e. loudly but gently slapping different parts of the body, mostly the outer limbs) is another way of creating a rhythm that students can learn to maintain and copy. A benefit of this technique is that it implements tactile and kinesthetic stimuli into the skill acquisition process, catering to more kinesthetically oriented learners.

Charts and song mapping are both techniques that help children connect with the sounds that correspond to the beats in a rhythm, by writing them out or drawing them visually. This connects with more visually oriented learners.
Simple technology that instructors can use to facilitate rhythmic-skills acquisition includes rhythm-keeping devices like metronomes that students can use as a sensory baseline for the beat of the rhythm that they are learning. More advanced technology includes software that simulates rhythmic activity and asks the student to respond at correct intervals.

USE OF TECHNOLOGY

Physical educators can use various technological tools to analyze student performance, fitness, and performance. Two important and interrelated technological tools are videotape and movement analysis software.

Videotape

Videotaping students participating in skill performance and fitness activities allows students and teachers to analyze technique closely. Instructors can identify and point out errors in form to the students. This visual reinforcement enhances the learning process. In addition, periodic videotaping allows instructors to monitor progress in skill performance and fitness over time.

Movement analysis software

Movement analysis software helps students and instructors analyze movement patterns captured on digital video cameras in great detail. For example, movement analysis software can distill the individual characteristics of a person's gate. Such high detailed analysis allows instructors and students to study individual patterns of movement, individual movement styles, and strategies for peak performance. Movement analysis software helps identify key elements of a movement that need improvement and helps track progress in development, maturation, and error correction.

SKILL 13.3 Distinguishing among similarities and differences in movement skills and motor patterns

Different activities require different motor skills and patterns. Students clearly learn the majority of this through repetition or practice, practice and practice. Our bodies will learn the movements this way and mentally will carry them over into other activities that involve similar type skills and patterns. For example, hitting a forehand in tennis and swinging a baseball bat may seem to have similar motor skills and patterns and on a beginner's level there are a few, however when a player reaches a more advanced level of play, they will learn that the motor skills and patterns involved in each movement have many more differences than similarities. Running is a motor skill that physical, in regard to the human body, is similar from sport to sport, however in a 5k (3.1 miles) a runner may use this skill in a different pattern say than a 220 sprinter.

Students learn to combine movements, to coordinate familiar patterns and movements while developing strength and control from sport to sport. They learn that their bodies are capable of moving in many different patterns and ways and that they can demonstrate whatever motor pattern they need to through a variety of movement skills.

SKILL 13.4 Demonstrating knowledge of movement principles and concepts (e.g., motion, stability, balance, force projection and absorption, buoyancy, rotation, acceleration) and their application to motor skills and movement tasks

Instructors can promote student understanding and application of movement concepts and biomechanical principles by using techniques that showcase a particular movement or action along with strategies for improvement. Sample applications of movement concepts and biomechanical principles include moving in pathways or at different levels, and adjusting throwing technique using principles of rotation and force application.

Moving in pathways means that students execute the training motions slowly, ensuring that the path of movement remains along the most efficient possible track (both to cut down wasted movement and to use muscles most effectively).

Adjusting throwing technique using principles of rotation and force application involves analyzing the action of the throw and focusing on discrete elements of the action, one at a time, that the student can improve by applying biomechanical processes (in terms of angle of rotation and muscular force application). Instructors can facilitate this process by recording student movements with a video camera and reviewing the film in slow motion with student. Ideally, instructors should ask the student to identify the areas that he or she believes need improvement before the instructor begins to make suggestions.

CONCEPT OF EFFORT QUALITIES APPLIED TO PHYSICAL EDUCATION

Effort qualities are the qualities of movement that apply the mechanical principles of balance, time, and force).

Balance - activities for balance include having children move on their hands and feet, lean, move on lines, and balance and hold shapes while moving.

Time - activities using the concept of time can include having children move as fast as they can and as slow as they can in specified, timed movement patterns.

Force - activities using the concept of force can include having students use their bodies to produce enough force to move them through space. They can also paddle balls against walls and jump over objects of various heights.

CONCEPTS OF EQUILIBRIUM AND CENTER OF GRAVITY APPLIED TO MOVEMENT

When body segments move independently, body mass redistributes, changing the location of the body's center of gravity. Segments also move to change the body's base of support from one moment to the next to cope with imminent loss of balance.

The entire center of gravity of the body shifts in the same direction of movement of the body's segments. As long as the center of gravity remains over the base of support, the body will remain in a state of equilibrium. The more the center of gravity is situated over the base, the greater the stability. A wider base of support and/or a lower center of gravity enhances stability. To be effective, the base of support must widen in the direction of the force produced or opposed by the body. Shifting weight in the direction of the force in conjunction with widening the base of support further enhances stability.

Constant interaction of forces that move the body in the elected direction results in dynamic balance. The smooth transition of the center of gravity changing from one base of support to the next produces speed.

CONCEPT OF FORCE APPLIED TO MOVEMENT

Force is any influence that can change the state of motion of an object; we must consider the objective of movement.

Magnitude of Force – force must overcome the inertia of the object and any other resisting forces for movement to occur.

For linear movement, force applied close to the center of gravity requires a smaller magnitude of force to move the object than does force applied farther from the center of gravity.

For rotational movement, force applied farther from the center of gravity requires a smaller magnitude of force to rotate the object than does force applied closer to the center of gravity.

For objects with a fixed point, force applied anywhere other than through the point of fixation results in object rotation.

Energy – the capacity to do work. (The more energy a body has the greater the force with which it can move something [or change its shape] and/or the farther it can move it).

Movement (mechanical energy) has two types:

1. Potential energy (energy possessed by virtue of position, absolute location in space or change in shape).

> **A. Gravitational potential energy** - potential energy of an object that is in a position where gravity can act on it.

> **B. Elastic (strain) potential energy** - energy potential of an object to do work while recoiling (or reforming) after stretching, compressing, or twisting.

2. Kinetic energy (energy possessed by virtue of motion that increases with speed).

Force Absorption - maintaining equilibrium while receiving a moving object's kinetic energy without sustaining injury or without losing balance while rebounding. The force of impact is dependent on an object's weight and speed. The more abruptly kinetic energy is lost, the more likely injury or rebound occurs. Thus, **absorbing force requires gradually decelerating a moving mass by utilization of smaller forces over a longer period**. Stability is greater when the object receives the force closer to the center of gravity.

Striking resistive surfaces - the force of impact per unit area decreases when the moving object's area of surface making contact increases and the surface area that the object strikes increases.

Striking non-resistive surfaces - the force of impact decreases if the moving object's area of surface making contact decreases because it is more likely to penetrate.

The more time and distance that motion stops for a moving object to strike any surface, the more gradually the surface absorbs the force of impact, and the reaction forces acting upon the moving object decrease.

Equilibrium returns easily when the moving body (striking a resistive surface) aligns the center of gravity more vertically over the base of support.

Angular force against a body decreases when the distance between a contacting object and the body decreases and the contact occurs closer to the center of gravity. Also, widening the base of support in the direction of the moving object increases stability.

CONCEPT OF LEVERAGE APPLIED TO MOVEMENT

First-class lever - the axis is between the points of application of the force and the resistance.

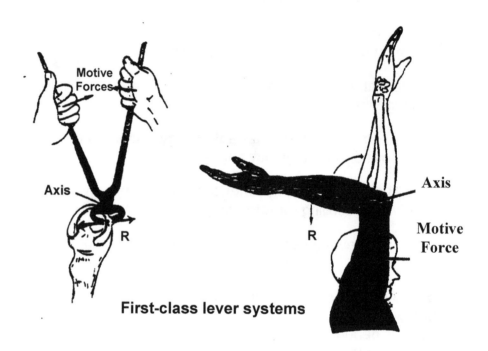

First-class lever systems

Second-class lever - the force arm is longer than the resistance arm (operator applies resistance between the axis and the point of application of force).

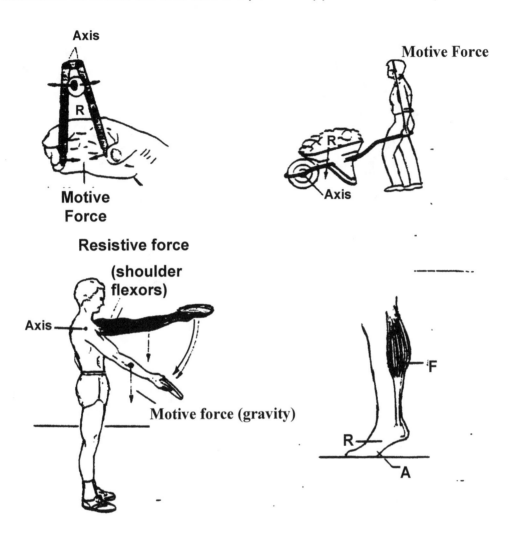

Second-class lever systems

Third-class lever - the force works at a point between the axis and the resistance (resistance arm is always longer than the force arm).

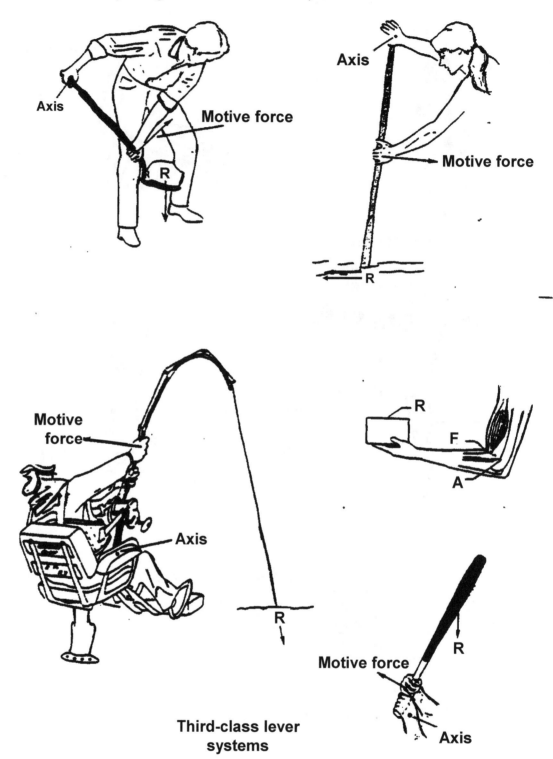

Third-class lever systems

Muscle force is applied where muscles insert on bones.

With a few exceptions, the body consists primarily of third-class levers, with bones functioning as the levers and contracting innervated muscles acting as the fulcrums or by gravity acting on various body masses. As a result, the human body favors speed and range of motion over force.

Because most human body levers are long, their distal ends can move rapidly. Thus, the body is capable of swift, wide movements at the expense of abundant muscle force.

The human body easily performs tasks involving rapid movement with light objects. Very heavy tasks require a device for the body to secure an advantage of force.

Sports instruments increase body levers, thereby increasing the speed of an object's imparting force. However, the use of sports instruments requires more muscle force.

The body's leverage rarely includes only one part of the body (a simple, singular lever). Movement of the body is an outcome of a system of levers operating together. However, levers do function in sequence when the force produced by the system of levers is dependent on the speed at the extremity. Many levers function simultaneously for a heavy task (e.g. pushing).

MECHANICAL PRINCIPLES OF MOTION APPLIED TO PHYSICAL EDUCATION ACTIVITIES

1. **Inertia** - tendency of a body or object to remain in its present state of motion; an object will stay in a prescribed straight path and will move at its given speed unless some force acts to change it.

2. **Projecting objects for vertical distance** - the forces of gravity and air resistance prevent vertically projected objects from continuing at their initial velocities. The downward, resistive force of gravity slows a projectile directed upward until it halts (at the peak of vertical path). At this point, the downward force of gravity becomes an incentive force that increases the speed of the object until it confronts another force (the earth or other external object) that slows the object until it stops. When the object stops ascending and begins to descend, gravity alters the object's direction of motion. Air resistance (of still air) always opposes the object's motion. Therefore, an ascending object's air resistance is downward and a descending object's air resistance is upward. An increase in velocity increases air-drag force that decreases the magnitude of the drag as the object moves upward, slowing in velocity. The magnitude of the drag increases as the object moves faster and faster downward. Moreover, the direction and magnitude of the object's acceleration, due to the force of gravity, are constant while direction and magnitude of changes, due to air resistance, are dependent on the object's speed and direction.

An object travels the highest when projected with the greatest velocity, and the object's weight affects neither gravity's upward deceleration nor its downward acceleration. The object's weight, however, is a factor in calculating the net force acting on the object's vertical movement through the air.

- **Projecting the body for vertical distance** - for these activities (e.g. vertical leaping), the height of reach of the hand from the ground is the significant factor. The following three factors determine the body's reach height: 1) the center of gravity's vertical velocity, 2) the center of gravity's height from the ground at takeoff, and 3) the vertical distance of the fingertips relative to the center of gravity at the peak of the jump.

- **Projecting for vertical distance with a horizontal component** - for these activities (e.g. high jumping), a running approach to the point of takeoff produces some horizontal velocity even with a 100% vertical takeoff.

- **Projecting for horizontal distance** - a body will continue to travel horizontally until an external force, usually the ground, halts it. Gravity stops vertical movement while ground friction eventually stops horizontal velocity, preventing any additional horizontal distance. "Air time" increases when the initial upward vertical velocity component is greater. There is a tradeoff between maximum "air time" (determined by vertical velocity) and maximum horizontal distance (determined by horizontal velocity).

- **Horizontal projections where takeoff and landing heights are equal** - maximum horizontal distance occurs when the projection angle is 45-degrees.

- **Horizontal projections where takeoff and landing heights are uneven** – the height of an object's center of gravity depends on a performer's height and his/her location in relation to the ground upon release or impact of the object. The greater the object's travel time forward, the farther the object's distance before landing. Hence, a taller performer has an automatic advantage over a shorter performer who throws with the same projection velocity. In addition, the greater the difference between takeoff and landing heights, the smaller the optimum angle of release - given equal projection velocities.

Projecting objects for accuracy:

- **Vertical plane targets** - accuracy is easiest when using a trajectory that is perpendicular to the target as it coincides with the target face. As projection distance increases, a more curved parabolic path is required.

- **Horizontal plane targets** - the more vertically the projectile arrives at the target (as close to 90 degrees as possible), the greater the likelihood of successfully hitting the target and preventing the object from rolling or sliding away from the target area.

Projecting the body for accuracy - for moving or positioning the body (or its segments) to achieve an ideal/model performance by body maneuvers, the performer projects his body's center of gravity to an imaginary target point in space.

Projecting objects for accuracy when speed may enhance the performance - the performer must increase the angle of projection for slower projection speeds (must consider participant's height).

- **Acceleration** - the movement response (acceleration) of a system depends not only on the net external force applied, but also depends on the resistance to movement change (inertia).

If an object's acceleration is proportional to the applied force, greater force produces greater acceleration. An object's acceleration is inversely proportional to its mass (the greater the mass, the less the acceleration).

- **Angular acceleration** (rate that an object's angular speed or direction changes) - angular acceleration is great when there is a large change in angular velocity in a short amount of time. A rigid body (or segment) encounters angular acceleration or deceleration only when a net external torque is applied. When torque stops, the body reaches and maintains a new velocity until another torque occurs. Acceleration is always in the direction of the acting torque, and the greater the torque, the greater the angular acceleration.

- **Linear acceleration** (time rate of change in velocity) - an object's magnitude of acceleration is significant if there is a large change of velocity in a small amount of time. When the same velocity changes over a longer period, acceleration is small. Acceleration occurs only when force is applied. When the force stops, the object/body reaches a new and the object/body continues at the new speed until that a force changes that speed or direction. In addition, the direction of acceleration is the same direction as the applied net force. A large force produces a large acceleration. A small force produces a modest acceleration.

- **Zero/Constant Acceleration** (constant velocity) - there is no change in a system's velocity when the object/body moves at a given velocity and encounters equal, opposing forces. Hence, velocity is constant since no force causes acceleration or deceleration.

- **Acceleration caused by gravity** - a falling object/body continues to accelerate at the rate of 9.8 m/sec. (32 ft/sec.) throughout its fall.

- **Radial acceleration (direction change caused by centripetal force)** - centripetal force is aimed along an illusory line (the circular path) at any instant. Therefore, it is the force responsible for change of direction. The bigger the mass, the greater the centripetal force required. A tighter turn magnifies direction change (radial acceleration), so friction must increase to offset the increased acceleration. Maximum friction (centrifugal force) reduces speed. A combination of the variables mass, radius of curvature, speed of travel, and centripetal force cause radial acceleration.

Action/Reaction - every action has an equal and opposite reaction.

- **Linear motion** - the larger the mass, the more it resists motion change initiated by an outside force.

Body segments exert forces against surfaces they contact. These forces and the reaction of the surfaces result in body movement. For example, a runner propels himself forward by exerting a force on the ground (as long as the surface has sufficient friction and resistance to slipping). The force of the contact of the runner's foot with the ground and the equal and opposite reaction of the ground produces movement. A canoe paddler or swimmer exerts a backward force by pushing the water backwards, causing a specific velocity that is dependent on the stroke's force - as well as the equal and opposite force made by the water pushing forward against the canoe paddle or arm moving the canoe or swimmer forward.

Every torque (angular motion) exerted by one body/object on another has another torque equal in magnitude and opposite direction exerted by the second body/object on the first. Changing angular momentum requires a force that is equal and opposite of the change in momentum.

Performing actions in a standing position requires the counter pressure of the ground against the feet for accurate movement of one or more parts of the body.

SKILL 13.5 Analyzing various movement patterns in terms of biomechanical efficiency and effectiveness

We can use movement concepts and biomechanical principles to analyze movement skills by first examining the movement skill in detail (often with the assistance of recording equipment that allows play back in slow motion), and then breaking down the motions involved. For each motion, we should note the angle through which the joints must move and the direction of force that the muscles must apply. We can then check this information against our knowledge of movement concepts and biomechanical principles. Finally, we can modify the motion to ensure that the joints move and the muscles apply force in the most efficient way.

Instructors can facilitate student acquisition and refinement of specific movements and sports skills by applying this same knowledge to the teaching and training process. Instructors should teach students both the correct way to execute the movement and the biomechanical principles that facilitate the movement. In effect, this helps students understand why they should not be perform the movement in ways that are incorrect (because the body cannot perform the movement as effectively in that way). This helps the student self-monitor their own progress, and focus on the elements that need improvement.

Instructors can encourage improvement of body mechanics for safe and efficient movement by giving students an understanding of what the underlying biomechanical principles really are. When students understand the way their bodies work, it is easier for them to modify their movement activities "on the fly" to correspond to more healthy and efficient movement. For example, when lifting a television – something not have covered or practiced in physical education classes – knowledge of correct spinal alignment and weight distribution for lifting purposes can help students deduce the best way to perform the lift.

IDENTIFYING MATURE AND IMMATURE MOTOR PATTERNS

In all physical activity or training, there are certain fundamental movement skills that involve patterns necessary for the development of the body. We define them as the foundation movements or precursor patterns to the more specialized complex skills that are useful in all types of sports, dance, and play.

Fundamental movement skills form an indispensable part of all physical activity and physical education. Such basic movement skills are extremely important for children in their early years. These particular skills include running, stopping, changing direction, starting, hopping, skipping, and rolling.

These fundamental movement skills play an important role in the physical well-being of all growing children and are important for adults as well. These skills create the framework of every physical activity and sport.

Physical education instructors should be able to identify mature and immature motor patterns. For example, when observing an overhand throw, there are certain universal characteristics of immature throwing patterns. These include stepping with the foot on the same side of the body as the throwing arm, using only the elbow to propel the object, and facing the target throughout the throwing process. Conversely, characteristics of a mature overhand throwing pattern include leading with the foot opposite the throwing hand, using the entire body and arm to propel the ball, and starting the throwing motion facing perpendicular to the target.

COMPETENCY 14.0   **UNDERSTAND PRINCIPLES AND ACTIVITIES FOR DEVELOPING LOCOMOTOR, NONLOCOMOTOR, MANIPULATIVE, AND RHYTHMIC MOVEMENT SKILLS**

SKILL 14.1   Identifying critical elements of basic movement patterns (i.e., locomotor, nonlocomotor, manipulative, and rhythmic movement)

o   *See Skill 13.1*

SKILL 14.2   Recognizing locomotor skills (e.g., run, hop), nonlocomotor skills (e.g., twist, sway, static balance, weight transfer), and rhythmic/spatial compositions (e.g., dance movements and techniques)

o   *See Skill 13.1*

SKILL 14.3   Identifying techniques and motor patterns for throwing, catching, dribbling, kicking, and striking skills and for combinations of manipulative skills (e.g., catch and throw)

ANALYSIS OF BASIC MOVEMENT PATTERNS: OVERHAND THROW, UNDERHAND THROW, KICK

Overhand Throw

The overhand throw consists of a sequence of four movements: a stride, hip rotation, trunk rotation, and forward arm movement. The thrower should align his body sideways to the target (with opposite shoulder pointing towards the target). The overhand throw begins with a step or stride with the opposite foot (i.e. left foot for a right-handed thrower). As the stride foot contacts the ground, the pivot foot braces against the ground and provides stability for the subsequent movements. Hip rotation is the natural turning of the hips toward the target. Trunk rotation follows hip rotation. The hips should rotate before the trunk because the stretching of the torso muscles allows for stronger muscle contraction during trunk rotation. Following trunk rotation, the arm moves forward in two phases. In the first phase the elbow is bent. In the second phase, the elbow joint straightens and the thrower releases the ball.

Development of the overhand throwing motion in children occurs in three stages: elementary, mature, and advanced. In the elementary stage, the child throws mainly with the arm and does not incorporate the other body movements. The signature characteristic of this stage is striding with the foot on the same side of the body as the throwing arm (i.e. placing the right foot in front when throwing with the right hand). In the mature stage, the thrower brings the arm backward in preparation for the throw. Use of body rotation is still limited. Children in the advanced stage incorporate all the elements of the overhand throw. The thrower displays an obvious stride and body rotation.

Underhand Throw

The thrower places the object in the dominant hand. When drawing the arm back the triceps straighten the elbow and, depending on the amount of power behind the throw, the shoulder extends or hyperextends using the posterior deltoid, latissimus dorsi, and the teres major. At the time of drawback, the thrower takes a step forward with the leg opposite of the throwing arm. When coming back down, the thrower moves the shoulder muscles (primarily the anterior deltoid) into flexion. When the object in hand moves in front of the body, the thrower releases the ball. The wrist may be firm or slightly flexed. The thrower releases the object shortly after the planting the foot and the biceps muscle contracts, moving the elbow into flexion during follow through.

Kick

In executing a kick, the object needs to be in front of the body and in front of the dominant leg. The kicker steps and plants with the opposite leg while drawing the kicking leg back. During draw back, the hamstring muscle group flexes the knee. When the kicker plants the opposite foot, the hips swing forward for power and the knee moves into extension using the quadriceps muscle group. The contact point is approximately even with the plant foot and a comfortable follow through completes the action.

SKILL 14.4 Recognizing combined or integrated use of locomotor, nonlocomotor, and manipulative skills and motor patterns (e.g., balancing patterns, jump and twist, pivot and throw)

Combinations of motor skills, demonstrations of agility and balance, and dance steps and sequences all involve the same key elements of body awareness (proprioception/kinesthesia) and control. Some specific elements include pivot and throw, and a variety of movement sequences that combine traveling, rolling, balancing, and weight transfer.

Pivot and throw are both skills that grow out of the individual's awareness and control of his body's positioning and weight distribution, both at rest and, especially, in motion. To properly execute this movement sequence (i.e., changing direction and continuing to move, maintaining fluid movement throughout the execution), the actor must efficiently distribute his body weight, and manage his weight distribution properly throughout the execution of the pivot. Poor execution will put the individual off-balance, preventing him from continuing the chain of movement without stumbling.

Movement sequences that combine traveling, rolling, balancing, and weight transfer, as with the pivot and throw skills described earlier, rely on the individual's awareness and control of his body's positioning and weight distribution. In order to travel across a space, execute rolls, balancing techniques, and the requisite weight transfers linked to those actions, the athlete must have a keen sense of where their weight is currently distributed, and how to move it in the desired direction with maximum efficiency.

SKILL 14.5   Selecting appropriate techniques, skills, sequences, equipment, and materials for complex rhythmic, aerobic, and dance activities (e.g., tumbling routines, dance sequences)

   o   *See also Competency 23.0*

GYMNASTIC MOVEMENTS – STUNTS, TUMBLING, APPARATUS WORK, AND FLOOR EXERCISE

Gymnastics is a sport involving the performance of sequences of movements requiring physical strength, flexibility, and kinesthetic awareness (e.g. handsprings, handstands, and forward rolls). Its roots lie in the fitness and beauty practices of ancient Greeks, including skills for mounting and dismounting a horse and circus performance skills. In ancient times the term implied exercise taken by men in a gymnasium, a venue for intellectual and physical education. It is often considered a dangerous sport, as the difficult acrobatic maneuvers often performed on equipment high above the ground puts the athlete at risk of serious injury.

Proper stretching and strength building exercises are necessary for gymnastics. A useful, brief warm-up can consist of push-ups, sit-ups, and flexibility exercises for hamstrings, back, ankles, neck, wrists, and shoulders. An aerial is one example of a stunt (i.e. difficult physical feat) in which the gymnast turns completely over in the air without touching the apparatus with his or her hands. Floor exercise and tumbling can include somersaults, backward and frontward rolls, cartwheels, forward straddle rolls, back tucks, back handsprings, and handstands. Gymnasts perform apparatus work on the vaulting horse, balance beam, and uneven bars. A strong run, dynamism, power, and precision in the rotations are characteristics of an efficient vault. The main characteristics for the beam are a well-developed sense of balance and great power of concentration. The uneven bars demand strength as well as concentration, courage, coordination, precision, and split-second timing.

RHYTHMIC GYMNASTICS AND EDUCATIONAL GYMNASTICS

Rhythmic gymnastics is a sport, which combines dance and gymnastics with the use of balls, hoops, ribbons, ropes, and clubs. Gymnasts perform on a carpet to music either individually or in a group of five. In competition, gymnasts perform leaps, pivots, balances, and other elements to demonstrate flexibility and coordination. The gymnast must completely integrate the apparatus into the routine and perform specific moves with each apparatus. Individual routines last from 1 minute and 15 seconds to 1 minute and 30 seconds, while group routines last from 2 minutes 15 seconds to 2 minutes and 30 seconds. The main difference between rhythmic and artistic gymnastics is that rhythmic gymnasts cannot incorporate acrobatic skill. In fact, judges penalize gymnasts for incorporating acrobatic skill into their routines. However, gymnasts may perform pre-acrobatic elements such as forward and backward shoulder rolls, fish-flops, and tah-dahs. In addition, the new Code of Points permits walkovers and cartwheels. Originality and risk are integral parts of this sport, and no two routines are ever the same.

In educational gymnastics, students learn to use and manage their bodies in safe, efficient and creative ways. Educational gymnastics can utilize certain fixed equipment such as mats, bars, ropes, and boxes and is also know as "body management" because the activities provide opportunities for students to learn to manage their own bodies. Instead of a series of gymnastics stunts, they select, refine and perform the six Basic Movement Patterns of Landings, Locomotions, Statics, Rotations, Swings, and Jumpsprings in a variety of contexts and environments. Emphasis is on challenges and problem solving. Instructors use the Movement Variables of Body, Space, Effort, and Relationships to design movement-learning experiences. Students work individually, in pairs, and in groups to create movement sequences and structures.

Elaborate facilities are not required in this approach. In fact, many good educational gymnastics programs take place out-of-doors in natural settings. While large-scale gymnastics equipment is not essential for providing students with quality movement-learning experiences, such equipment is certainly advantageous. Another advantage of educational gymnastics is that it provides for the development of the upper body. It is much easier and more common to develop strength in the lower body than in the upper body. Many everyday events such as walking and running and jumping enhance lower body strength. Most team games and sports emphasize lower body strength and tend to neglect upper body development. Gymnastics also help to build overall muscular strength and flexibility. There is also equal development of both left and right sides of the body because most gymnastics activities involve simultaneous use of both arms (e.g. rolls, hangs, swings, supports) or both legs (e.g. springs, tumbling). In contrast, many game activities that involve the use of an implement (e.g., bat, racquet, stick) or object (e.g., beanbag, ball, Frisbee) tend to favor the development of one side of the body more than the other does.

Finally, if educational gymnastics experiences are to be truly "educational," then we must ask in what ways are they educational? In short, these experiences are educational because they start with the needs of students. The instructor presents the students with movement problems , which the students must solve, asks questions to gain the cognitive involvement of students, offers various solutions in the form of movement sequences, and guides students to reflect upon and synthesize their experiences. Students gain knowledge and understandings of the mechanical principles associated with the Basic Movement Patterns of gymnastics and they increase their ability to apply these principles.

COMPETENCY 15.0 **UNDERSTAND THE ROLE OF MOVEMENT ACTIVITIES IN THE DEVELOPMENT OF SELF-MANAGEMENT SKILLS AND POSITIVE PERSONAL AND SOCIAL BEHAVIORS**

SKILL 15.1 Recognizing how physical education settings, activities, rules, procedures, and practices promote self-management skills (e.g., taking turns, following directions, sharing space and equipment with others)

For most people, the development of social roles and appropriate social behaviors occurs during childhood. Physical play between parents and children, as well as between siblings and peers, serves as a strong regulator in the developmental process. Chasing games, roughhousing, wrestling, or practicing sport skills such as jumping, throwing, catching, and striking, are some examples of childhood play. These activities may be competitive or non-competitive and are important for promoting social and moral development of both boys and girls. Unfortunately, fathers will often engage in this sort of activity more with their sons than their daughters. Regardless of the sex of the child, both boys and girls enjoy these types of activities.

Physical play during infancy and early childhood is central to the development of social and emotional competence. Research shows that children who engage in play that is more physical with their parents, particularly with parents who are sensitive and responsive to the child, exhibited greater enjoyment during the play sessions and were more popular with their peers. Likewise, these early interactions with parents, siblings, and peers are important in helping children become more aware of their emotions and to learn to monitor and regulate their own emotional responses. Children learn quickly through watching the responses of their parents which behaviors make their parents smile and laugh and which behaviors cause their parents to frown and disengage from the activity.

If children want the fun to continue, they engage in the behaviors that please others. As children near adolescence, they learn through rough-and-tumble play that there are limits to how far they can go before hurting someone (physically or emotionally), which results in termination of the activity or later rejection of the child by peers. These early interactions with parents and siblings are important in helping children learn appropriate behavior in the social situations of sport and physical activity.

Children learn to assess their social competence (i.e., ability to get along with and acceptance by peers, family members, teachers and coaches) in sport through the feedback received from parents and coaches. Initially, authority figures teach children, "You can't do that because I said so." As children approach school age, parents begin the process of explaining why a behavior is right or wrong because children continuously ask, "why?"

Similarly, when children engage in sports, they learn about taking turns with their teammates, sharing playing time, and valuing rules. They understand that rules are important for everyone, and without these regulations, the game would become unfair. The learning of social competence is continuous as we expand our social arena and learn about different cultures. A constant in the learning process is the role of feedback as we assess the responses of others to our behaviors and comments.

In addition to the development of social competence, sport participation can help youth develop other forms of self-competence. Most important among these self-competencies is self-esteem. Self-esteem is how we judge our worth and indicates the extent to which an individual believes he is capable, significant, successful and worthy. Educators have suggested that one of the biggest barriers to success in the classroom today is low self-esteem.

Children develop self-esteem by evaluating abilities and by evaluating the responses of others. Children actively observe parents' and coaches' responses to their performances, looking for signs of approval or disapproval of their behavior. Children often interpret feedback and criticism as either a negative or a positive response to the behavior. In sports, research shows that the coach is a critical source of information that influences the self-esteem of children.

Little League baseball players whose coaches use a "positive approach" to coaching (e.g. more frequent encouragement, positive reinforcement for effort and corrective, instructional feedback), had significantly higher self-esteem ratings over the course of a season than children whose coaches used these techniques less frequently. The most compelling evidence supporting the importance of coaches' feedback was found for those children who started the season with the lowest self-esteem ratings and increased considerably their self-assessment and self-worth. In addition to evaluating themselves more positively, low self-esteem children evaluated their coaches more positively than did children with higher self-esteem who played for coaches who used the "positive approach." Moreover, studies show that 95 percent of children who played for coaches trained to use the positive approach signed up to play baseball the next year, compared with 75 percent of the youth who played for untrained adult coaches.

We cannot overlook the importance of enhanced self-esteem on future participation. A major part of the development of high self-esteem is the pride and joy that children experience as their physical skills improve. Children will feel good about themselves as long as their skills are improving. If children feel that their performance during a game or practice is not as good as that of others, or as good as they think mom and dad would want, they often experience shame and disappointment.

Some children will view mistakes made during a game as a failure and will look for ways to avoid participating in the task if they receive no encouragement to continue. At this point, it is critical that adults (e.g., parents and coaches) intervene to help children to interpret the mistake or "failure." We must teach children that a mistake is not synonymous with failure. Rather, a mistake shows us that we need a new strategy, more practice, and/or greater effort to succeed at the task.

Fairness is another trait that physical activities, especially rules-based sports, can foster and strengthen. Children are by nature very rules-oriented, and have a keen sense of what they believe is and isn't fair. Fair play, teamwork, and sportsmanship are all values that stem from proper practice of the spirit of physical education classes. Of course, a pleasurable physical education experience goes a long way towards promoting an understanding of the innate value of physical activity throughout the life cycle.

SKILL 15.2 Identifying techniques and activities that promote cooperation and collaboration skills

By participating in physical activities, students develop various aspects of the self that are easily applicable to other settings (e.g., the workplace). Communication is one skill that improves enormously through participation in sports and games. Students will come to understand that skillful communication can contribute to a better all-around outcome, whether it be winning the game or successfully completing a team project. They will see that effective communication helps to develop and maintain healthy personal relationships, organize and convey information, and reduce or avoid conflict.

Physical activities also teach students how to set personal goals. At first, one can set a physical goal such as running one mile in eight minutes. After accomplishing that specific feat, the student will feel capable and will be more willing to set greater goals in various fields within his life.

Finally, physical activities teach perseverance, the importance of following directions, leadership, and teamwork. Recovering from competitive loses and withstanding personal and team setbacks help develop perseverance. All games and sports have rules that participants must follow in order to participate. Leadership and teamwork are both integral parts of team sports. In the team sport setting, participants learn how to work together and lead others to achieve a common goal. These skills are invaluable in real life and the workplace.

Examples of activities that promote cooperation and collaboration are all team sports. Basketball, baseball, softball, volleyball, soccer and football are all team sports. There has to be cooperation and collaboration among the teammates, otherwise there would be absolutely no success. Whereas individual sports such as tennis, swimming, wrestling, track and field (with the exception of relays) and golf are not as dependent on collaboration and cooperation in order for the athletes in these sports achieving successes. Irregardless of a team or individual sports, all organized physical activities involve some element of cooperation and collaboration. Rules, regulations, schedules and sportsmanship are fundamental requirements of physical activity and sports.

SKILL 15.3 Identifying movement activities that promote awareness of etiquette and safe interaction with others

The movement activities that promote awareness of etiquette and safe interaction with others are partner and team sports, physical movement activities where there is a possibility of injury, and, especially, those activities that tend to be more formal and regimented in their execution.

For example, wrestling and boxing are both sports where practice generally involves sparring with a partner. In these activities, practitioners will tend to develop a very keen sense of the guidelines regarding etiquette and safe interaction with the others surrounding them. This grows from the fact that safe interaction and etiquette is necessary at all times during training, otherwise serious injury may occur. Imagine, for example, a wrestler who does not observe the etiquette of a tap-out (i.e. he has manipulated his partner into a pin or lock, but does not release when they signal their surrender). No coach would tolerate such a wrestler.

Examples of disciplines that are more formal and regimented in their execution are many of the martial arts practiced in America today. In all cases, the etiquette and rules regarding safe interactions are so fundamental to the art, and so strictly observed (for example, bowing to your opponent and instructor as a gesture of respect) that they grow to become almost second nature.

SKILL 15.4 Analyzing ways in which movement activities can promote positive personal attitudes and behaviors (e.g., independence, responsibility, confidence, honesty, self-control, perseverance)

   o   *See Skill 15.1*

SKILL 15.5 Analyzing ways in which movement activities can promote positive social attitudes and behaviors (e.g., teamwork, sportsmanship, leadership, consideration of others, fairness, respect for diversity, loyalty, compassion)

Physical education activities can promote positive social behaviors and traits in a number of different ways. Instructors can foster improved relations with adults and peers by making students active partners in the learning process and delegating responsibilities within the class environment to students. Giving students leadership positions (e.g. team captain) can give them a heightened understanding of the responsibilities and challenges facing educators.

Team-based physical activities like team sports promote collaboration and cooperation. In such activities, students learn to work together, both pooling their talents and minimizing the weaknesses of different team members, in order to achieve a common goal. The experience of functioning as a team can be very productive for development of loyalty between children, and seeing their peers in stressful situations that they can relate to can promote a more compassionate and considerate attitude among students. Similarly, the need to maximize the strengths of each student on a team (who can complement each other and compensate for weaknesses) is a powerful lesson about valuing and respecting diversity and individual differences. Varying students between leading and following positions in a team hierarchy are good ways to help students gain a comfort level being both followers and leaders.

Physical fitness activities incorporate group processes, group dynamics, and a wide range of cooperation and competition. Ranging from team sports (which are both competitive and cooperative in nature) to individual competitive sports (like racing), to cooperative team activities without a winner and loser (like a gymnastics team working together to create a human pyramid), there is a great deal of room for the development of mutual respect and support among the students, safe cooperative participation, and analytical, problem solving, teamwork, and leadership skills.

Teamwork situations are beneficial to students because they create opportunities for them to see classmates with whom they might not generally socialize, and with whom they may not even get along, in a new light. It also creates opportunities for students to develop reliance on each other and practice interdependence. Cooperation and competition can also offer opportunities for children to practice group work. These situations provide good opportunities to practice analytical thinking and problem solving in a practical setting.

The social skills and values gained from participation in physical activities include:

- The ability to make adjustments to both self and others by an integration of the individual to society and the environment.

- The ability to make judgments in a group situation.

- Learning to communicate with others and be cooperative.

- The development of the social phases of personality, attitudes, and values in order to become a functioning member of society such as being considerate.

- The development of a sense of belonging and acceptance by society.

- The development of positive personality traits.

- Learning for constructive use of leisure time.

- A development of attitude that reflects good moral character.

- Respect of school rules and property.

The above list represents a sample of the socio-cultural benefits of participating in physical activity with others. Physical activity serves as a very important part of the socialization process. Physical activity during the socialization process creates an opportunity for children to define personal comfort levels with different types of physical interaction, as well as to establish guidelines for what is (and is not) acceptable physical behavior as related to their relationship with other individuals.

Participating in physical activity with others is also a step away from the trend of "playground to PlayStation", where students are less and less physically active, and spend less and less time engaging in outdoor physical activity. Physical activity on a socio-cultural level is an important aspect of the struggle against rising obesity levels in the United States, as well as related problems (like heart disease).

FAIRNESS, EQUITY, DIVERSITY

Physical activity and related games can introduce children to the concepts of equity and fairness. In addition, physical activity provides a venue for the interaction of diverse groups of people, allowing participants to observe and appreciate cultural differences and similarities.

- **Human Growth and Development** – Movement activities promote personal growth and development physically, by way of stimulating muscular development, and emotionally, by raising personal confidence levels among children and by allowing them to explore concepts of inter-group equity that may at first seem threatening. To the insecure child, the concept that another group may be equal to his own may seem to 'demote' his group and the child by extension.

- **Psychology** – Observation and interaction with the behavior of children from diverse backgrounds in a training environment (where the training activities tend to focus more on 'doing', which feels more genuine to children than the classroom setting of raising hands and answering questions) allows the child to see in others the same sorts of behavioral reasoning processes that he sees in himself. This humanizes others from diverse backgrounds, and promotes concepts of equity among diverse groups.

- **Aesthetics** – Human movement activities create an opportunity for individual participation in activities with intrinsic aesthetic qualities. A gymnastic technique or a perfectly executed swing of a baseball bat relies on both physical training and a level of intuitive action. This is an artistic form of expression that is readily accessible to children. Recognizing beauty in the activities and performances of others (in some cases from groups different from that of the viewing student) is a humanizing experience.

COMPETENCY 16.0   **UNDERSTAND EXERCISE PHYSIOLOGY, PRINCIPLES OF FITNESS TRAINING, AND THE ROLE OF PHYSICAL FITNESS IN THE PROMOTION OF PERSONAL HEALTH**

SKILL 16.1   **Analyzing how major body systems produce movement, use energy, adapt to physical activity, and contribute to fitness**

    o   *See also Skill 2.1*

PRODUCTION OF MOVEMENT AND ADAPTATIONS TO PHYSICAL ACTIVITY

The structure and function of the human body adapts greatly to physical activity and exertion. When challenged with any physical task, the human body responds through a series of integrated changes in function that involve most, if not all, of its physiological systems. Movement requires activation and control of the musculoskeletal system. The cardiovascular and respiratory systems provide the ability to sustain this movement over extended periods. When the body engages in exercise training several times, each of these physiological systems undergoes specific adaptations that increase the body's efficiency and capacity.

When the body works, it makes great demand on every muscle of the body. Either the muscles have to 'shut down' or they have to do work. The heart beats faster during strenuous exercise so that it can pump more blood to the muscles, and the stomach shuts down during strenuous exercise so that it does not waste energy that the muscles need. Exercising makes the muscles work like motor that use up energy in order to generate force. Muscles, also known as 'biochemical motors', use the chemical adenosine triphosphate (ATP) as an energy source.

Different types of systems, such as the glycogen-lactic acid system, help muscles perform. Such systems help in producing ATP, which is extremely vital to working muscles. Aerobic respiration, which also helps in releasing ATP, uses the fatty acids from fat reserves in muscle and helps produce ATP for a much longer period.

The following points summarize the process of bodily adaptation to exercise:

• Muscle cells use the ATP they have floating around in about 3 seconds.

• The phosphagen system kicks in and supplies energy for 8 to 10 seconds.

• If exercise continues longer, the glycogen-lactic acid system kicks in.

• Finally, if exercise continues, aerobic respiration takes over. This would occur in endurance events such as an 800-meter dash, marathon run, rowing, cross-country skiing, or distance skating.

Physical activity affects the cardiovascular and musculoskeletal systems the most. However, it also helps in proper functioning of metabolic, endocrine, and immune systems.

SKILL 16.2   Identifying the physiological changes that result from regular participation in physical activity

   o   *See Skill 2.4*

SKILL 16.3   Recognizing the components of health-related physical fitness, activities and strategies for achieving and maintaining physical fitness, and the relationship between physical activity and the prevention of disease

There are five health-related components of physical fitness: **cardio-respiratory or cardiovascular endurance, muscle strength, muscle endurance, flexibility, and body composition.**

Cardiovascular endurance – the ability of the body to sustain aerobic activities (activities requiring oxygen utilization) for extended periods.

Muscle strength – the ability of muscle groups to contract and support a given amount of weight.

Muscle endurance – the ability of muscle groups to contract continually over a period of time and support a given amount of weight.

Flexibility – the ability of muscle groups to stretch and bend.

Body composition – an essential measure of health and fitness. The most important aspects of body composition are body fat percentage and ratio of body fat to muscle.

Physical activity improves each of the components of physical fitness. Aerobic training improves cardiovascular endurance. Weight training, body support activities, and calisthenics increase muscular strength and endurance. Stretching improves flexibility. Finally, all types of physical activity improve body composition by increasing muscle and decreasing body fat.

SKILL 16.4 Distinguishing among types, components, and principles of physical fitness training

BASIC TRAINING PRINCIPLES

The **Overload Principle** is exercising at an above normal level to improve physical or physiological capacity (a higher than normal workload).

The **Specificity Principle** is overloading a particular fitness component. In order to improve a component of fitness, you must isolate and specifically work on a single component. Metabolic and physiological adaptations depend on the type of overload; hence, specific exercise produces specific adaptations, creating specific training effects.

The **Progression Principle** states that once the body adapts to the original load/stress, no further improvement of a component of fitness will occur without the addition of an additional load.

There is also a **Reversibility-of-Training Principle** in which all gains in fitness are lost with the discontinuance of a training program.

MODIFICATIONS OF OVERLOAD

We can modify overload by varying **frequency, intensity, and time**. Frequency is the number of times we implement a training program in a given period (e.g. three days per week). Intensity is the amount of effort put forth or the amount of stress placed on the body. Time is the duration of each training session.

PRINCIPLES OF OVERLOAD, PROGRESSION, AND SPECIFICITY APPLIED TO IMPROVEMENT OF HEALTH-RELATED COMPONENTS OF FITNESS

1. Cardio-respiratory Fitness:

Overloading for cardio-respiratory fitness:

- **Frequency** = minimum of 3 days/week

- **Intensity** = exercising in target heart-rate zone

- **Time** = minimum of 15 minutes rate

Progression for cardiovascular fitness:

- begin at a frequency of 3 days/week and work up to no more than 6 days/week

- begin at an intensity near THR threshold and work up to 80% of THR

- begin at 15 minutes and work up to 60 minutes

Specificity for cardiovascular fitness:

- To develop cardiovascular fitness, you must perform aerobic (with oxygen) activities for at least fifteen minutes without developing an oxygen debt. Aerobic activities include, but are not limited to brisk walking, jogging, bicycling, and swimming.

2. Muscle Strength:

Overloading for muscle strength:

- **Frequency** = every other day

- **Intensity** = 60% to 90% of assessed muscle strength

- **Time** = 3 sets of 3 - 8 reps (high resistance with a low number of repetitions)

Progression for muscle strength:

- begin 3 days/week and work up to every other day

- begin near 60% of determined muscle strength and work up to no more than 90% of muscle strength

- begin with 1 set with 3 reps and work up to 3 sets with 8 reps

Specificity for muscle strength:

- to increase muscle strength for a specific part(s) of the body, you must target that/those part(s) of the body

3. Muscle endurance:

Overloading for muscle endurance:

- **Frequency** = every other day

- **Intensity** = 30% to 60% of assessed muscle strength

- **Time** = 3 sets of 12 - 20 reps (low resistance with a high number of repetitions)

Progression for muscle endurance:

- begin 3 days/week and work up to every other day

- begin at 20% to 30% of muscle strength and work up to no more than 60% of muscle strength

- begin with 1 set with 12 reps and work up to 3 sets with 20 reps

Specificity for muscle endurance:

- same as muscle strength

4. Flexibility:

Overloading for flexibility:

- **Frequency**: 3 to 7 days/week

- **Intensity**: stretch muscle beyond its normal length

- **Time**: 3 sets of 3 reps holding stretch 15 to 60 seconds

Progression for flexibility:

- begin 3 days/week and work up to every day

- begin stretching with slow movement as far as possible without pain, holding at the end of the range of motion (ROM) and work up to stretching no more than 10% beyond the normal ROM

- begin with 1 set with 1 rep, holding stretches 15 seconds, and work up to 3 sets with 3 reps, holding stretches for 60 seconds

Specificity for flexibility:

- ROM is joint specific

5. Body composition:

Overloading to improve body composition:

- **Frequency**: daily aerobic exercise

- **Intensity**: low

- **Time**: approximately one hour

Progression to improve body composition:

- begin daily

- begin a low aerobic intensity and work up to a longer duration (see cardio-respiratory progression)

- begin low-intensity aerobic exercise for 30 minutes and work up to 60 minutes

Specificity to improve body composition:

Increase aerobic exercise and decrease caloric intake

TECHNIQUES AND BENEFITS OF WARMING UP AND COOLING DOWN

A warm-up should consist of 5 to 10 minutes of aerobic activity in which the participant uses the muscles needed in the activity to follow (similar movements at a lower activity). Warm-ups also include stretching of major muscle groups after the gradual warm-up.

The benefits of warming up are:

- preparing the body for physical activity

- reducing the risk of musculoskeletal injuries

- releasing oxygen from myoglobin

- warming the body's inner core

- increasing the reaction of muscles

- bringing the heart rate to an aerobic conditioning level

Cooling down is similar to warming up - a moderate to light tapering-off vigorous activity at the end of an exercise session.

The benefits of cooling down are:

- redistributing circulation of the blood throughout the body to prevent pooling of blood

- preventing dizziness

- facilitating the removal of lactic acid

SKILL 16.5 Recognizing differences between health- and skill-related fitness, ranges of individual variation, and levels of readiness for fitness

INDIVIDUAL HEALTH AND SELF-ASSESSMENT

Naturally, variations in levels of health and fitness exist no two individual are exactly alike. These variations are apparent in all areas of physical fitness including body composition, cardiovascular endurance, muscular strength and endurance, and flexibility.

Body composition describes the physical make-up of the body. The two components of body composition are fat tissue and lean tissue (i.e., muscle, bone, etc.). We can measure body mass by circumference and skinfold measurements. A more practical method of measuring body composition is the Body Mass Index (BMI). We use the BMI to assess body weight relative to height. BMI equals weight in kilograms divided by height in meters, squared (kg/m^2). Although this method does not distinguish between fat mass and muscle mass, a BMI of 25 and higher increases many health risks such as high blood pressure, high cholesterol, type 2 diabetes, heart attack and stroke. Normal values fall between 18.5 and 24.9.

Cardiovascular fitness relates to the ability to perform moderate to high intensity exercise for a prolonged period. Peak levels of cardiovascular fitness usually occur around age 20-25 and decrease by approximately 10% each decade thereafter (one percent per year). Low levels of fitness increases the risk of premature death from cardiovascular disease. A high level of fitness reduces the risk of premature death from many causes and provides many health benefits. Men often have higher levels of cardiovascular fitness than women do. Everyone should engage in cardiovascular exercise three to five days per week, for 20-60 minutes, at an intensity of 55-90% of maximum heart rate (220 – age). The mode of exercise should engage large muscle groups in a continuous, rhythmic motion. In addition, everyone should choose a mode they enjoy to increase adherence to an exercise routine.

Muscular fitness relates to how much force a muscle group can generate (strength) and how effectively the muscle group can sustain that force over a period of time (endurance). Gains in strength, muscle mass, and endurance require different training methods. Lifting heavy weights 4 to 8 repetitions per exercise encourages strength development. Lifting moderate weight with 8 to 12 repetitions per exercise leads to an increase in muscle size (hypertrophy). Lifting light weights 12 to 15 repetitions per exercise develops muscular endurance. A minimum weight-training regimen consists of one set of eight to twelve repetitions using ten of the primary muscle groups (four lower body, six upper body) on two non-consecutive days of the week. Generally, men show greater muscular fitness levels than women, but with age, the margin becomes smaller. Peak levels of muscular fitness occur in the second decade of life.

Flexibility is the ability of a joint to move through its range of motion (ROM). Measurements of flexibility are joint specific, so it is difficult to establish overall flexibility by just one test. Like cardiovascular and muscular fitness, flexibility decreases with age. Minimal requirements to improve flexibility include stretching each major joint to tightness, holding for 15-30 seconds, repeating each stretch 2 to 4 times per session, and engaging in flexibility training 2 to 4 days per week.

Improvement in each of these categories leads to a decreased risk of injury and disease and allows performance of normal, everyday activities with greater ease. Strategies for enhancing adherence to these fitness programs include appropriately maintained facilities/equipment, emphasizing short-term goals, minimizing injuries, encouraging group participation, emphasizing variety and enjoyment, and recruiting support and motivation from family and friends.

LEVELS OF READINESS AND EXPECTED DEVELOPMENTAL PROGRESSIONS FOR IMPROVEMENTS IN FITNESS

A normal three-year-old should be able to walk up and down the stairs, jump from the lowest step, and land on both the feet without falling. They should also be capable of standing on one foot and balancing and kicking a large ball (though not with a lot of force). A three-year-old can jump on the same spot, ride on a small tricycle, and throw a ball (although not very straight and with limited distance). The large motor skills are more or less developed, but fine motor skills and hand-eye coordination need refining. For example, a three-year-old may not be able to dodge a ball or play games like badminton, which require greater hand-eye coordination, speed, and balance, but a three-year-old can catch a big ball thrown to him/her from a short distance.

A four-year-old is capable of walking on a straight line, hopping using one foot, and pedaling a tricycle with confidence. A four-year-old can climb ladders and trees with relative ease. A four-year-old child can run around obstacles, maneuver, and stop when necessary. A four-year-old can throw a ball a greater distance and is capable of running around in circles.

A five-year-old is capable of walking backwards, using the heel and then the toe, and is able to easily climb up and down steps by alternating feet without any outside help. Five-year-olds can touch their toes without bending at the knee and balance on a beam. They may be able to do somersaults provided it is taught in a proper and safe manner. A five-year-old can ride a tricycle with speed and dexterity, make almost ten jumps or hops without losing balance and falling, and stand on one foot for about ten senconds.

Early elementary school children have already acquired many large motor and fine motor skills. Their movement is more accurate and with purpose, though some clumsiness may persist. An elementary student is always on the run and restless. A child older than five finds pleasure in more energetic and vigorous activities. He/she can jump, hop, and throw with relative accuracy and concentrate on an activity which sustains his/her interest. However, concentration on a single activity usually does not last long. Early elementary students enjoy challenges and can benefit greatly from them.

When proper and appropriate physical education is available, by the time a child finishes the fourth grade he is able to demonstrate well-developed locomotor movements. He is also capable of manipulative and nonlocomotor movement skills like kicking and catching. He is capable of living up to challenges like balancing a number of objects or controlling a variety of things simultaneously. Children at this developmental age begin to acquire specialized movement skills like dribbling. When a child has finished eighth grade, he is able to exhibit expertise in a variety of fine and modified movements (e.g. dance steps). Children begin to develop the necessary skills for competitive and strategic games. Despite a lack of competency in a game, they learn to enjoy the pleasure of physical activity. By the time the children finish the twelfth grade they can demonstrate competency in a number of complex and modified movements with relative ease (e.g. gymnastics, dual sports, and dance). Students at this age display their interest in gaining a greater degree of competency at their favorite game or activity.

ACTIVITIES FOR VARIOUS OBJECTIVES, SITUATIONS, AND DEVELOPMENTAL LEVELS

The following is a list of physical activities that may reduce specific health risks, improve overall health, and develop skill-related components of physical activity. Some of these activities, such as walking and calisthenics, are more suitable to students at beginning developmental levels, while other, such as circuit training and rowing are best suited for students at more advanced levels of development.

1. **Aerobic Dance**:
Health-related components of fitness = *cardio-respiratory, body composition.*
Skill-related components of fitness = *agility, coordination.*

2. **Bicycling**:
Health-related components of fitness = *cardio-respiratory, muscle strength, muscle endurance, body composition.*   **Skill-related components of fitness** = *balance.*

3. **Calisthenics**:
Health-related components of fitness = *cardio-respiratory, muscle strength, muscle endurance, flexibility, body composition.*
Skill-related components of fitness = *agility.*

4. Circuit Training:
Health-related components of fitness = *cardio-respiratory, muscle strength, muscle endurance, body composition.* **Skill-related components of fitness** = *power.*

5. Cross Country Skiing:
Health-related component of fitness = *cardio-respiratory, muscle strength, muscle endurance, body composition.* **Skill-related components of fitness** = *agility, coordination,; power.*

6. Jogging/Running:
Health-related components of fitness = *cardio-respiratory, body composition.*

7. Rope Jumping:
Health-related components of fitness = *cardio-respiratory, body composition.*
Skill-related components of fitness = *agility, coordination, reaction time, speed.*

8. Rowing:
Health-related components of fitness = *cardio-respiratory, muscle strength, muscle endurance, body composition.*
Skill-related components of fitness = *agility, coordination, power.*

9. Skating:
Health-related components of fitness = *cardio-respiratory, body composition.* **Skill-related components of fitness** = *agility, balance, coordination, speed.*

10. Swimming/Water Exercises:
Health-related components of fitness = *cardio-respiratory, muscle strength, muscle endurance, flexibility, body composition.* **Skill-related components of fitness** = *agility, coordination.*

11. Walking (brisk):
Health-related components of fitness = *cardio-respiratory, body composition.*

In general, teachers may need to modify instructional methods to accommodate students with disabilities participating in physical education class. The physical educator should ensure that students with disabilities understand the purpose of the lesson before the activity begins. The teacher should design lesson plans that include alternate activities in the event that the originally planned activity does not work well for the student(s) with disabilities. Teachers should not place students with disabilities in activities where they have no chance of success. Thus, teachers should avoid elimination games. The physical educator should praise even minor displays of progress and achievement. The teacher should work with the student(s) with disabilities to set achievable goals, as goal attainment is a wonderful motivator.

Physical educators must have a strong, working knowledge of specific disabilities and how they affect a student's ability to learn. When working with students mentally retarded students, instructors should emphasize progressive gross motor movement. Teacher instruction should focus on demonstration rather than oral explanation. Instructors should reward effort displayed by students. Additionally, the practice periods for students with mental retardation should be short to alleviate boredom and aggravation. Instructors should also make modifications for the visually impaired student. Lesson planning for the visually impaired student should focus on individual movement activities. The physical educator should use a whistle or loud verbal cues in class. If the visually impaired student has some residual eyesight, the teacher might have the student utilize a brightly colored ball against a contrasting backdrop. When working with a student with a hearing impairment, the physical education teacher should use visual cues. The instructor or other students must read all written instructions aloud. During all stages of instruction, the hearing-impaired student should be close to the teacher.

If a student with an orthopedic disability is present in class, lesson plans should focus on individual and dual sports to maximize the student's chance of success. Lastly, instructors may need to make modifications for students with emotional disabilities. Students with emotional disabilities can succeed in a stable, organized setting. The teacher should praise individual accomplishments. In order to avoid or minimize behavior disruptions, the instructor should clearly identify and consistently enforce rules and expectations. Finally, when working with a student with any given disability, it is crucial that the physical education teacher follows the physician instructions exactly.

Instructors may also need to modify instructional methods to accommodate students from diverse cultural and linguistic backgrounds. When working with students from diverse cultural backgrounds, the physical educator should self-educate regarding the cultural values and norms of the culture from which the students originate. When delivering instruction, the teacher should highlight information regarding participation in the activity in the student's home country. Often English is not the primary language for students from diverse cultural backgrounds. When working with students who utilize English as their second language, teachers should repeat instructions a number of times. The teacher should have knowledge of basic words relating to physical education in the language of the students present in class. The teacher should use precise English and avoid slang. During skill practice, the teacher could pair the student with others that might help them in their skill development. Finally, it is important that the teacher knows how to pronounce all students' names properly, especially the names of students from a diverse cultural background.

SKILL 16.6 Demonstrating awareness of resources, time, cost, accessibility, media influences, and other factors that affect participation in fitness activities

Many factors influence a student's participation in a particular activity. For instance, a boy may not wish to participate in a ballet dance because he perceives ballet dancing to be something for girls only. Or his cultural or ethnic norms may dictate that boys are too "macho" for that kind of dance (or any kind of dance for that matter). Similarly, a girl may not be interested in playing football because she believes football is a sport only boys play. Or perhaps her background and culture may suggest that any participation in sports or game is inappropriate for females. She may also think that she is not strong or big enough to participate in football. She may have been told that girls should play non-contact sports like tennis or participate in a dance group. The fact that only men play organized football at the highest levels reinforces the perception that women cannot play football. Perhaps contact sports are sports that her older brother(s) play and, even if she (or a boy) were interested, she (or he) is too young to participate.

In any of the above cases, the emphasis should be impartiality in terms of requirements for participation regardless of age, gender, ethnicity, and disability. We should also note that everyone is good at something and that nobody is good at everything. Those who are disabled may believe that they cannot play anything at all because of their disability. For those disabled students, many games and sports are strictly prohibited. However, instructors can modify many others to a point where the disabled student may participate and gain satisfaction.

Self-concept and motor performance are two important factors that affect student attitudes toward and engagement in physical activity. Students with more developed motor skills and healthier self-concepts are more likely to pursue participation in physical activities. We will now discuss several of the environmental and cultural factors that affect the development of self-concept and motor skills.

BIOLOGICAL AND ENVIRONMENTAL INFLUENCES ON GENDER DIFFERENCES IN MOTOR PERFORMANCES

The differences between males and females in motor performance result from certain biological and environmental influences. Generally, people perceive the males as stronger, faster, and more active than females. This higher activity level can stem from childhood behaviors influenced by certain environmental factors and superior motor performance results largely from the biological make up of males versus females.

In most cases, the male body contains less fat mass and more muscle mass than the female body. In addition, the type of muscle differs between males and females. Males have more fast-twitch muscle fibers allowing for more short duration, high intensity movements such as jumping and sprinting. In addition, males generally, but not always, display better coordination. Females have proved their superiority at certain activities, such as skipping, and tend to display better fine movements, such as neater handwriting.

Certain environmental factors also contribute to the gender differences in motor performance. As children, boys tend to be more physically active. Society expects boys to participate in sports and play games that involve running around, such as tag and foot races. On the other hand, society expects girls to be more social and less active. They participate in activities such as playing with dolls. In addition, parents rarely ask girls to perform tasks involving manual labor.

While these sedentary tasks have value, it is important for both males and females to participate in an adequate amount of physical activity each day. If children develop this type of active lifestyle early in life, they are more likely to maintain it throughout adulthood.

PSYCHOLOGICAL FACTORS

Certain psychological aspects may hinder participation in certain physical activities. These factors can depend on the individual, the group the individual will participate with, and the activity itself.

An individual's personality type and interests can determine their level of participation. Outgoing, energetic, and aggressive personality types usually exhibit increased levels of participation. Reserved or lazy personality types are sometimes difficult to work with and motivate. Shy individuals are usually compliant, but may not feel completely comfortable in participation, especially activities involving larger groups.

Physical education instructors often overlook the importance of activity groups to the psychological well-being of students. Instructors must construct groups with certain factors in mind. Children may feel intimidated by participating in activities with older individuals. In addition, girls may not feel comfortable participating with boys, and vise versa. Grouping students by age, gender, and skill level helps maintain self-confidence.

The type of activity can also affect participation. Every one has different interests and instructors should not necessarily force students to participate in activities they do not enjoy. Such action can lead to a diminished physical activity level throughout life. Instructors should introduce alternate activities to increase levels of participation for all individuals.

TECHNIQUES TO MAXIMIZE PARTICIPATION

There are three options for maximizing participation: activity modification, multi-activity designs, and homogeneous or heterogeneous grouping.

Activity modification is the first option to achieve maximum participation by simply modifying the type of equipment used or the activity rules. However, keep activity as close to the original as possible (i.e. substitute a yarn ball for a birdie for badminton).

Multi-activity designs permit greater diversification of equipment and more efficient use of available facilities (keeps all students involved).

Homogeneous and heterogeneous grouping for the purpose of individualized instruction, enhancing self-concepts, equalizing competition, and promoting cooperation among classmates.

Furthermore, instructors should plan activities that encourage the greatest amount of participation by utilizing all available facilities and equipment, involving students in planning class work/activities, and being flexible. Instructors can also use tangible rewards and praise.

Family resources and time availability also play a major role in physical activity. An awareness of this will help open new opportunities through agencies and communities in offering and providing assistance to families in these types of situations. So many families depend on dual incomes with parents, guardians and/or older siblings working just to make ends meet. To throw in the mix getting a school age child to an after school activity, finding the resources to pay for all the necessary equipment needed for their child's participation in the activity can become an unattainable opportunity for their child. Community and social resources, thankfully are stepping up more and more to the plate to assist this type of situations by providing after school transportation to activities and assisting with paying for the needed equipment for the activity.

COMPETENCY 17.0   **UNDERSTAND PRINCIPLES, TECHNIQUES, AND ACTIVITIES FOR DEVELOPING AND MAINTAINING HEALTHY LEVELS OF CARDIOVASCULAR FITNESS**

SKILL 17.1   **Demonstrating knowledge of principles, skills, and activities for cardiovascular strength and endurance conditioning**

PRINCIPLES AND ACTIVITIES FOR DEVELOPING AEROBIC ENDURANCE

The term aerobic refers to conditioning or exercise that requires the use of oxygen to derive energy. Aerobic conditioning is essential for fat loss, energy production, and effective functioning of the cardiovascular system. Aerobic exercise is difficult to perform for many people and participants must follow certain principles and activities in order to develop aerobic endurance.

Slow twitch muscle tissue, fueled by oxygen, powers aerobic activities. For the body to sustain aerobic activity for an extended period, the heart must pump oxygen-rich blood to the muscles of the body. When the heart tires due to insufficient cardiorespiratory fitness, the quantities of oxygen delivered to the muscles decreases to levels that cannot sustain the activity.

Other physiological processes involved in aerobic endurance include the respiratory system (which must take sufficient air into the body and efficiently supply oxygen to the blood), the blood itself (which must efficiently carry oxygen), the circulatory system (that takes blood to the muscles and then returns it to the heart), and the muscles themselves (which must efficiently extract oxygen from the blood).

Tips that aid in developing and building aerobic endurance include working out for extended periods at the target heart rate, slowly increasing aerobic exercises, exercising for three or four times per week, and taking adequate rest to help the body recover.

Exercising in the target heart rate zone for 30-45 minute periods is the most important principle in the development of aerobic endurance. Submaximal intensity activities, such as walking and slow jogging, are effective aerobic activities that improve aerobic endurance without unnecessary strain on the body.

The following is an example of a **cardio-respiratory fitness** program design:

- **mode:** aerobic activities (e.g. walking, jogging, swimming, cycling, rowing)

- **frequency:** 3 to 5 days/week

- **intensity:** 60% to 90% of maximum oxygen uptake or 60% to 80% THR

- **time:** 20 to 60 minutes of continuous or interval (non-continuous) activity (time depends on intensity level)

- **progression:** instructor adjusts prescription according to an individual's fitness level and conditioning effects.

ACTIVITY SELECTION

Aerobics are a fundamental component of every physical education or training program. Aerobic activities are necessary for all because they are central to weight reduction, cardiovascular fitness, muscular strength development, and performance in all sports events.

Appropriate aerobic activities for various developmental levels vary from low and moderate intensity exercises to high intensity ones. Low and moderate intensity activities include doing household work, walking, playing with children, and working on the lawn. High-intensity aerobic activities include jogging, cycling, participating in sports like ice or roller-skating, downhill skiing, and swimming. Treadmills and other equipment help create strenuous aerobic exercises.

Instructors and students must take care while undertaking such high-intensity aerobic exercises, because they can be highly strenuous and taxing on muscles, especially during the initial stages. At this beginning stage, the exercise intensity must be low. With passage of time and development towards higher stages, the student can increase the level and intensity of aerobic exercises.

Whether the goal is to develop the body's ability to undergo high levels of muscular activity or just to remain fit, there are aerobic activities suited to every developmental stage and for every person.

CARDIOVASCULAR ACTIVITIES

Walking is a good generic cardiorespiratory activity for promoting basic fitness. Instructors can incorporate it into a variety of class settings (not only physical education instructors – for example, a Biology class might include a field trip to a natural setting that would involve a great deal of walking). Walking is appropriate for practically all age groups, but can only serve as noteworthy exercise for students who lead a fairly sedentary lifestyle (athletic students who train regularly or participate in some sport will not benefit greatly from walking).

Jogging or **Running** is a classic cardiorespiratory activity in which instructors can adjust the difficulty level by modifying the running speed or the incline of the track. It is important to stress proper footwear and gradual increase of intensity to prevent overuse injuries (e.g. stress fractures or shin splints).

Bicycling is another good cardiorespiratory activity that is appropriate for most age groups. Obviously, knowing how to ride a bicycle is a prerequisite, and it is important to follow safety procedures (e.g. ensuring that students wear helmets). An additional benefit of bicycle riding is that it places less strain on the knee joints than walking or running.

Swimming is an excellent cardiorespiratory activity that has the added benefit of working more of the body's muscles, more evenly than most other exercises, without excessive resistance to any one part of the body that could result in an overuse injury. To use swimming as an educational cardiorespiratory activity, there must be qualified lifeguards present, and all students must have passed basic tests of swimming ability.

There are many alternatives for cardiorespiratory activities, like **inline skating** and **cross-country skiing**. More importantly, instructors should modify the above exercises to match the developmental needs of the students – for example, younger students should receive most of their exercise in the form of games. An instructor could incorporate running in the form of a game of tag, soccer, or a relay race.

SKILL 17.2 Demonstrating knowledge of techniques for assessing and monitoring cardiovascular endurance levels

We can measure cardiorespiratory fitness in a number of ways. The simplest way is for the students to check their resting heart rate. To do this, the students should:

- Find their pulse in any point of the body where an artery is close to the surface (e.g., wrist [radial artery], neck [Carotid artery], or the elbow [brachial artery]).

- Count how many heartbeats they feel in one minute's time.

We usually express resting heart rate in "beats per minute" (bpm). For males, the norm is about 70 bpm. For women, the norm is about 75 bpm. This rate varies between people and the reference range is normally between 60 bpm and 100 bpm. It is important to note that resting heart rates can be significantly lower in athletes, and significantly higher in the obese.

Another way to measure cardiorespiratory fitness is by having students determine their Target Heart Rate (THR). The Target Heart Rate, or Training Heart Rate, is a desired range of heart rate reached during aerobic exercise, which allows a student's heart and lungs to receive the most benefit from a workout. Students should check their heart rates frequently during activity to ensure they train within their THR zones.

Finally, another useful technique for self-assessment, which instructors can combine with the pulse-rate monitoring mentioned above, is to instruct the students to keep a training log. The indicators tracked in the log may be very concrete (e.g. heart rate during exertion, duration of exertion, or resting heart rate and blood pressure), or more subjective (e.g. how students feel during and after their workouts). Instructors should also encourage older students to devise their own training benchmarks based on their knowledge of cardiorespiratory fitness training processes and their personal fitness goals.

TARGET HEART RATE ZONE AND HEART RATE MONITORS

The target heart rate (THR) zone is another common measure of aerobic exercise intensity. Participants find their THR and attempt to raise their heart rate to the desired level for a certain period. Students can use electronic heart rate monitors that constantly track heart rate during physical activity. Such monitors often alert students when they enter and leave their THR, allowing for adjustment of activity level. There are three ways to calculate the target heart rate.

1. METs (maximum oxygen uptake), which is 60% to 90% of functional capacity.

2. Karvonean Formula = [Maximum heart rate (MHR) – Resting heart rate (RHR)] x intensity + RHR.   MHR= 220 - Age
Intensity = Target Heart Range (which is 60% - 80% of MHR - RHR + RHR).

THR = (MHR - RHR) x .60 + RHR to (MHR - RHR) x .80 + RHR

3. Cooper's Formula to determine target heart range is:
THR = (220 - AGE) x .60 to (220 - AGE) x .80.

PERCEIVED EXERTION

Perceived exertion is another method of monitoring intensity of aerobic activities. Participants describe how hard they feel they are working based on physical sensations such as muscle fatigue, sweating, heart rate, and breathing rate. The Borg Scale is a quantitative rating system of perceived exertion. The following is an example of the Borg Scale, which ranges from 6 to 20, with corresponding descriptions.

6	No exertion at all
7	Extremely light
9	Very light (e.g. walking slowly at own pace for several minutes)
11	Light
13	Somewhat hard
15	Hard (heavy)
17	Very hard (i.e. a healthy person can still continue, but with great difficulty)
19	Extremely hard (i.e. most strenuous exercise most have ever experienced)
20	Maximum exertion

SKILL 17.3 Recognizing appropriate levels of intensity, frequency, and duration in cardiovascular strength and endurance conditioning activities

Cardiovascular fitness relates to the ability to perform moderate to high intensity exercise for a prolonged period. Performance of this type of exercise relies on the function of the respiratory, cardiovascular, and skeletal muscle systems. The function of the respiratory system is to take oxygen into the lungs. The function of the cardiovascular system is the delivery of deoxygenated blood to the lungs and oxygenated blood out to the rest of the body. The pumping of the heart accomplishes this task. Finally, the skeletal muscle absorbs the oxygen from the blood and uses it to produce energy.

To improve cardiovascular endurance, one must perform continuous and rhythmic exercise involving large muscle groups for at least 20 minutes per day, at least three days per week, at an intensity of at least 55% of maximum heart rate. As endurance improves, the duration, frequency, and intensity of exercise must increase, as the cardiovascular system will adapt to training.

Examples of activities promoting enhancement of cardiovascular endurance include, but are not limited to, walking, running, cycling, swimming, stair climbing, dancing, skating, and skiing. Certain sports such as basketball, tennis, hockey, and racquetball also have the potential to increase cardiovascular endurance provided they are performed at a sufficient duration and intensity. Factors involved in choosing a mode of exercise include level of enjoyment and status of health/injury. Instructors should allow individuals to choose the modes of exercise they enjoy in order to increase adherence to an exercise program. Orthopedic complications such as sprains, strains, arthritis, and osteoporosis can contraindicate certain exercises like walking, running, and stair climbing. Those with orthopedic complications should participate in non-weight bearing activities, such as swimming and cycling.

An important factor to understand about cardiovascular fitness is the specificity of training principle. This principle states that performance of a certain mode of exercise will not necessarily carry over to other modes. For example, let's say a person trains by **cycling** for 30 minutes a day, five days a week, at an intensity of 75% of their maximum heart rate. The results from such training when performing a **running** program at the same duration, frequency, and intensity do not fully transfer. In other words, the cyclist will not necessarily be able to perform a running program with the same elements of frequency, intensity, and time.

SKILL 17.4 Selecting appropriate cardiovascular fitness activities for various developmental levels and purposes

o *See Skill 17.1*

SKILL 17.5 Recognizing the benefits of regular participation in cardiovascular fitness activities and strategies for integrating cardiovascular fitness activities into daily life

○   *See also Skill 8.2*

Listed below are simple ways to integrate cardiorespiratory activities into your daily life:

- Do housework. Vacuuming, dusting, and mopping all add more steps to your day. There chores also involve lifting and stretching.
- Do yard work. Rake leaves, use a push mower to mow the lawn, dig holes to plant flowers or pick up trash.
- Go for a short walk before breakfast or after dinner. Start with a 5-10 minute walk and work up to 30 minutes.
- If possible, walk or bike when doing chores rather than driving.
- Walk the dog.
- Take the stairs instead of using the elevator.
- Plan fun activities with friends that require physical activity (e.g., hiking, swimming, backpacking, etc.)

COMPETENCY 18.0   **UNDERSTAND PRINCIPLES, TECHNIQUES, AND ACTIVITIES FOR DEVELOPING AND MAINTAINING FLEXIBILITY AND MUSCULAR STRENGTH AND ENDURANCE**

SKILL 18.1   **Recognizing the components of flexibility (e.g., muscles, joints, ligaments, tendons) and principles, techniques, and activities for promoting flexibility of the major joints and areas of the body**

COMPONENTS OF FLEXIBILITY

To effectively select, adapt, and modify flexibility activities, instructors must understand the components of flexibility. The components of flexibility are muscles, joints, tendons, and ligaments. Each of these components has unique characteristics and limitations that we must consider when planning a flexibility training program.

Muscles – Muscle is the body's contractile tissue. Its function is to produce force and cause motion (movement within the internal organs and, especially for our purposes, locomotion). Muscles are generally split into Type I (slow twitch) which carries more oxygen and sustains aerobic activity, and Type II (fast twitch), which carries less oxygen and powers anaerobic activity. Muscles that are too short can limit flexibility, and failing to stretch after resistance training can cause the muscles to shorten. The stretch reflex, whereby the opposing muscle will contract in order to prevent over-expansion, can also curtail flexibility (this contraction is generally premature, and part of flexibility training is to re-train the opposing muscle not to contract as quickly).

Joints – Joints are the locations at which two bones make contact. Their construction allows movement and provides functional mechanical support. We can classify joints as fibrous (connected by collagen), cartilaginous (connected by cartilage), or synovial (capped by cartilage, supported by ligaments, enveloped by the synovial membrane, and filled with synovial fluid). The limits of its range of motion, imposed by the joint's physical structure or, more often, by lack of flexibility of the muscles, ligaments and tendons, define a joint's flexibility.

Ligaments – A ligament is a short band of tough fibrous connective tissue composed mainly of long, stringy collagen fibers. They connect bones to other bones to form a joint. Ligaments can limit the mobility of a joint or prevent certain movements altogether. Ligaments are slightly elastic and under tension, they will gradually lengthen. Ligaments that are too short may curtail flexibility by limiting a joint's range of motion.

Tendons – A tendon (or sinew) is a tough band of fibrous connective tissue (similar in structure to ligaments) that connects muscle to bone or muscle to muscle. Tendons are composed mainly of water, type-I collagen, and cells called tenocytes. Most of the strength of tendons stems from the parallel, hierarchical arrangement of densely packed collagen fibrils, which have great strength, little extensibility, and no ability to contract.

FLEXIBILITY TRAINING

Flexibility is the range of motion around a joint or muscle. Flexibility has two major components: static and dynamic. Static flexibility is the range of motion without a consideration for speed of movement. Dynamic flexibility is the use of the desired range of motion at a desired velocity. These movements are useful for most athletes.

Good flexibility can help prevent injuries during all stages of life and can keep an athlete safe. To improve flexibility, you can lengthen muscles through activities such as swimming, a basic stretching program, or Pilates. These activities all improve your muscles' range of motion. While joints also consist of ligaments and tendons, muscles are the main target of flexibility training. Muscles are the most elastic component of joints while ligaments and tendons are less elastic and resist elongation. Overstretching tendons and ligaments can weaken joint stability and lead to injury.

Coaches, athletes and sports medicine personnel use stretching methods as part of their training routine for athletes. They help the body to relax and to warm-up for more intense fitness activities.

The following is an example of a **flexibility** program design:

- **mode:** stretching

- **frequency:** 3 to 7 days/week

- **intensity:** just below individual's threshold of pain

- **time:** 3 sets with 3 reps holding stretches 15 to 30 seconds, with a 60 rest interval between sets

Flexibility training is perhaps the most undervalued component of conditioning. Dynamic flexibility is the ability to perform dynamic movements within the full range of motion of the specified joint. Static active flexibility refers to the ability to stretch an antagonist muscle using only the tension in the antagonist muscle. Static-passive flexibility is the ability to hold a stretch using body weight or some other external force.

Dynamic stretching is generally very safe and very effective for warming up muscle groups and moderately improving flexibility. When performing dynamic stretches, participants must be careful to avoid sudden, jerky movements.

Static stretching is also safe, if the participant warms up the muscles prior to stretching. Because cold muscles are less elastic, static stretching without adequate warm up can lead to injury. Static stretching is very effective in increasing muscle flexibility.

Isometric, PNF, and ballistic stretching are more advanced techniques that require extreme caution and supervision. Most physical trainers believe ballistic stretching, bouncing into stretches, is ineffective and dangerous. Most trainers do not recommend ballistic stretching. PNF and isometric stretching are effective in certain situations such as rehabilitation and advanced training, but require close supervision.

SKILL 18.2   Recognizing the major muscle groups and principles, techniques, and activities for developing strength and endurance of the major muscle groups and areas of the body

MAJOR MUSCLE GROUPS

Shoulder
>   Deltoids – Military/Shoulder Press

Arms
>   Biceps Brachii – Front of upper arm - Curls
>   Triceps Brachii – Back of upper arm - Triceps Extension

Legs
>   Quadriceps – Front of upper leg – Leg Extensions
>   Hamstrings – Back of upper leg – Leg Curls
>   Gastrocnemius – Back of lower leg (calves) – Calf Raises
>   Gluteus Maximus – Buttocks – Squats

Chest
>   Pectoralis Major – Bench Press

Back
>   Latissimus Dorsi – Chin-ups, Pull-ups

Waist
>   Rectus Abdominis – Stomach/Abdominals – Sit-ups

MUSCULAR STRENGTH

Muscular strength is the ability of the muscles to exert force during an activity. It also helps the muscles to perform without fatigue. The activities that can help improve muscular endurance include walking, jogging, bicycling or dancing. Muscle strength is a measure of how much you can lift one time in a maximal effort situation. Larger people tend to have an edge over smaller people in terms of pounds lifted. The exercises that can help build muscular strength are push-ups(keep body straight, one leg raised), back lunges(keep tummy tight, back straight, head up), and two-point oblique (lie on back with back pushed into floor, right hand behind right ear, right knee bent with foot flat on floor).

The following is an example of a **muscle strength** program design:

- **mode:** weight training (isotonic/dynamic)

- **frequency:** minimum 3 days/week to a maximum of every other day

- **intensity:** 60% to 90% of maximum muscle strength (1-RM)

- **time:** 3 sets with 3 to 8 reps and a 60 second rest interval

- **progression:** increase workload (overload) when individual can perform 15 reps at 10 RM level

The following is an example of a **muscle endurance** program design:

- **mode:** weight training

- **frequency:** minimum 3 days/week up to every other day

- **intensity:** 30% to 60% of maximum muscle strength (1-RM)

- **time:** 3 sets with 12 to 20 reps, or until point of muscle fatigue with a 15 to 60 second rest interval

- **progression:** increase workload (overload) periodically based on number of continuous repetitions

MUSCULAR STRENGTH AND ENDURANCE ACTIVITIES

Possessing the strength and ability to overcome any resistance in one single effort or in repeated efforts over a period of time is muscular strength and endurance. It represents the ability to complete a heavy task in a single effort. Muscular strength and endurance not only helps in keeping body ailments in check, but also in enabling better performance in any sporting event.
Most fitness experts regard calisthenics as the best form of exercises in order to increase muscular development and strength. Although calisthenics are good beginning exercises, later on participants should complement them with progressive resistance training so that there will be an increase in bone mass and connective tissue strength. Such a combination would also help in minimizing any damages or injuries that are apt to occur at the beginning or initial training stages.

Besides calisthenics and progressive resistance training, aerobics can also help in maintaining muscular strength and endurance.

Muscular strength is the maximum amount of force that one can generate in an isolated movement. Muscular endurance is the ability of the muscles to perform a submaximal task repeatedly or to maintain a submaximal muscle contraction for extended periods. Body-support activities (e.g. push-ups and sit-ups) and callisthenic activities (e.g. rope jumping) are good exercises for young students or beginners of all ages. Such exercises use multiple muscle groups and have minimal risk of injury. At more advanced levels of development and for those students interested in developing higher levels of strength and muscle mass, weight lifting is the optimal activity.

To improve muscular strength and endurance a student can:

- Train with free weights
- Perform exercised that use an individual's body weight for resistance (e.g., push-ups, sit-ups, dips, etc.)
- Do strength training exercises two times per week that incorporate all major muscle groups

SKILL 18.3   Identifying types and uses of equipment for flexibility training and progressive-resistance exercise

FLEXIBILITY DEVELOPMENTAL PROGRESSIONS

When starting any exercise program, the best way to begin is by stretching or flexing muscles as a warm up. This will allow the body to adapt to exercise. Flexibility activities are necessary for any physical training or exercising program as they help prevent against injuries.

Activities that can improve flexibility include stretching, bending, doing yoga, dancing, martial arts, and even other muscle work that is gentle and not strenuous at all. The different classifications of stretching and flexibility exercises include proprioceptive neuromuscular facilitation (PNF), static, dynamic, and partner resistance.

Static and dynamic stretching are the two most traditional classifications of flexibility training. Static stretching involves holding a position. In other words, the participant stretches to the farthest point possible and holds for several seconds. Dynamic stretching, on the other hand, involves slow, steady movements through a range of motion. Examples of dynamic stretches include arm and leg swings. Both static and dynamic stretching is suitable to individuals of all developmental levels. Static stretching is effective for improving range of flexibility. A warm up is necessary prior to static stretching to reduce the risk of injury. Dynamic stretching is an excellent warm up in itself because it involves slow, gradual movements.

Proprioceptive neuromuscular facilitation (PNF) is a more advanced form of flexibility training that combines traditional stretching with muscle contraction. Particularly effective for rehabilitation, PNF can also target specific muscle groups and increase muscular strength. PNF is best suited for individuals training at higher levels of fitness. PNF is not suitable for children or any persons whose bones are still growing.

Finally, in partner resistance stretching a partner applies resistance to a specific body part to stretch the targeted muscle actively. This is a more advanced technique that is a key component of PNF. Partner resistance stretching is best suited for more advanced athletes and caution is necessary to avoid injury. Because the partner cannot feel the stretch, he or she must communicate with the participant to prevent overextension.

EXERCISES THAT BENEFIT THE MAJOR MUSCLE GROUPS OF THE BODY

Some of the major muscle groups of the body important to physical fitness are the traps, delts, pecs, lats, obliques, abs, biceps, quadriceps, hamstrings, adductors, triceps, biceps, and gluts.

Dumbbell Shoulder Shrug
(Trapezius)

Seated Bent-Over Rear Deltoid Raise
(Rear Deltoids)

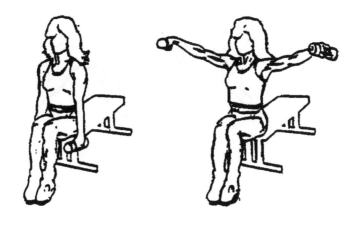

Seated Side Lateral Raise
(Front and Outer Deltoids)

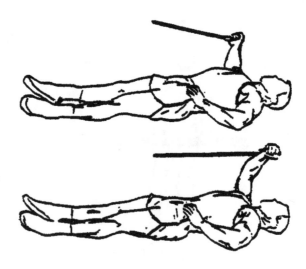

Lying Low-Pulley One-Arm Chest
(Lateral Pectorals)

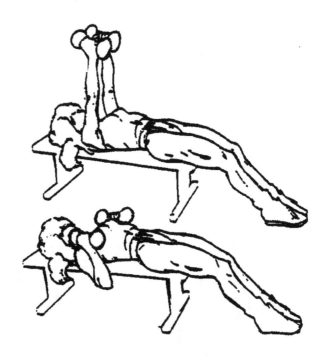

Flat Dumbbell Press
(Pectorals)

Medium-Grip Front-to-Rear Lat Pull Down
(Lats)

Straight-Arm Close-Grip Lat Pull Down
(Lats)

Dumbbell Side Bend
(Obliques)

Seated Barbell Twist
(Obliques)

Leg Pull-In
(Lower Abdominals)

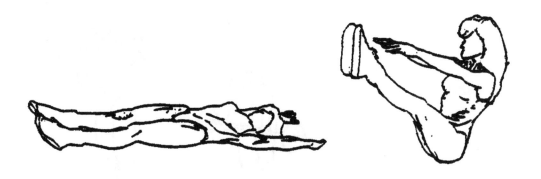

Jackknife Sit-Up
(Upper and Lower Abdominals)

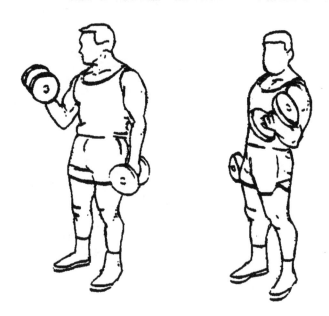

Standing Alternated Dumbbell Curl
(Biceps)

Standing Medium-Grip Barbell Curl
(Biceps)

Standing Close-Grip Easy-Curl-Bar Triceps Curl
(Triceps)

Standing Bent-Over One-Arm-Dumbbell Triceps Extension
(Triceps)

Flat-Footed Medium-Stance Barbell Half-Squat
(Thighs)

Freehand Front Lunge
(Thighs and Hamstrings)

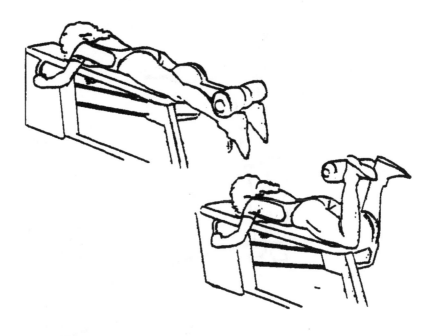

Thigh Curl on Leg Extension Machine
(Hamstrings)

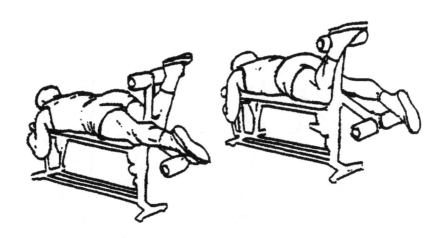

One-at-a-Time Thigh Curl on Leg Extension Machine
(Hamstrings)

Hip Abduction
(Hips)

Hip Adduction
(Inner Thigh)

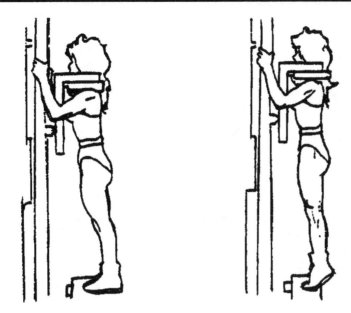

Standing Toe Raise on Wall Calf Machine
(Main Calf Muscles)

Standing Barbell Toe Raise
(Main Calf Muscles)

Hip Extension
(Hips and Thighs)

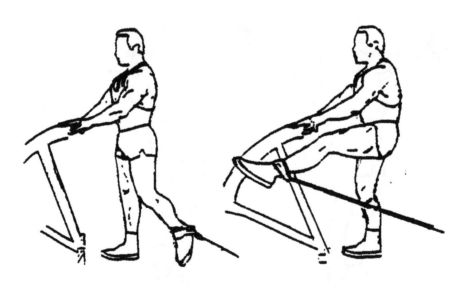

Hip Flexion
(Hip Flexors)

SKILL 18.4   Evaluating the safety and effectiveness of various types of flexibility and strength training and of various exercises

The practice of progressive resistance is an integral part of individual physical development and training programs. As with all other forms of exercise, participants should always follow certain principles and safety practices when performing progressive-resistance exercises.

As a safety precaution, instructors should formulate a health or medical questionnaire for students to complete. This can serve as a screening tool before enrolling a student into a progressive-resistance program. When beginning a weight-training program, novices should not attempt to lift too much weight.

Other principles and guidelines that participants should follow include:
- Warm-up prior to performing resistance exercises
- Gradually increase the number of repetitions for each exercise
- Exercise at least two days and receive adequate rest to achieve proper muscle development
- Perform exercises in a controlled manner
- Perform each exercise through a functional range of motion
- Work in conjunction with instructors who provide adequate feedback and guidance

Apart from the aforementioned principles, other basic principles of progressive resistance training include careful monitoring of types of lifts, intensity, volume, and variety of lifts, and taking adequate rest for recovery.

The equipment used for progressive resistance training or exercise include fit strips, dumbbells or barbells, and weight machines. Circuit training involves engaging in a variety of fitness exercises to achieve a full-body workout.

Partner-Resistance Exercises

For partner-resistance exercises, instructors should instruct students to pair-up with classmates of comparable size and strength, to ensure that the activity is productive and both training partners can apply sufficient resistance. Safety procedures for partner-resistance activities include properly demonstrating the required activity and clarifying to students that excessive competitiveness (to the extent of risking damage to another student) is not acceptable. In partner-resistance activities, the paired students serve as spotters for each other.

Weight Training

Weight training involves the use of weights (e.g. barbells or dumbbells) to create resistance to physical motion of body parts. In the case of weight training, properly demonstrating the required activity is fundamental, as the physical weights can present a heightened possibility for injuries. Instructors should instruct students to err on the side of less weight when unsure how much to use. A spotter should monitor students at all times. In order for students to make an educated decision about weight training, they need to have an understanding of the risks and benefits for personal muscular strength and endurance development.

Circuit Training

Athletes use circuit training to increase the efficiency and intensity of a training routine by alternating exercises that target different muscle groups instead of alternating exercises with rest-periods. This form of workout promotes muscular endurance development, but is more taxing on the students. Only those students who already exercising regularly and have proven their ability to remain disciplined and follow directions should attempt circuit training.

Proper Technique

Instructors should stress proper exercise technique at all times, especially with beginners to prevent development of bad habits. Whether it is weightlifting, running, or stretching, participants should not force any body part beyond the normal range of motion. Pain is a good indicator of overextension. Living by the phrase, "No pain, no gain", is potentially dangerous. Participants should use slow and controlled movements. In addition, participants must engage in a proper warm-up and cool-down before and after exercise. When lifting weights, it is always important to make sure that one has a spotter to assist them, should the need arise. A spotter can help correct the lifter's technique and help lift the weight to safety if the lifter is unable to do so. A partner can also offer encouragement and motivation. Flexibility is an often overlooked, yet important, part of exercise that can play a key role in injury prevention. Participants should perform stretching exercises after each workout session.

SAFETY – FLEXIBILITY ACTIVITIES

Safety and proper form are important considerations when engaging in flexibility exercises. The following is a list of rules that participants should follow when performing stretches:

- Always warm up before stretching: perform light to moderate cardiovascular activity prior to stretching to increase muscle elasticity – stretching while "cold" can cause injury because the muscles are tight and less elastic

- Stop if you feel pain: stretching should not cause acute pain, mild discomfort or a mild pulling sensation is acceptable

- Move into each stretch slowly and steadily – don't bounce

- Avoid "locking" joints by completely straightening them during stretches – always allow a small amount of bend when stretching

- Relax the shoulders, hands, and feet while stretching

- Maintain proper posture

INDICATED AND CONTRAINDICATED EXERCISES AND BODY POSITIONS

Contraindicated exercises and body positions (i.e. those positions that participants should avoid) in physical education activities are those that could result in injury. This includes exercises that may result in injury if performed incorrectly, where it is difficult to execute the technique properly without experience and careful supervision. Exercises that participants should avoid include sit-ups and any exercise in which the knee exceeds a 90-degree angle.

Participants should avoid sit-ups primarily because they don't work the abdominal muscles very much (since they emphasize sitting up instead of just pulling the sternum towards the pelvis, the hip flexors do most of the actual work). More significantly, though, sit-ups can damage the lower back because when the abdominal muscles contract, they attempt to round the lower back, whereas contraction of the hip flexors encourages an exaggerated arch. This opposite motion creates a grinding effect on the lowest vertebrae, which can eventually lead to chronic lower back pain.

The reason why exercises should never involve bending the knee in excess of a 90-degree angle is that bending it further puts the knee in a position where it can't safely bear weight, and greatly increases the chance of injury. Participants should also avoid exercises that involve twisting the knee. It is better to rotate the foot on the ball or heel than to twist the knee.

Indicated exercises and body positions (i.e. those that participants should use) in physical education activities are safe and they offer the maximum benefit to the student's physical development. These exercises are easy to perform and target major muscle groups. Good example exercises include push-ups, pull-ups, and abdominal crunches.

SKILL 18.5 Recognizing the benefits of regular participation in flexibility and strength training activities and strategies for integrating these activities into daily life

STRENGTH TRAINING

The benefits of regular participation in muscular strength and endurance activities include:

- Increased bone density
- Increased connective tissues strength
- Increased lean body mass
- Anaerobic power and capacity
- Improved blood-lipid ratios
- Aids in body composition management

Strategies for integrating strength and endurance activities into daily life include:

- Doing yard work
- Climbing stairs
- Lifting objects (e.g. children, laundry baskets, etc.)

FLEXIBILITY TRAINING

Flexibility training helps the muscle groups to balance. It is important that a person understand the many benefits that result from a good flexibility program.
Flexibility also improves the muscular balance and posture. Stretching activities that you can do include the hamstring stretch, calf, chest, shoulder, quadriceps, inner thigh, triceps, and forearm stretch.

Stretching promotes muscular relaxation. It also increases blood supply and nutrient flow to joints. Flexibility enhances enjoyment and is a fun, healthy activity.

People can easily integrate stretching into their daily lives. It is easy to perform basic stretches while sitting at a desk in class or at work. Such simple activities can improve well-being while enhancing flexibility.

COMPETENCY 19.0   UNDERSTAND ASSESSMENT OF HEALTH-RELATED
FITNESS AND PRINCIPLES AND PROCEDURES FOR
DEVELOPING PERSONAL FITNESS PLANS BASED ON
ASSESSMENT RESULTS

SKILL 19.1   Recognizing uses, components, characteristics, advantages,
limitations, and techniques associated with various types of
fitness assessment methods and instruments (e.g.,
FITNESSGRAM, peer assessment)

Evaluations determine the value of a particular activity. Instructors should integrate the
continuous process of evaluation into the teaching-learning experience. The goal of an
evaluation should not be limited to the school setting and the students' experiences.
Rather, we should also think of it in terms of a community's progress. Measurements for
evaluation provide other valuable services that instructors can use to classify students,
determine students' status for grading, and aid in the diagnosis of students' weaknesses
in relation to fitness skill development.

A renowned guide for educators includes the following three principles:

- Students should accept evaluations as an integral part of the teaching process.
- Instructors should use evaluations to assist students in achieving terminal
  competencies (psychomotor, cognitive, and affective).
- Instructors should base evaluations on the status of the individual student.

The Office of Instructional Services enumerates achievement standards for children in
elementary school. An individualized, well-executed physical education program should
enable a student to:

- Walk 500 yards without stopping.
- Run 30 yards dash in six seconds or less.
- Jump a standing broad jump a distance of approximately their height plus three
  inches.
- Bounce a ball to 2/4 or 4/4 music count.

Portfolio assessments are evaluations of the learning that happens in a natural setting.
They can capitalize on student work, enhance both teacher and student involvement in
evaluation, and satisfy the accountability needed to prompt school reform. Portfolio
assessment includes active diaries, attitude inventories, entry-level skill test, and
teacher/peer rating forms.

Interactive health subject area CD's allow students and instructors to enter personal fitness data and evaluation results and receive immediate feedback and suggestions for improvement.

SELECTING, CONSTRUCTING, ADAPTING, AND IMPLEMENTING ASSESSMENTS

Physical educators should construct assessments that evaluate all three domains of physical education: psychomotor, cognitive, and affective. Teachers should divide assessments in the psychomotor domain into two groups: skill-related fitness and sport-specific skills. The physical education teacher can objectively measure skill-related fitness utilizing assessments specifically designed to evaluate each component. Speed, agility, coordination, balance, and reaction time are the components of skill-related fitness. Teachers may choose to use standardized tests developed to assess each of these components. Most of these tests also include normative data. Similarly, many standardized tests are also available as an objective assessment of sport-specific skills. Many of these tests also include normative data.

Teachers should thoroughly evaluate an assessment before choosing to utilize it, as some of the existing tests are quite complicated and burdensome to implement. If a teacher chooses not to use an existing assessment, adaptation of an existing assessment is always an option. To adapt an existing assessment, the physical educator can evaluate the assessment and determine which components of the assessment are reasonable to implement and provide a valid assessment of the specified skill. The teacher would delete the remaining components from the assessment prior to implementation. In addition to the option of deleting segments of the existing assessment, the teacher might choose to make general modifications to the overall assessment. The physical educator can measure both skill-related fitness and sport-specific skills subjectively through informal assessments. Examples of informal assessments include student interviews, student self-evaluation, and checklists.

In addition to psychomotor skills, the physical educator also assesses development of the cognitive domain. Evaluation of the cognitive domain includes formal written assessments. When constructing a written assessment, the physical educator should design the assessment at an age appropriate level, include all written instructions on the test, and arrange similarly formatted questions together. Sample types of written test questions include matching, multiple choice, true-false, fill-in-the-blank, short answer, and essay. When possible, the physical educator should administer written assessments in a classroom setting, rather than on the gymnasium floor. Assessment of both the psychomotor and cognitive domains will occur at the end of each unit of instruction.

Finally, the physical educator should assess development in the affective domain. Informal assessment of the affective domain might include checklists similar to the informal checklists utilized to assess development in the psychomotor domain. Utilizing these affective checklists clarifies behavioral expectations. Additionally, standardized attitude scales are also available to physical educators. Instructors should measure development in the affective domain at various intervals throughout the school year.

METHODS OF ASSESSMENT

There are many methods of assessment available to the physical education instructor. Standardized tests are traditional assessment tools that have limited effectiveness in physical education. Because students differ greatly in natural ability and fitness, measurement against personal standards is more useful than measurement against generic standards. Some of the tools for personal assessment include observational checklists, portfolios, journals, peer assessments, and rating scales.

ASSESSMENT IN THE COGNITIVE DOMAIN

1. **Standardized Tests** – scientifically constructed test with established validity and reliability.

2. **Teacher-made Tests** – developed personally by the teacher.

3. **Essay Tests/Written Assignments** – tests the ability to organize information presented logically in written paragraphs.

4. **Objective Tests** – true/false, multiple choice, matching, diagrams, completion, or short written response.

5. **Norm-Referenced Tests** – compares individual's score to the scores of others.

6. **Criterion-Referenced Tests** – Interpreting a score by comparing it to a predetermined standard.

The trend in physical education assessment is to move increasingly away from norm- and criterion-referenced evaluations (i.e. measuring a student's achievements against the achievements of a normative group or against criteria that are arbitrarily set by either the educator or the governing educational body), and towards performance-based, or "authentic" evaluations. This creates difficulty for physical educators because it eliminates preset reference points.

The advantage of performance-based evaluations is they are equally fair to individuals with diverse backgrounds, special needs, and disabilities. In all cases, the instructor evaluates students based on their personal performance.

Portfolio construction is one way of assessing the performance of a student. The student chooses the achievements to add to the portfolio. This creates a tool that assesses current abilities and serves as a benchmark against which the instructor can measure future performance (thus evaluating progress over time, and not just a localized achievement).

TYPES OF EVALUATION

Summative evaluation strategies involve assigning the student a letter or number grade, which can reflect both the student's performance and progress. Examples include:

- Performance evaluations – the instructor assigns a letter or number grade based on the student's performance on a task or set of tasks (e.g. push-ups and sit-ups, time to run one mile, etc.).

- Progress evaluations – the instructor assigns a letter or number grade based on the student's improvement in the ability to perform a task or set of tasks.

- Effort evaluations – the instructor assigns a letter or number grade based on the student's effort in working towards training goals.

- Behavior evaluations – the instructor assigns a letter or number grade based on the student's behavior in and attitude towards training and the training environment.

Formative evaluation strategies do not provide a letter or number grade to the student, but rather focus on a textual analysis of the student's performance and progress. Examples include a written analysis of the student's performance, progress, effort, attitude, and behavior.

NATIONAL ASSESSMENT PROGRAMS

To help realize fitness goals, several organizations exist to educate and encourage physical fitness. Three such programs include Physical Best, President's Challenge, and Fitnessgram.

Physical Best is a comprehensive health-related fitness education program developed by physical educators for physical educators. The purpose of Physical Best is to educate, challenge, and encourage all children to develop the knowledge, skills, and attitudes for a healthy and fit life. The goal of the program is to move students from dependence to independence for their own fitness and health by promoting regular, enjoyable physical activity. The focus of Physical Best is to educate ALL children regardless of athletic talent, physical, and mental abilities or disabilities. (1)

The President's Challenge is a program that encourages all Americans to make regular physical activity a part of their everyday lives. No matter what your activity and fitness level, the President's Challenge can help motivate you to improve. (2)

The Cooper Institute in Dallas, Texas introduced Fitnessgram in 1982. The objective was to increase parental awareness of children's fitness levels by developing an easy way for physical education teachers to report the results of physical fitness assessments. (3)

1) http://www.aahperd.org/NASPE/physicalbest/
2) http://www.presidentschallenge.org/
3) http://www.cooperinst.org/ftginfo.asp#Overview

SKILL 19.2 Identifying developmentally appropriate assessment strategies for various fitness goals, purposes, and situations

EVALUATING MUSCULAR STRENGTH AND ENDURANCE

The standard procedure for evaluating muscular strength and endurance is measurement of repetitions performed and/or amount of weight used for various resistance exercises. For example, the instructor may ask students to perform as many pull-ups as they can or bench press a given weight as many times as they can. Comparing individual results to age- and size-based norms allows instructors to tailor fitness programs to meet the needs of each student.

Muscle strength tests – dynamometers (hand, back, and leg), cable tensiometer, the 1-RM Test (repetition maximum: bench press, standing press, arm curl, and leg press), bench-squat, sit-ups (one sit up holding a weight plate behind the neck), and lateral pull-down.

Muscle endurance tests – squat-thrust, pull-ups, sit-ups, lateral pull-down, bench-press, arm curl, push-ups, and dips.

EVALUATING FLEXIBILITY

Standard methods of evaluating flexibility include the sit and reach test and having students try to touch their hands behind their backs. Instructors can devise additional flexibility tests to evaluate the range of motion of specific joints. In these cases, the tests should reflect practical function.

Flexibility tests – sit and reach, Kraus-Webber Floor Touch Test, trunk extension, forward bend of trunk, Leighton Flexometer, shoulder rotation/flexion, and goniometer.

ASSESSING AND INTERPRETING FITNESS DATA AND MOTOR SKILL
PERFORMANCE

In this section, we will discuss methods for assessing and interpreting student fitness
data and motor skill performance. First, we introduce examples of fitness and skill tests.
Next, we discuss fitness prescriptions and feedback. Finally, we discuss interpretation
of test results and communication of results to various audiences.

Specific physical fitness appraisals

The following is a list of tests that instructors can use to assess the physical fitness of
students.

Cardio-respiratory fitness tests – maximal stress test, sub maximal stress test, Bruce
Protocol, Balke Protocol, Astrand and Rhyming Test, PWC Test, Bench Step Test,
Rockport Walking Fitness Test, and Cooper 1.5 Mile Run/Walk Fitness Test.

Body Composition determination – Hydrostatic weighing, skin fold measurements,
limb/girth circumference, and body mass index.

Agility tests – Illinois Agility Run.

Balance tests – Bass Test of Dynamic Balance (lengthwise and crosswise), Johnson
Modification of the Bass Test of Dynamic Balance, modified sideward leap, and balance
beam walk.

Coordination tests – Stick test of Coordination.

Power tests – vertical jump.

Speed tests – 50-yard dash.

Skill assessment in the evaluation of student performance

A. General Skills:

1. **Iowa Brace Test** – measures motor educability.

2. **AAHPERD Youth Fitness Test** – measures motor capacity.

3. **AAHPERD Health Related Physical Fitness Test** – measures physical capacity.

4. **McCloy's General Motor Ability and Capacity Test** – measures motor ability and
motor efficiency.

5. **Rodgers Strength Test** – measures muscular strength.

6. **Texas PE Test** – measures motor ability.

7. **Skills tests for accuracy** – involve kicking, throwing, or striking an object toward a goal; activities include volleyball serves, basketball free throws, badminton short serves, and basketball passing (e.g. AAHPERD Basketball Passing Test for Accuracy).

8. **Skills test for total bodily movement** – requires performing a test course with movements similar to the sport (e.g. AAHPERD Basketball Control Test).

9. **Wall Volley Test** - measures the number of consecutive successful time/trials to pass, kick, throw, or strike an object at a wall in a given time (e.g. AAHPERD Basketball Passing Test).

10. **Skills Tests for Power or Distance** - involve kicks, throws, or strokes to measure the ability to kick, throw, or strike an object (e.g. Badminton Drive for Distance, Cornish Handball Power Test).

11. **Combination Tests** - composed of previous groupings to assess speed and accuracy.

B. Teacher Ratings: instructors create a numerical scale from one to five and rank performance based on specific, observable movements. An example is evaluating the use of space, use of focus, and variety of movements in a creative movement class.

C. Student Progress: score improvements (e.g. archery, badminton) and charting (e.g. basketball shots missed).

Instructors can administer skills tests for specific sports in one of two ways. First, rate individual performance based on a specified number of trials. Alternatively, evaluate skills using norm-referenced scales for a specific grade level.
Two problems with skill tests are that they take too much time to administer and the reliability is suspect.

Basic statistical applications

Statistical applications for physical education assessment purposes allow us to evaluate where the score of a given assessment stands in comparison to other assessments and compare different assessments of the same student's abilities (in other fields – tracking intra-individual differences, or in the same field over time – tracking the student's progress).

Central tendency and variability determine where a range of scores cluster on the assessment scale and whether they are all highly localized around one point on the scale, or spread out over a range.

Standard scores and norms allow us to evaluate where assessment results stand in relation to the 'normal' expected achievement level.

Correlations allow us to evaluate the frequency at which two assessment trends appear in conjunction. Note that correlation does not imply causation.

Instructors must always understand that their physical assessments must be in direct correlation to the standards required by the state.

SKILL 19.3   Demonstrating knowledge of how to use fitness assessment results to establish individual goals for health-related fitness

FITNESS PRESCRIPTIONS

Physical fitness assessments are an important tool for physical education instructors and students. Instructors must be careful not to overemphasize fitness assessments, as students that score poorly may become discouraged and students that perform well may become complacent. When used correctly, however, the results of fitness assessments are valuable tools in the development of exercise prescriptions. For example, an instructor can use the results of a multi-faceted fitness assessment to determine the fitness strengths and weaknesses of each student and the areas that each student needs to improve.

Simple exercises to improve aerobic endurance include walking, jogging, and bicycling. Exercises to improve muscular strength and endurance include push-ups, pull-ups, sit-ups, and weight lifting. Exercises to improve flexibility are stretches for various parts of the body. The exercises that help improve aerobic endurance, muscular strength, and muscular endurance also help improve body composition.

APPLYING AND COMMUNICATING ASSESSMENT DATA

Instructors should compare assessment data to grade equivalency norms to determine where each child is relative to where he should be. However, the instructor should place the most emphasis on evaluating the child relative to past performance. Progress is more important than current achievement. A learning-disabled child might display below average levels of achievement despite having made a great deal of progress, while a gifted child might be above grade equivalency norms despite stagnation.

Instructors should communicate assessment data should differently to students, parents, and school board members.

- **Assessment data communicated to students** should be encouraging, and should be limited to a textual analysis of the child's progress and effort (it is not helpful or encouraging to remind a child that he is below grade level norms, especially if he has worked hard and made progress). The ultimate purpose of assessment data communicated to a child is to encourage further hard work.

- **Assessment data communicated to parents** should also be encouraging and should focus on the child's progress and effort. That said, it is also important that a parent receive an accurate picture of the child's status relative to grade level norms, especially if the child is in need of remedial assistance.

- **Assessment data communicated to school board members** is generally more summative in nature (a letter or number grade). Since school board members will generally see evaluations of entire classes at a time without knowing the individual children, it is not important for them to receive an encouraging picture of an individual child's progress. It is more important for them to see both current achievement levels and rates of progress to properly assess curriculum design, lesson planning, and program evaluation.

SKILL 19.4 Interpreting fitness test results to identify strengths and weaknesses in relation to fitness components and to select fitness activities for a personal fitness plan

   o   See Skill 19.3

SKILL 19.5   Applying knowledge of principles and techniques for designing and implementing individualized fitness and weight management plans (e.g., setting realistic short-term goals, monitoring caloric intake and expenditure)

   o   See also Skill 16.5

GOAL SETTING

Goal setting is an effective way of achieving progress. In order to preserve and/or increase self-confidence, you and your students must set goals that are frequently reachable. One such way of achieving this is to set several small, short-term goals to attain one long-term goal. Be realistic in goal setting to increase fitness levels gradually and always make sure that the goals that are set are measurable. As students reach their goals, set more in order to continue performance improvement. Keep in mind that maintaining a current fitness level is an adequate goal provided the individual is in a healthy state. Reward your students when they reach goals. Rewards serve as motivation to reach the next goal. Also, be sure to prepare for lapses. Try to get back on track as soon as possible.

SKILL 19.6   Recognizing ways in which activity participation patterns change throughout the life span and strategies for motivating individuals to persevere in personal fitness plans

INTRINSIC MOTIVATION

Intrinsic motivation refers to the motivation to engage in an activity without any compelling external reason. It is when performing the activity is "its own reward". An understanding of the factors related to intrinsic motivation combines elements of attribution theory, self-efficacy, and research related to goal orientation. Some specific factors include:

- Attribution of educational results to internal factors that are under the control of the student (for example, the amount of effort that they put in, as opposed to their skill level, which students see as a fixed quantity).

- Belief that they are able to perform the desired tasks effectively because of their effort and skill-set (i.e. that positive results of their actions are not the result of luck).

- A connection with the subject matter – the student will either enjoy the activity for the sake of the activity or enjoy the personal feeling of gaining skill in performing the activity (as opposed to rote-learning situations or receiving rewards for performance, such as good grades).

MOTIVATIONAL METHODS

Physical education instructors should give students homework just as academic teachers do. For example, when teaching the overhand throw, the instructor may ask his students to practice throwing with a friend during recess or a parent at home. Instructors should also be familiar with local sports leagues and other opportunities for physical activity in the community. The instructor can inform students of such opportunities and promote participation in physical activities throughout the year.

MOTIVATIONAL STRATEGIES

Motivation is essential to student learning in physical education and all academic disciplines. Physical education instructors should recognize and understand the important elements of student motivation. Important theories and concepts in student motivation include attribution theory, social learning theory, learned helplessness, and self-efficacy.

Attribution theory describes how people make causal explanations and how they answer questions beginning with 'Why?' The theory deals with the information people use in making causal inferences and with how they utilize this information to answer causal questions. For instance, a student's aggressively competitive behavior may reflect her personality, or it may be a response to situational pressures. Attribution theory describes the processes of explaining events and the behavioral and emotional consequences of those explanations. Attribution theory also claims that students perceptions of their educational experience affects their motivation more than the experience itself.

Social learning theory focuses on the learning that occurs within a social context. It emphasizes that people learn from one another and includes such concepts as observational learning, imitation, and modeling. Social learning theory asserts that people can learn by observing the behavior of others and the outcomes of those behaviors. It further states that learning can occur without a permanent change in behavior. Physical education instructors should also be note that cognition plays an important role in learning. Awareness and expectations of future rewards or punishments can have a major effect on the behaviors that people exhibit. Thus, socialization and reward/punishment can motivate students to learn.

Learned helplessness occurs in situations where continued failure may inhibit somebody from trying again and can also lead to many forms of depression. Thus, it is very important how physical education instructors respond to children's failures and successes. If a student feels as though he cannot control his environment, this lack of control will impair learning in certain situations. That is, learned helplessness often occurs in environments where people experience events in which they have, or feel as though they have, no control over what happens to them.

Self-efficacy describes a person's belief about his/her capability to produce designated levels of performance that exercise influence over events that affect their lives. Self-efficacy beliefs determine how people feel, think, motivate themselves, and behave. Such beliefs produce these diverse effects through cognitive, motivational, affective, and selection processes. A strong sense of efficacy enhances human accomplishment and personal well-being in many ways. People with high assurance in their capabilities view difficult tasks as challenges rather than threats. A student with high self-efficacy will be highly motivated to participate in sports and game related activities. To build efficacy, the instructor must not only raise the student's belief in his/her capabilities, but also structure situations that breed success and limit repeated failure. Students with high self-efficacy measure success in terms of self-improvement rather than by triumphs over others.

SELF-MOTIVATION

Finding intrinsic motivation for study is the main factor promoting the development of self-motivated learners. Helping learners become self-motivated is a process that revolves around connecting them personally with the material that they are studying, and instilling a belief in the their ability to control the outcome of their studies (if they believe they are not capable of mastering the material, they cannot become self-motivated learners).

This process begins with the cultivation of a positive attitude about the study of the subject matter in question. Instructors should emphasize to students that they are capable of mastering the material. Instructors can reinforce this belief by setting small, incremental milestones in the educational plan that show the students the progress they are making.

Having convinced the students of their ability to learn the subject matter and master their goals, instructors should teach the students to become increasingly goal-oriented. This begins with students setting their own short-term goals and, after they begin developing a pattern of meeting their goals, longer-term goals. As students set goals, instructors should teach students to accept and assume responsibility for their decisions, actions, and outcomes.

SUBAREA VI.   SPORTS AND LIFETIME ACTIVITIES

COMPETENCY 20.0   UNDERSTAND TECHNIQUES, SKILLS, RULES, STRATEGIES, ETIQUETTE, EQUIPMENT, AND SAFETY PRACTICES FOR INDIVIDUAL, DUAL, AND LIFETIME SPORTS AND ACTIVITIES (E.G., BADMINTON, BOWLING, GOLF, TUMBLING, TENNIS, TRACK AND FIELD)

SKILL 20.1   Recognizing skills, rules, strategies, and performance assessment techniques for individual, dual, and lifetime sports and activities

INDIVIDUAL AND DUAL SPORTS AND ACTIVITIES – OVERVIEW

Archery – Skills that students study in archery classes include proper care for their equipment, properly stringing the bow, drawing, and shooting with accuracy (including compensating for distance, angle, and wind).

Safety practices in archery include respectful handling of the equipment (which is potentially dangerous) and ensuring that students only draw bows when pointed at a (non-living) target. Finally, instructors should keep students away from the path between firing students and their targets at all times.

Proper equipment for archery classes include a bow and arrows, which can vary greatly in technical complexity and cost, and a target.

Badminton – Students in a badminton class will have to master the strokes as basic skills and should learn at least some of them by name (e.g. types of serves, net shot, net kills, drive, push, lift). Students should also know which strokes are appropriate from which areas of the court.

Bocce ball – Requires a flat, level playing surface (packed dirt, gravel or grass are ideal). The instructor divides students into two teams of one, two, or four players each. Each team gets four balls, divided equally among the players. A player from the starting team stands behind the foul line (10 feet from the throwing end of the court) and throws the small ball ("pallina") toward the opposite end of the playing surface. The player then throws one of the larger balls ("boccia"), trying to get it as close to the pallina as possible without touching it. Players from the opposing team take turns throwing their balls until one of the balls stops closer to the pallina than the starting player's ball. If they fail to do so, the starting team tries to outdo its first attempt. Teams continue to take turns in this manner until they have thrown all the balls. The team with closest ball gets a point. This game emphasizes throwing skills (coordination, gross and fine motor skills).

Bowling – Skills that students will learn in bowling classes include learning to select a ball of comfortable weight and appropriate for the shot they need to make, properly controlling the ball so it hits the pins they are aiming for, and learning the dynamics of pin interaction to plan the proper angle of entry for the ball.

Safety practices in bowling include wearing proper footwear, handling the balls cautiously, and preventing horseplay (to avoid situations where a heavy bowling ball may drop inopportunely and cause injury).
Equipment needed for a bowling class includes proper footwear, a bowling ball, pins, and a lane.

Cross-country running – Much like track and field, cross-country running will teach the students proper running form, the ability to pace their energy expenditure relative to the length of the course, and the ability to adapt their running technique to the terrain.

Cross-country running strategy focuses on adapting energy expenditure relative to the length of the course and psychological training to minimize responsiveness to physical exhaustion. Runners should familiarize themselves with a course before running it.

Safety practices, like other running sports, focus on proper attention to warm-ups and cool-downs and remaining attentive to the course, which may be quite rugged. Because cross-country running often takes place in fairly remote, natural settings, it is important to coordinate the availability of first aid.

Equipment required for cross-country running includes proper footwear and water to prevent dehydration on longer runs.

Frisbee Golf – Skills that students will acquire in a Frisbee golf class include methods of throwing the Frisbee (primarily forehand, side arm, and backhand throws). Students will also gain an intuitive sense for the physics governing the movement of the Frisbee (e.g. stability and speed range).

Frisbee golf strategy focuses on gauging distances and the amount of force and angle of throw required to land the disc in the target.

Frisbee golf safety practices involve ensuring that students don't wander in areas where a disc is in play, as this may result in injury. Instructors should also instruct students to remain alert and not throw the disc if they perceive there is a possibility that they might hit an individual.

Equipment needed for Frisbee golf include a proper disc (though you can substitute a regular Frisbee for school purposes), target nets, and a playing area large enough to accommodate the game without excessive risk of the Frisbee flying irretrievably out of bounds.

Golf – The most fundamental skills for students to learn when studying golf include the correct way to execute a golf swing with proper posture and how to judge distance for shot selection correctly. Further, students should learn specific shots and their names (e.g. tee shot, fairway shot, bunker shot, and putt).

Strategy in golf centers on properly gauging distances and required force to control the ball to the best extent possible.

Safety practices in golf, especially with students, involve ensuring that the course is clear and there are no students nearby when players are swinging. Instructors should also remind students that golf clubs are not toys, and that misuse can result in injury.

Equipment necessary for a golf class includes a proper set of clubs and golf balls (a golf course or open area for hitting balls is also necessary).

Handball – Skills that students will learn in a handball class will include catching and accurately throwing the ball, taking steps while bouncing it (similar to basketball's dribble), and quick analysis of the playing situation to determine who the best target is for a pass.

Strategy in handball centers on staying one step ahead of the opposing team. Keep them guessing and have multiple contingencies for given situations, so that game play doesn't become predictable (and easier to counter). Specific tactics can include types of shots that are harder for the opponent to hit, and shots that will put the ball out of play (when it is advantageous to do so).

Pickleball – Skills that students will learn in pickleball classes include manipulation of the ball with the racket and the variety of strokes.

Pickleball strategy is similar to tennis. Students should learn to vary their strokes to keep their opponents guessing, with the goal of reaching the frontcourt in a net volley position first. This places the students in the best position to win the point.

Table Tennis (Ping Pong) – Skills that students will study when learning table tennis include the variety of grips (e.g. penhold, shakehand, V-grip), and the various types of offensive and defensive strokes. Students will also learn to gauge the force needed to manipulate the ball properly.

Strategies for success in table tennis involve manipulating and minimizing the opponent's ability to return a shot – this includes learning to hit to the opponent's weak side, putting a spin on the ball so as to make its movement less predictable, and setting the opponent up to receive a shot that he cannot return.

Tennis – Skills that students will learn when studying tennis include the proper grips of the racket and stroke techniques, which they should know by name (e.g. flat serve, topspin serve, forehand, backhand, volley, overhead).

Shuffleboard – Depending on whether students are playing deck shuffleboard or table shuffleboard, they will learn to manipulate the discs, either with or without sticks.

Strategy requires students to properly gauge and apply the force needed to propel the disc accurately to a particular spot on the playing area.

Safety practices in shuffleboard include properly instructing and monitoring students to avoid horseplay, which may result in injury caused by the playing equipment.

Equipment needed for a shuffleboard class include a disc with which to play, the equipment to manipulate the disc (this will vary depending on whether the shuffleboard game is played on a deck or on a table), and the appropriate playing area.

Track and field – In track and field practice, students will acquire proper running form, the ability to pace their energy expenditure relative to the length of the track, and the ability to manipulate objects in field events.

Track and field strategy focuses on learning to pace energy expenditure relative to the length of the track and analyzing the psychological interaction with other racers and competitors.

Safety practices in track and field include adhering to proper warm up and cool down procedures to prevent injury and handling field equipment (e.g. discus, javelin, and shot) with care.

Equipment that is important to track events is minimal, with the only important requirement being appropriate footwear. Field events require specialized equipment. For example, throwing events require a discus, shot, or javelin. Jumping events require a landing area and height or length measuring device.

INDIVIDUAL AND DUAL SPORT STRATEGIES

Archery strategies for correcting errors in aiming and releasing:

- Shifting position.

- Relaxing both the arms and shoulders at the moment of release.

- Reaching point of aim before releasing string.

- Pointing aim to the right or left of direct line between the archer and the target's center.

- Aiming with the left eye.

- Sighting with both eyes.

- Using the proper arrow.

Bowling for spares strategies:

- Identifying the key pin and determining where to hit it to pick up remaining pins.

- Using the three basic alignments: center position for center pins, left position for left pins, and right position for right pins.

- Rolling the spare ball in the same manner as rolled for the first ball of frame.

- Concentrating harder for the spare ball because of the reduced opportunity for pin action and margin of error.

Badminton Strategies:

Strategies for Return of Service

- Returning serves with shots that are straight ahead.

- Returning service so that opponent must move out of his/her starting position.

- Returning long serves with an overhead clear or drop shot to near corner.

- Returning short serves with underhand clear or a net drop to near corner.

Strategies for Serving

- Serving long to the backcourt near centerline.

- Serving short when opponent is standing too deep in his/her receiving court to return the serve, or using a short serve to eliminate a smash return if opponent has a powerful smash from the backcourt.

Handball or Racquetball Strategies:

- Identifying opponent's strengths and weaknesses.

- Making opponent use less dominant hand or backhand shots if they are weaker.

- Frequently alternating fastballs and lobs to change the pace (changing the pace is particularly effective for serving).

- Maintaining position near middle of court (the well) that is close enough to play low balls and corner shots.

- Placing shots that keep opponent's position at a disadvantage to return cross-court and angle shots.

- Using high lob shots that go overhead but do not hit the back wall with enough force to rebound to drive an opponent out of position when he/she persistently plays close to the front wall.

Tennis Strategies:

- Lobbing – using a high, lob shot for defense giving the player more time to get back into position. Lobbing is also a great change-up in order to break the other players concentration.

- Identifying opponent's weaknesses, attacking them, and recognizing and protecting one's own weaknesses by not allowing the other player to be able to identify them.

- Be quicker and out-think an opponent.

- Using change of pace, lobs, spins, approaching the net, and deception at the correct time.

- Hitting cross-court (from corner to corner of the court) for maximum safety and opportunity to regain position.

- Directing the ball where the opponent is not.

- Let the opposing player make the mistakes. Keep the ball in play.

RULES OF INDIVIDUAL AND DUAL SPORTS

ARCHERY:

- Arrows that bounce off the target or go through the target count as 7 points.

- Arrows landing on lines between two rings receive the higher score of the two rings.

- Arrows hitting the petticoat receive no score.

BADMINTON:

- Intentionally balking opponent or making preliminary feints results in a fault (side in = loss of serve; side out = point awarded to side in).

- When a shuttlecock falls on a line, it is in play (i.e. a fair play).

- If the striking team hits shuttlecock before it crosses net it is a fault.

- Touching the net when the shuttlecock is in play is a fault.

- The same player hitting the shuttlecock twice is a fault.

- The shuttlecock going through the net is a fault.

BOWLING:

- No score for a pin knocked down by a pinsetter (human or mechanical).

- There is no score for the pins when any part of the foot, hand, or arm extends or crosses over the foul line (even after ball leaves the hand) or if any part of the body contacts division boards, walls, or uprights that are beyond the foul line.

- There is no count for pins displaced or knocked down by a ball leaving the lane before it reaches the pins.

- There is no count when balls rebound from the rear cushion.

RACQUETBALL/HANDBALL:

- A server stepping outside service area when serving faults.

- The server is out (relinquishes serve) if he/she steps outside of serving zone twice in succession while serving.

- Server is out if he/she fails to hit the ball rebounding off the floor during the serve.

- The opponent must have a chance to take a position or the referee must call for play before the server can serve the ball.

- The server re-serves the ball if the receiver is not behind the short line at the time of the serve.

- A served ball that hits the front line and does not land back of the short line is "short"; therefore, it is a fault. The ball is also short when it hits the front wall and two sidewalls before it lands on the floor back of the short line.

- A serve is a fault when the ball touches the ceiling from rebounding off the front wall.

- A fault occurs when any part of the foot steps over the outer edges of the service or the short line while serving.

- A hinder (dead ball) is called when a returned ball hits an opponent on its way to the front wall - even if the ball continues to the front wall.

- A hinder is any intentional or unintentional interference of an opponent's opportunity to return the ball.

TENNIS:

A player loses a point when:

- The ball bounces twice on her side of the net.

- The player returns the ball to any place outside of designated areas.

- The player stops or touches the ball in the air before it lands out-of-bounds.

- The player intentionally strikes the ball twice with the racket.

- The ball strikes any part of a player or racket after initial attempt to hit the ball.

- A player reaches over the net to hit the ball.

- A player throws his racket at the ball.

- The ball strikes any permanent fixture that is out-of-bounds (other than the net).

- A ball touching the net and landing inside the boundary lines is in play (except on the serve, where a ball contacting the net results in a "let" – replay of the serve)

- A player fails, on two consecutive attempts, to serve the ball into the designated area (i.e. double fault).

TERMINOLOGY OF TARGET SPORTS

Archery Terminology:

- Addressing the target – standing ready to shoot with a proper shooting stance.

- Anchor point – specific location on the archer's face to which index finger comes while holding and aiming.

- Archery golf (adaptation of golf to archery) – players shoot for holes, scoring according to the number of shots required to hit the target.

- Arm guard – a piece of leather or plastic worn on the inside of the forearm, protecting the arm from the bowstring.

- Arrow plate – a protective piece of hard material set into the bow where the arrow crosses it.

- Arrow rest – a small projection at the top of the bow handle where the arrow rests.

- Back – the side of the bow away from the shooter.

- Bow arm – the arm that holds the bow.

- Bow sight – a device attached to the bow through which the archer sights when aiming.

- Bow weight – designates the amount of effort needed to pull a bowstring a specific distance.

- Cant – shooting while holding the bow slightly turned or tilted.

- Cast – the distance a bow can shoot an arrow.

- Clout shooting – a type of shooting using a target 48 feet in diameter laid on the ground at a distance of 180 yards for men and 120 or 140 yards for women. Participants usually shoot 36 arrows per round.

- Cock/Index feather – the feather that is set at a right angle to the arrow nock; differently colored than the other two feathers.

- Creeping – letting the drawing hand move forward at the release.

- Crest – the archer's identifying marks located just below the fletchings.

- Draw – pulling the bowstring back into the anchor position.

- End – a specific number of arrows shot at one time or from one position before retrieval of arrows.

- Face – the part of the bow facing the shooter.

- Finger tab – a leather flap worn on the drawing hand protecting the fingers and providing a smooth release of the bowstring.

- Fletchings – the feathers of the arrow that give guidance to its flight.

- Flight shooting – shooting an arrow the farthest possible distance.

- Handle – the grip at the midsection of the bow.

- Hen feathers – the two feathers that are not set at right angles to the arrow nock.

- Instinctive shooting – aiming and shooting instinctively rather than using a bow sight or point-of-aim method.

- Limbs – upper and lower parts of the bow divided by the handle.

- Nock – the groove in the arrow's end where the string is placed.

- Nocking point – the point on the string where the arrow is placed.

- Notch – the grooves of the upper and lower tips of the limbs where the bowstring is fitted.

- Over bow – using too strong a bow that is too powerful to pull a bowstring the proper distance.

- Overdraw – drawing the bow so that the pile of the arrow is inside the bow.

- Petticoat – the part of the target face outside the white ring.

- Pile/point – the arrow's pointed, metal tip.

- Plucking – jerking the drawing hand laterally away from the face on the release causing the arrow's flight to veer to the left.

- Point-blank range – the distance from the target where the point of aim is right on the bull's eye.

- Point-of-aim – a method of aiming that aligns the pile of the arrow with the target.

- Quiver – a receptacle for carrying or holding arrows.

- Recurve bow – a bow that is curved on the ends.

- Release – the act of letting the bowstring slip off the fingertips.

- Round – the term used to indicate shooting a specified number of arrows at a designated distance or distances.

- Roving – an outdoor archery game that uses natural targets (trees, bushes, stumps, etc.) for competition.

- Serving – the thread wrapped around the bowstring at the nocking point.

- Shaft – the long, body part of the arrow.

- Spine – the rigidity and flexibility characteristics of an arrow.

- Tackle – archery equipment referred to in its entirety.

- Target face – the painted front of a target.

- Trajectory – the flight path of the arrow.

- Vane – an arrow's plastic feather.

Bowling Terminology:

- Anchor – the teammate who shoots last.

- Baby split – the 1-7 or 3-10 pin railroads.

- Backup – a reverse hook rotating to the right for a right-handed bowler.

- Bed posts – the 7-10 railroad.

- Blow – an error or missing a spare that is not split.

- Box – a frame.

- Brooklyn – a crossover ball striking the 1-2 pocket.

- Bucket – the 2-4-5-8 or 3-5-6-9 leaves.

- Cherry – chopping off the front pin on a spare.

- Double – two consecutive strikes.

- Double pinochle – the 7-6 and 4-10 split.

- Crossover – same as a Brooklyn.

- Dutch 200 (Dutchman) – a score of 200 made by alternating strikes and spares for the entire game.

- Error – same as a "blow."

- Foul – touching or going beyond the foul line in delivering the ball.

- Frame – the box where scores are entered.

- Gutter ball – a ball that falls into either gutter.

- Handicap – awarding an individual or team a bonus score or score adjustment that is based on averages.

- Head pin – the number one pin.

- Hook – a ball that breaks to the left for a right-handed bowler and breaks to the right for a left-handed bowler.

- Jersey side – same as a Brooklyn.

- Kegler – synonym for a bowler.

- Lane – a bowling alley.

- Leave – pin or pins left standing after a throw.

- Light hit – hitting the head pin lightly to the right or left side.

- Line – a complete game as recorded on the score sheet.

- Mark – getting a strike or spare.

- Open frame – a frame in which no mark is made, leaving at least one pin standing after rolling both balls in a frame.

- Pocket – space between the head pin and pins on either side.

- Railroad – synonym for a split.

- Sleeper – a pin hidden from view.

- Spare – knocking all pins down with two balls.

- Split – a leave, after throwing the first ball, in which the number one pin plus a second pin are down, and when seven pins remain standing.

- Spot – a bowler's point of aim on the alley.

- Striking out – obtaining three strikes in the last frame.

- Tap – a pin that remains standing after an apparently perfect hit.

- Turkey – three consecutive strikes.

TERMINOLOGY OF NET/WALL SPORTS

Badminton Terminology:

- Alley – the area on each side of the court used for doubles that is 1.5 feet wide.

- Around the head stroke – an overhead stroke used to hit a forehand-like overhead stroke that is on the backhand side of the body.

- Back alley – the area between the baseline and the doubles long service line.

- Backcourt – the back third of the court.

- Backhand – a stroke made on the non-racket side of the body.

- Baseline – the back boundary line of the court.

- Bird – another name for the shuttlecock/shuttle.

- Block – a soft shot used mainly to defend a smash; intercepting opponent's smash and returning it back over the net.

- Carry/Throw – a call when the shuttle remains on the racket during a stroke. It is legal if the racket follows the intended line of flight.

- Centerline – the mid-line separating the service courts.

- Clear – a high shot that goes over the opponent's head and lands close to the baseline.

- Combination alignment – partners playing both up-and-back and side-by-side during doubles games and/or volleys.

- Crosscourt – a diagonal shot hit into the opposite court.

- Defense – the team or player hitting the shuttle upwards.

- Double hit – an illegal shot where the player contacts the shuttle twice with the racket in one swing.

- Doubles service court – the short, wide area to which the server must serve in doubles play.

- Down the line shot – a straight-ahead shot (usually down the sideline).

- Drive – a hard, driven shot traveling parallel to the floor (clears net but does not have enough height for opponent to smash).

- Drop – a shot just clearing the net and then falling close to it.

- Face – the racket's string area.

- Fault – an infraction of the rules resulting in loss of serve or a point awarded to the server.

- First serve – a term used in doubles play to indicate that the server is the "first server" during an inning.

- Foot fault – Illegal movement/position of the feet by either the server or receiver.

- Forecourt – the front area of the court (between the net and the short service line).

- Forehand – a stroke made on the racket side of the body.

- Game point – the point, if won, that allows the server to win the game.

- Hand in – a term indicating that the server retains the serve.

- Hand out – the term used in doubles to denote that one player has lost the service.

- Home base – a center court position where a player can best play any shot hit by an opponent.

- Inning – the period a player or team holds service.

- Let – stopping the point because of some type of outside interference. Players replay the point.

- Lifting the shuttle – stroking the shuttle underhanded and hitting it upward.

- Long serve – a high, deep serve landing near the long service line in doubles or the back boundary line in singles.

- Love – the term used to indicate a zero score.

- Match – a series of games. Winning two out of three games wins the match.

- Match point – the point, if won by the server, which makes that person the winner of the match.

- Midcourt – the middle-third of the court (between short service line and long service line for doubles).

- Net shot – a shot taken near the net.

- Non-racket side – the opposite side of the hand holding the racket.

- Offense – the team or player that is stroking the shuttle downward.

- Overhead – a motion used to strike the shuttle when it is above the head.

- Racket foot or leg – the foot or leg on the same side as the hand holding the racket.

- Ready position – the position a player assumes to be ready to move in any direction.

- Receiver – the player to whom the shuttle is served.

- Second serve – in doubles, the term indicates that one partner has lost the serve, and the other partner is now serving.

- Server – the player putting the shuttle into play.

- Setting – choosing the amount of additional points to play when certain tie scores occur.

- Short-serve – a serve barely clearing the net and landing just beyond the short service line.

- Shuttlecock/Shuttle – the feathered, plastic or nylon object that players volley back and forth over the net.

- Side Alley – see alley.

- Smash – an overhead stroke hit downward with great velocity and angle.

- "T" – the intersection of the centerline and the short service line.

- Underhand – an upward stroke to hit the shuttle when it has fallen below shoulder level.

- Unsight – illegal position taken by the server's partner so the receiver cannot see the shuttle.

- Up-and-back – an offensive alignment used in doubles. The "up" player is responsible for the forecourt and the "back" player is responsible for both.

Racquetball/Handball Terminology:

- Ace – a serve that completely eludes the receiver.

- Back-wall shot – a shot made from a rebound off the back wall.

- Box – see service box.

- Ceiling shot – a shot that first strikes the ceiling, then the front wall.

- Crotch – the junction of any two playing surfaces, as between the floor and any wall.

- Crotch shot – a ball that simultaneously strikes the front wall and floor (not good).

- Cut throat – a three-man game in which the server plays against the other two players. Each player keeps an individual score.

- Drive shot – a power shot against the front wall rebounding in a fast, low, and straight line.

- Fault – an illegally served ball.

- Handout – retiring the server who fails to serve legally or when the serving team fails to return a ball that is in play.

- Hinder – interference or obstruction of the flight of the ball during play.

- Kill – a ball rebounded off the front wall so close to the floor that it is impossible to return.

- Passing shot – a shot placed out of an opponent's reach on either side.

- Rally – continuous play of the ball by opponents.

- Receiving line – the broken line parallel to the short line on a racquetball court.

- Run-around shot – a ball striking one sidewall, the rear wall, and the other sidewall.

- Safety zone – a five-foot area bounded by the back edge of the short line and receiving line that is only observed during the serve in racquetball.

- Screen – a hinder due to obstruction of the opponent's vision.

- Server – person in the "hand-in" position and eligible to serve.

- Service box – the service zone bounded by the sidewall and a parallel line 18 inches away; denotes where server's partner must stand in doubles during the serve.

- Service court – the area where the ball must land when it is returned from the front wall on the serve.

- Service line – the line that is parallel to and five feet in front of the short line.

- Service zone – the area where the ball must be served.

- Short line – the line on the floor parallel to front wall and equidistant from front and back wall. The serve must go over this line when returning from the front wall.

- Shoot – attempt kill shots.

- Side out – loss of serve.

- Thong – the strap on the bottom handle of the racquetball racquet that is worn around the player's wrist.

- Volley – returning the ball to the front wall before it bounces on the floor.

- Z-ball – defensive shot that strikes the front wall, a sidewall, and then the opposite sidewall.

Tennis Terminology:

- Ace – serving a ball untouched by the opponent's racket.

- Advantage (Ad) – a scoring term. The next point won after the score is "deuce."

- Alley – the 4.5-foot strip on either side of the singles court that enlarges the court for doubles.

- Approach shot – a shot hit inside the baseline while approaching the net.

- Backcourt – the area between the service line and the baseline.

- Backhand – strokes hit on the left side of a right-handed player.

- Backspin – spin placed on a ball that causes the ball to bounce back toward the hitter.

- Back swing – the beginning of all groundstrokes and service motion requiring a back swing to gather energy for the forward swing.

- Baseline – the end line of a tennis court.

- Break – winning a game in when the opponent serves.

- Center mark – a short mark bisecting the baseline.

- Center service line – the perpendicular line to the net dividing the two service courts in halves.

- Center strap – the strap at the center of the net anchored to the court to facilitate a constant 3-foot height for the net at its center.

- Center stripe – same as the center service line.

- Chip – a short chopping motion of the racket against the back and bottom side of the ball imparting backspin.

- Chop – placing backspin on the ball with a short, high-to-low forward swing.

- Cross-court – a shot hit diagonally from one corner of the court over the net into the opposite corner of the court.

- Cut off the angle – moving forward quickly against an opponent's cross-court shot, allowing the player to hit the ball near the center of the court rather than near the sidelines.

- Deep (depth) – a shot bouncing near the baseline on groundstrokes and near the service line on serves.

- Default – a player who forfeits his/her position in a tournament by not playing a scheduled match.

- Deuce – a term used when the game score is 40-40.

- Dink – a ball hit very softly and relatively high to ensure its safe landing.

- Double fault – two consecutive out-of-bounds serves on the same point resulting in loss of the point.

- Doubles lines – the outside sidelines on a court used only for doubles.

- Down the line – a shot hit near a sideline traveling close to, and parallel to, the same line from which the shot was initially hit.

- Drive – an offensive shot hit with extra force.

- Drop shot – a groundstroke hit so that it drops just over the net with little or no forward bounce.

- Drop volley – a volley hit in such a manner that it drops just over the net with little or no forward bounce.

- Error – a mistake made by a player during competition.

- Flat shot – a ball hit in a way where there is no rotation or spin when traveling through the air.

- Foot fault – illegal foot movement before service, penalized by losing that particular serve. Common foot faults are stepping on or ahead of the baseline before contacting the ball and running along the baseline before serving.

- Forecourt – the area between the net and the service line.

- Forehand – the stroke hit on the right side of a right-handed player.

- Frame – the rim of the racket head plus the handle of the racket.

- Game – scoring term when a player wins 4 points before an opponent while holding a minimum 2-point lead.

- Grip – the portion of the racket that the player grasps in his hand.

- Groundstroke – any ball hit after it has bounced.

- Half volley – a ball hit inches away from the court's surface after the ball has bounced.

- Hold serve – winning your own serve. If you lose your own serve, your serve has been "broken."

- Let (ball) – a point replayed because of some kind of interference.

- Let serve – a serve that touches the net tape, falls into the proper square, and is played over.

- Linesman – a match official who calls balls "in" or "out."

- Lob – a ball hit with sufficient height to pass over the out-stretched arm of a net player.

- Lob volley – a shot hit high into the air from a volleying position.

- Love – scoring term that means zero points or games.

- Match – a contest between two or four opponents.

- Match point – the point immediately before the final point of a match.

- Midcourt – the area in front of the baseline or behind the service line of the playing court.

- Netball – a ball that hits the net, falling on the same side as the hitter.

- No man's land – a general area within the baseline and proper net position area. When caught in that area, the player must volley or hit ground strokes near his/her feet.

- Offensive lob – a ball hit just above the racket reach of an opposing net player.

- Open face racket – a racket whose face is moving under the ball. A wide- open racket face is parallel to the court surface.

- Overhead – a shot hit from a position higher than the player's head.

- Over-hitting – hitting shots with too much force; over-hitting usually results in errors.

- Pace – the speed of the ball.

- Passing shot – a shot passing beyond the reach of the net player landing inbounds.

- Poach – to cross over into your partner's territory in doubles in an attempt to intercept the ball.

- Racket face – the racket's hitting surface.

- Racket head – the top portion of the racket frame that includes the strings.

- Rally – opponents hitting balls back and forth across the net.

- Receiver – the player about to return the opponent's serve.

- Server – the player initiating play.

- Service line – the line at the end of the service courts parallel to the net.

- Set – a scoring term meaning the first player to win six games with a minimum two-game lead.

- Set point – the point, if won, which will give the player the set.

- Sidespin – a ball hit rotating on a horizontal plane.

- Signals in doubles – signaling your partner that you are going to poach at the net.

- Singles line – the sideline closest to the center mark that runs the entire length of the court.

- Slice – motion of the racket head going around the side of the ball, producing a horizontal spin on ball.

- Tape – the band of cloth or plastic running across the top of the net.

- Telegraphing the play – indicating the direction of one's intended target before hitting the ball.

- Topspin – forward rotation of the ball.

- Touch – the ability to make delicate, soft shots from several positions on the court.

- Twist – a special rotation applied to the ball during the serve causing the ball to jump to the left (of right-handed server).

- Umpire – the official that calls lines.

- Under spin – a counterclockwise spin placed on the ball (i.e. backspin).

- Volley – hitting the ball in the air before it bounces on the court.

SKILL 20.2   Demonstrating knowledge of appropriate etiquette, interactions, care of equipment, and safety practices for individual, dual, and lifetime sports and activities

Rules and etiquette are of great importance to sports and physical activities. Rules help ensure fair play, equity, and safety for all participants. Teamwork is another important aspect of sports. Team sports require individual players to come together, merge individual skill sets, and pool individual strengths and weaknesses to achieve team success.

APPROPRIATE BEHAVIOR IN PHYSICAL EDUCATION ACTIVITIES

Appropriate Student Etiquette/Behaviors include: following the rules and accepting the consequences of unfair action, good sportsmanship, respecting the rights of other students, reporting own accidents and mishaps, not engaging in inappropriate behavior under peer pressure encouragement, cooperation, paying attention to instructions and demonstrations, moving to assigned places and remaining in own space, complying with directions, practicing as instructed to do so, properly using equipment, and not interfering with the practice of others.

Appropriate Content Etiquette/Behaviors include the teacher describing the performance of tasks and students engaging in the task, the teacher assisting students with task performance, and the teacher modifying and developing tasks. Players must be taught and learn how to keep their emotions in check. It is inappropriate behavior, irregardless of the sport, for a player to lose control of their emotions and lash out verbally at themselves or any opponent.

Appropriate Management Etiquette/Behaviors include the teacher directing the management of equipment, students, and space prior to practicing tasks; students getting equipment and partners; the teacher requesting that students stop "fooling around."

SAFETY

There are several safety practices specific to net/wall sports. First, because most of these sports involve swinging a racket or paddle and hitting a ball with a great deal of force, monitoring the area of play is very important. Instructors must ensure that students only swing rackets and hit balls at appropriate times. Second, instructors and students must keep the playing area clear of stray balls and other obstacles to prevent injuries. Finally, some of the net/wall sports, such as handball, require use of protective eyewear.

The following is a list of sport-specific equipment for net/wall sports:

- Badminton – rackets, nets, shuttlecocks
- Handball – a wall, handballs, protective eyewear
- Pickleball – wood paddle rackets, plastic balls, nets, a paved surface
- Table Tennis – paddles, balls, table, nets
- Tennis – court, nets, rackets, tennis balls
- Volleyball – nets, volleyballs

SKILL 20.3 Identifying critical elements essential to competent performance in activities such as badminton, bowling, golf, tumbling, tennis, and track and field

Skills necessary for successful participation in sports and fitness activities include proprioception, spatial orientation, hand-eye coordination, and movement skills.

Proprioception – Proprioception is the sense of the relative position of neighboring parts of the body. Unlike the six external senses (sight, taste, smell, touch, hearing, and balance) by which we perceive the outside world, proprioception is an internal sense that provides feedback solely on the status of the body internally. It is the sense that indicates whether the body is moving with required effort, as well as where the various parts of the body are located in relation to each other. We can improve proprioception by training.

Spatial orientation – Spatial orientation refers to the process of aligning or positioning oneself with respect to a specific direction or reference system. Specifically, it is the relationship established between the body's self-oriented coordinate system and an external reference frame. This happens via the integration of sensory signals from the visual, vestibular, tactile, and proprioceptive systems.

Hand-eye coordination – Hand-eye coordination is the ability of the visual perception system to coordinate the information received through the eyes to control, guide, and direct the hands in the accomplishment of a given task (examples include handwriting or catching a ball). Hand-eye coordination uses the eyes to direct attention and the hands to execute a task.

Movement skills – Movement skills center on the integration of balance and proprioceptive skills to produce movement that effectively manages the weight distribution of the body.

In addition to these generic skills, successful performance in individual, dual, and team sports requires many specific physical and social skills, which we will now discuss.

KEY PERFORMANCE ELEMENTS

Key elements of successful performance in individual, dual, and team sports and activities include discipline and dedication, athletic ability, technical skills, and communication. These elements are all interconnected. Without discipline and dedication, the proper levels of athletic ability and technical skills will not develop (natural talent will only carry one so far). Without communication, the athlete will not be able to coordinate their efforts with their partners or teammates (in dual or team sports, respectively), nor will they be able to effectively interact with their coaches and instructors to improve their own performance abilities.

Students can improve performance in sports and physical activities by engaging in regular, varied, and knowledge-based training on both athletic aspects and technical skills. Training must be regular and frequent (but varied, so as not to result in over-training and injury). In addition, training must also be knowledge-based, to ensure that it produces the maximum benefits to the athlete, both in terms of physical athletic development, and development of technical skills and reflexes.

Instructors can promote improvement of students' teamwork in sports and physical activities by creating varied training situations in which entire teams practice together (as opposed to individual training activities that promote the development of technical and athletic skills of individual team members). Effective teamwork stems from two sources. The first is the ability of all the team members to communicate and cooperate with each other (instructors can develop this by teamwork and communication training). The second source is the closer ties that develop between team members that train together for an extended period. For example, the ability to anticipate their teammates' next move.

Students can improve their skill combinations in sports and physical activities by engaging in training activities that focus on the practice and refinement of specific skill aspects individually, without removing them from a realistic training setting or context. In other words, students should practice skills individually, but not in isolation, as they must remain in the context of the game or sport.

SKILL 20.4 Demonstrating knowledge of principles of training and conditioning appropriate to specific individual, dual, and lifetime sports and activities

Following appropriate principles of training and conditioning is an important aspect of devising an athletic training program. Programs and principles vary based on the specific individual, dual, and lifelong sports and activities for which the athlete is preparing. Training for all types of activities, however, should address endurance, strength, flexibility, and integration of these components.

Concerning endurance training, when devising the program it is important to examine both the degree (i.e., how long and how much effort) and type of endurance (i.e., muscular or cardiovascular) required by the activity in question. Further, there is the question of which muscles need to develop endurance – for example, tennis focuses the endurance needs on the legs (running) and arms (swinging), whereas gymnastics emphasizes more general muscular endurance.

Concerning strength training, we must consider both how much strength a sport and activity requires, and in which muscles. For example, gymnastics is highly demanding of all the muscles and a tennis player will need to be able to swing a racket with considerable force. An aerobic dancer, on the other hand, while requiring a great deal of endurance, has less need of intensive strength training.

Concerning flexibility training, again we must consider the type of flexibility required (i.e., dynamic, active-static, or passive-static) required. Gymnasts, for example, require all kinds of flexibility. A tennis player, however, requires mostly dynamic flexibility, that will allow him to stretch his muscles quickly while they are in motion.

Concerning overall program construction, we must devise training cycles with that allow the body time to develop and adapt. Similarly, depending on the intensity and type of the training, the athlete may require more rest time, or they may have to vary the training practices to a greater extent.

COMPETENCY 21.0   **UNDERSTAND TECHNIQUES, SKILLS, RULES, STRATEGIES, ETIQUETTE, EQUIPMENT, AND SAFETY PRACTICES FOR TEAM SPORTS AND ACTIVITIES (E.G., BASKETBALL, FLAG FOOTBALL, SOCCER, SOFTBALL, TEAM HANDBALL, VOLLEYBALL)**

SKILL 21.1   Recognizing skills, rules, strategies, and performance assessment techniques for team sports and activities

TEAM PASSING SPORTS – OVERVIEW

Basketball – The fundamental skills of basketball include passing, dribbling, and shooting. As students' skills improve, they may begin to specialize in playing a specific position (point guard, shooting guard, small forward, power forward or center).

Touch/Flag Football – Skills that students will practice include running and passing – tackling is not relevant in touch or flag football situations. As students improve, they may begin to specialize in playing specific positions (e.g. quarterbacks or receivers). They may also become more involved in the study and implementation of strategy.

The main goal of offensive strategy in football is to move closer to the opposing team's end zone, to the point where the ball is close enough to score either a touchdown or a field goal. The aim of defensive strategies is to prevent this same movement towards the end zone by the opposition. Both offensive and defensive strategies make important use of concepts of time management and the possibility of "running out the clock". Formations are central to football strategy, both on offense and on defense, and students should become familiar with simple formations for both.

Lacrosse – Lacrosse players must master the skills of catching and throwing the ball with their sticks and cradling (the motion that allows players to run with the ball in their stick).

Lacrosse strategy has many parallels with other team sports like basketball, soccer, and field hockey. In all of these sports, the team of players has to maneuver to outflank and outsmart their opponents in order to score a goal.

Soccer – Soccer players must master the skills of running, accurate kicking, manipulation of the ball, and footwork that allows the student to maneuver when in motion.

The key to soccer strategy is for students to understand that the goal is to get the ball to the right person's feet – the one who has the most time and space (facing the least pressure) and is in the most advantageous position to score (or make a goal-scoring pass). Broadly, offensive strategy will spread the team out, to allow for coverage of more of the field. Defensive strategy will have the team compress to a compact unit that is able to cover the goal effectively.

Team Handball – Skills that students will learn in a handball class will include catching and accurately throwing the ball, taking steps while bouncing the ball (similar to basketball's dribble), and quick analysis of the playing situation to ascertain who the best target is for a pass.

Strategy in handball centers around staying one step ahead of the opposing team, keeping them guessing, and having multiple contingencies for given situations so that game play doesn't become predictable (and easier to counter). Specific tactics can include types of shots that are harder for the opponent to hit and shots that will put the ball out of play (when it is advantageous to do so).

Ultimate Frisbee – Skills that students must acquire to play ultimate Frisbee proficiently include catching the Frisbee, accurately throwing the Frisbee, and running. Instructors should also emphasize strategic thinking, as there is limited time to select a destination for and execute a throw.

The goal of offensive strategy in ultimate Frisbee is to create open lanes in the field that are free of defenders. Common offensive strategies include the 'vertical stack' and 'horizontal stack' (similar to a spread offense in football). Defensive strategy aims to gain control of the Frisbee and deflect passes made by the opposing team. A basic defensive principle is the 'force', which calls for the defense to cut off the handler's access to half of the field, thereby forcing the offensive player to throw the Frisbee to the other side of the field.

TEAM STRIKING/FIELDING SPORTS – OVERVIEW

Baseball – Skills that students studying baseball will acquire include accurate throwing and catching, and the correct way to swing and hit with a baseball bat.

Defensive strategy in baseball focuses on the actions of the pitcher, who is responsible for trying to strike out the team that is at bat. Offensive strategy in baseball centers on batting, and attempting to turn batters into runners.

Safety practices in baseball include maintaining discipline among the students, as horseplay and lack of attentiveness can lead to injury, (e.g. a ball could hit a student who isn't paying attention). In addition, instructors should remind students the baseball bat is not a toy, and they should handle it with care and not swing it near other students.

Equipment required for baseball practice includes baseball bats, baseballs, baseball gloves (though for some educational situations, the gloves are not necessary), base markers of some kind, and protective padding for the catcher.

Cricket – Skills that students in cricket class will acquire include accurate throwing and catching, swinging the bat correctly, and the proper form for the execution of an effective pitch.

Unlike baseball and softball, where pitching controls the game, in cricket, batting controls the game. Since in cricket the batter can hit in any direction around him, he will focus on weak spots in the opposing team's field deployment, and the defensive strategy of the opposing team will focus on minimizing weak spots for the batter to exploit.

Safety practices in cricket are similar to baseball and softball; enforcing discipline and maximizing attentiveness to prevent the chance of injury, and reminding students that they should not swing the bat when other students are in the vicinity.

Equipment required for cricket practice includes cricket bats, cricket balls, appropriate protective gear, and base markers.

Field hockey – Skills that students of field hockey will acquire include running, tactical thinking on the field, and the ability to manipulate the ball with the stick (including running with the ball and different types of shots).

Offensive strategy in field hockey focuses on maneuvering the ball between team members to prevent the opposing team from intercepting, in order to get close enough to the opposing team's net to score a goal. Defensive strategy will strive to create solid coverage of the advancing team, to enable interception of the ball.

Safety practices include emphasizing mindfulness on the part of the students to prevent accidents, and reinforcing the safety regulations of the game concerning legal use of the hockey stick.

Equipment needed for the practice of field hockey with students includes an appropriate ball, sticks for the students, and appropriate protective gear.

Softball – Skills students in softball classes will acquire include accurate throwing and catching, and the correct way to swing and hit with a softball bat.

Softball is similar in strategy to baseball. Defensive strategy focuses on the pitcher, who is responsible for trying to strike out the team that is at bat. Offensive strategy centers on batting, and attempting to turn batters into runners.

Safety practices in softball are also similar to baseball. Enforcing discipline and maintaining student attentiveness to prevent the chance of injury is of utmost importance. Instructors must also emphasize to the students that they should not swing the bat when other students are in the area.

Equipment required for softball practice includes a softball bat and softball, fielding gloves, appropriate protective gear, and base markers of some sort.

TEAM SPORT STRATEGIES

Basketball Strategies:

Use a Zone Defense

- To prevent drive-ins for easy lay-up shots.

- When playing area is small.

- When team is in foul trouble.

- To keep an excellent rebounder near opponent's basket.

- When opponents' outside shooting is weak.

- When opponents have an advantage in height.

- When opponents have an exceptional offensive player, or when the best defenders cannot handle one-on-one defense.

Offensive Strategies Against Zone Defense

- Using quick, sharp passing to penetrate zone forcing opposing player out of assigned position.

- Overloading and mismatching.

Offensive Strategies for One-On-One Defense

- Using the "pick-and-roll" and the "give-and-go" to screen defensive players to open up offensive players for shot attempts.

- Teams may use free-lancing (spontaneous one-one-one offense), but more commonly they use "sets" of plays.

Soccer Strategies:

- **Heading** – using the head to pass, to shoot, or to clear the ball.

- **Tackling** – objective is to take possession of the ball from an opponent. Successful play requires knowledgeable utilization of space.

Volleyball Strategies:

- Using forearm passes (bumps, digs, or passes) to play balls below the waist, to play balls that are driven hard, to pass the serve, and to contact balls distant from a player.

RULES OF TEAM SPORTS

BASKETBALL:

- A player touching the floor on or outside the boundary line is out-of-bounds.

- The ball is out of bounds if it touches anything (a player, the floor, an object, or any person) that is on or outside the boundary line.

- An offensive player remaining in the three-second zone of the free-throw lane for more than three seconds is a violation.

- A ball firmly held by two opposing players results in a jump ball.

- A throw-in is awarded to the opposing team of the last player touching a ball that goes out-of-bounds.

SOCCER:

The following are direct free-kick offenses:

- Hand or arm contact with the ball

- Using hands to hold an opponent

- Pushing an opponent

- Striking/kicking/tripping or attempting to strike/kick/trip an opponent

- Goalie using the ball to strike an opponent

- Jumping at or charging an opponent

- Kneeing an opponent

- Any contact fouls

The following are indirect free-kick offenses:

- Same player playing the ball twice at the kickoff, on a throw-in, on a goal kick, on a free kick, or on a corner kick.

- The goalie delaying the game by holding the ball or carrying the ball more than four steps.

- Failure to notify the referee of substitutions/re-substitutions and that player then handling the ball in the penalty area.

- Any person, who is not a player, entering playing field without a referee's permission.

- Unsportsmanlike actions or words in reference to a referee's decision.

- Dangerously lowering the head or raising the foot too high to make a play.

- A player resuming play after being ordered off the field.

- Offsides – an offensive player must have two defenders between him and the goal when a teammate passes the ball to him or else he is offsides.

- Attempting to kick the ball when the goalkeeper has possession or interference with the goalkeeper to hinder him/her from releasing the ball.

- Illegal charging.

- Leaving the playing field without referee's permission while the ball is in play.

SOFTBALL:

- Each team plays nine players in the field (sometimes 10 for slow pitch).

- Field positions are one pitcher, one catcher, four infielders, and three outfielders (four outfielders in ten player formats).

- The four bases are 60 feet apart.

- Any ball hit outside of the first or third base line is a foul ball (i.e. runners cannot advance and the pitch counts as a strike against the batter)

- If a batter receives three strikes (i.e. failed attempts at hitting the ball) in a single at bat he/she strikes out.

- The pitcher must start with both feet on the pitcher's rubber and can only take one step forward when delivering the underhand pitch.

- A base runner is out if:

  - A. The opposition tags him with the ball before he reaches a base.
  - B. The ball reaches first base before he does.
  - C. He runs outside of the base path to avoid a tag.
  - D. A batted ball strikes him in fair territory.

- A team must maintain the same batting order throughout the game.

- Runners cannot lead off and base stealing is illegal.

- Runners may overrun first base, but can be tagged out if off any other base.

VOLLEYBALL:

The following infractions by the receiving team result in a point awarded to the serving side and an infraction by serving team results in side-out:

- Illegal serves or serving out of turn.

- Illegal returns or catching or holding the ball.

- Dribbling or a player touching the ball twice in succession.

- Contact with the net (two opposing players making contact with the net at the same time results in a replay of the point).

- Touching the ball after it has been played three times without passing over the net.

- A player's foot completely touching the floor over the centerline.

- Reaching under the net and touching a player or the ball while the ball is in play.

- The players changing positions prior to the serve.

SAMPLE OFFICIATING SITUATIONS

NOTE: Since rules change yearly, acquiring new rulebooks every year is necessary for proper officiating.

Basketball situation: Actions of the spectators interfere with the progression of the game.

Ruling: An official may call a foul on the team whose supporters are interfering with the game.

Basketball situation: A1 is attempting a field goal and B1 fouls him. A1 continues with the field goal attempt and, before releasing the ball, crashes into B2 who has a legal position on the floor. A1 successfully completes the field goal.

Ruling: The ball was immediately dead when A1 fouled B2; therefore, field goal does not count. However, since B1 fouled A1 while attempting the field goal, A1 receives two free throws.

Basketball situation: The official in the frontcourt runs into a pass thrown from the backcourt by A1 and goes out-of-bounds.

Ruling: B receives a throw-in. The official is part of the court.

Basketball Situation: A1 catches the ball in mid-air and lands with the right foot first and then the left foot. A1 pivots on the left foot.

Ruling: A violation has occurred because A1 can only pivot on the foot that first lands on the floor, which was the right foot.

Soccer situation: The ball is alive when a substitute enters the playing field.

Ruling: A non-player fouls. Referee can either penalize at location of the next dead ball or at the place of entry (usually when the team offended is at an advantage).

Soccer situation: B1 charges A1's goalie in A1's penalty area.

Ruling: Team A receives a direct free kick at the spot of foul. A flagrant charge awards team A, a penalty-kick at the other end of the field, and B1 is disqualified.

Soccer situation: The goalie is out of position when a back on team B heads the ball out and falls into the net. A2 gets the ball, passes it to A1, and has only the goalie to beat.

Ruling: A1 is not offside because the B back left the field during legal play.

Volleyball situation: Team A's second volley hits an obstruction directly over the net, returns to A's playing area, and team A plays it again.

Ruling: Fair play and the next play is team A's third play.

Volleyball situation: The serving team has three front line players standing close together in front of the server at the spiking line.

Ruling: Illegal alignment is called for intentional screening.

Volleyball situation: RB and CB on the receiving team are overlapping when at the time of the serve, and the serve lands out-of-bounds.

Ruling: Serving team receives a point because of receiving team's illegal alignment.

Volleyball situation: LB on team B saves a spiked ball and it deflects off his/her shoulder.

Ruling: A legal hit.

TERMINOLOGY OF TEAM PASSING SPORTS

Basketball Terminology:

- Backcourt players (Guards) – players who set up a team's offensive pattern and bring the ball up the court.

- Backdoor – an offensive maneuver in which a player cuts toward the baseline to the basket, behind the defenders, and receives a ball for a field goal attempt.

- Baseline – the end line of the court.

- Blocking/Boxing out – a term used when a player is under the backboard to prevent an opposing player from achieving a good rebounding position.

- Charging – personal contact by a player with the ball against the body of a defensive opponent.

- Corner players (Forwards) – tall players that make up the sides of the offensive set-up who are responsible for the rebounding and shooting phases of the team's offense.

- Cut – a quick, offensive move by a player attempting to get free for a pass.

- Denial defense – aggressive individual defense to keep an offensive player from receiving a pass.

- Double foul – two opponents committing personal fouls against each other simultaneously.

- Dribble – ball movement by a player in control who throws or taps the ball in the air or onto the floor and then touches it. The dribble ends when the dribbler touches the ball with both hands concurrently, loses control, or permits it to come to rest while in contact with it.

- Drive – an aggressive move by a player with the ball toward the basket.

- Fake (Feint) – using a deceptive move with the ball pulling the defensive player out of position.

- Fast break – quickly moving the ball down court to score before the defense has a chance to set up.

- Field goal – a basket scored from the field.

- Freelance – no structure or set plays in the offense.

- Free throw – the right given a player to score one or two points by unhindered shots for a goal from within the free throw circle and behind the free throw line.

- Give-and-go – a maneuver when the offensive player passes to a teammate and then immediately cuts in toward the basket for a return pass.

- Held ball – occurs when two opponents have one or both hands firmly on the ball and neither can gain possession without undue roughness.

- Inside player (Center, Post, Pivot) – this player is usually the tallest team player who is situated near the basket, around the three-second lane area, and is responsible for rebounding and close-range shooting.

- Jump ball – a method of putting the ball into play by tossing it up between two opponents in the center circle to start the game or any overtime periods.

- Outlet pass – a term used that designates a direct pass from a rebounder to a teammate (the main objective is starting a fast break).

- Overtime period – an additional period of playing time when the score is tied at the end of the regulation game.

- Personal foul – a player foul that involves contact with an opponent while the ball is alive or after the ball is in possession of a player for a throw-in.

- Pick – a special type of screen where a player stands so the defensive player slides to make contact to free an offensive teammate for a shot or drive.

- Pivot – occurs when a player who is holding the ball steps once or more than once in any direction with the same foot while the other foot, called the pivot foot, remains at its point of contact with the floor. Also, another term for the inside player.

- Posting up – a player cutting to the three-second lane area, pausing, and anticipating a pass.

- Rebound – when the ball bounces off the backboard or basket.

- Restraining circles – three circles with a six-foot radius. One is located in the center of the court, and the others are located at each of the free-throw lines.

- Running time – not stopping the clock for fouls or violations.

- Screen – an offensive maneuver positioning a player between the defender and a teammate to free the teammate for an uncontested shot.

- Switching – defensive guards reversing their guarding assignments.

- Technical foul – a non-contact foul by a player, team, or coach for unsportsmanlike behavior or failing to abide by rules regarding submission of lineups, uniform numbering, and substitution procedures.

- Telegraphing a pass – a look or signal to indicate where the ball is going to be passed.

- Throw-in – a method of putting the ball in play from out-of-bounds.

- Traveling – illegal movement, in any direction, of a player in possession of the ball within bounds. Moving with the ball without dribbling.

- Violation – an infraction of the rules resulting in a throw-in from out-of-bounds.

Soccer Terminology:

- Center – passing from the outside of the field near the sideline into the center.

- Charge – illegal or legal body contact between opponents.

- Chip – lofting the ball into the air using the instep kick technique; contacting the ball very low causing it to loft quickly with backspin.

- Clear – attempting to move the ball out of danger by playing the ball a great distance.

- Corner kick – a direct free kick from the corner arc awarded to the attacking players when the defending team last played the ball over their own end line.

- Cross – a pass from the outside of the field near the end line to a position in front of the goal.

- Dead ball situation – the organized restarting of the game after stopping play.

- Direct free kick – a free kick whereby the kicker may score immediately from that initial contact.

- Dribble – the technique of a player self-propelling the ball with the foot in order to maintain control of the ball while moving from one spot to another.

- Drop ball – the method used to restart the game after temporary suspension of play when the ball is still in play.

- Goal area – the rectangular area in front of the goal where the ball is placed for a goal kick.

- Half volley – contacting the ball just as it hits the ground after being airborne.

- Head – playing the ball with the head.

- Indirect free kick – a free kick from which a player, other than the kicker, must contact the ball before the team can score a goal.

- Kickoff – the free kick starting play at the beginning of the game, after each period, or after a score.

- Obstruction – illegally using the body to shield an opponent from reaching the ball.

- One-touch – immediately passing or shooting a received ball without stopping it.

- Penalty area – the large rectangular area in front of the goal where the goalkeeper may use the hands to play the ball.

- Penalty kick – a direct free kick awarded in the penalty area against the defending team for a Direct Free Kick foul.

- Settle – taking a ball out of the air and settling it on the ground so that it is rolling and no longer bouncing.

- Square pass – a pass directed toward the side of a player.

- Tackle – a technique to take the ball away from the opponents.

- Through pass – a pass penetrating between and past the defenders.

- Throw-in – the technique to restart the game when the ball goes out of play over the sideline.

- Touchline – the side line of the field.

- Trap – the technique used for receiving the ball and bringing it under control.

- Two-touch- receiving – trapping and immediately re-passing the ball.

Volleyball Terminology:

- Attack – returning the ball across the net in an attempt to put the opponents at a disadvantage.

- Ball handling – executing any passing fundamental.

- Block – intercepting the ball just before or as it crosses the net.

- Bump – see forearm pass.

- Court coverage – a defensive player's court assignment.

- Dig – an emergency pass usually used to defend a hard-driven attack.

- Dink – a soft shot off the fingertips to lob the ball over a block.

- Double foul – infraction of rules by both teams during the same play.

- Drive – an attacking shot contacted in the center that attempts to hit the ball off the blocker's hands.

- Fault – any infraction of the rules.

- Forearm pass – a pass made off the forearms to play served balls, hard-driven spikes, or any low ball.

- Free ball – a ball returned by the opponent that is easily handled.

- Frontcourt – the playing area where it is legal to block or attack.

- Held ball – a ball that opponents simultaneously contact and momentarily hold above the net.

- Kill – an attack that the opposition cannot return.

- Lob – a soft attack contacted on the back bottom-quarter of the ball causing an upward trajectory.

- Overhand pass – a pass made by contacting the ball above the head with the fingers.

- Overlap – an illegal foot position when the ball is dead, with an adjacent player putting another out of position.

- Play over – replaying the rally because of a held ball or the official prematurely suspending play. The server re-serves with no point awarded.

- Point – a point is scored when the receiving team fails to return the ball to the opponents' court legally.

- Rotation – clockwise rotation of the players upon gaining the ball from the opponents.

- Serve – putting the ball in play over the net by striking it with the hand.

- Set – placing the ball near the net to facilitate attacking.

- Setter – the player assigned to set the ball.

- Side out – side is out when the serving team fails to win a point or plays the ball illegally.

- Spike – a ball hit with top spin and with a strong downward force into the opponents' court.

- Spiker – the player assigned to attack the ball.

- Spike-roll – an attack that first takes an upward trajectory using the spiking action (with or without jumping).

- Topspin (Overspin) – applying forward spin to the ball during the serve, spike, or spike roll.

SKILL 21.2 Demonstrating knowledge of appropriate etiquette, interactions, care of equipment, and safety practices for team sports and activities

o   *See also Skill 20.2*

SAFETY – TEAM PASSING SPORTS

Important safety considerations for team passing sports include proper maintenance of facilities and playing fields, use of protective equipment, and proper enforcement of the rules of play. Enforcement of rules is particularly important to prevent participants from injuring other participants either intentionally or unintentionally through reckless play.

The following is a list of sport-specific equipment for team passing sports:

- Basketball – basketballs, goals, appropriate shoes
- Touch or Flag Football – footballs, flags and flag belts, cones to mark boundaries and end zones
- Lacrosse – lacrosse sticks and balls, protective pads, goals (nets)
- Soccer – soccer balls, goals, field markers, protective shin guards
- Team Handball – handballs and goals
- Ultimate Frisbee – Frisbees and an open playing field

SKILL 21.3 Identifying critical elements essential to competent performance in activities such as basketball, flag football, soccer, softball, team handball, and volleyball

- ○ *See Skill 20.3*

SKILL 21.4 Demonstrating knowledge of principles of training and conditioning appropriate to specific team sports and activities

Following appropriate principles of training and conditioning is an important aspect of devising an athletic training program. Programs and principles vary based on the team sports and activities for which the athlete is preparing. Training for all types of activities, however, should address endurance, strength, flexibility, and integration of these components.

Concerning endurance training, the training should match the sport in question. For example, most team sports require a great deal of running, but the type of running should match the sport. That is to say, for example, in soccer, basketball, and softball, players often have to transition from standing to sprinting full speed. Training should match this reality, and incorporate sprints rather than a long jog.

Concerning strength training, team sports often require strength for very particular actions. For example, a softball player needs to swing the bat powerfully, a basketball player needs to throw the ball powerfully – in both cases, accuracy is required in addition to power. For this reason, we should select exercises to develop strength in the correct muscles. In addition, muscles should function the same way they do in the motion for which the athlete is preparing.

Concerning flexibility training, it is important to consider that most team sports require somewhat less flexibility than individual activities, but flexibility is also important for ensuring that movements remain fluid and unencumbered. For this reason, it is important to incorporate flexibility training into a training program.

Concerning overall program construction, there is often an off-season and an on-season over the course of a year. In these cases, it is best to develop the foundation of fitness during the off-season, and focus on finer, sport-specific skills as the on-season approaches.

SKILL 21.5 Analyzing the effect of participation in physical activity in promoting appreciation of cultural, ethnic, gender, and physical diversity in team sports and activities

○   *See Skill 15.5*

COMPETENCY 22.0   UNDERSTAND TECHNIQUES, SKILLS, RULES, STRATEGIES, ETIQUETTE, EQUIPMENT, AND SAFETY PRACTICES FOR OUTDOOR ACTIVITIES (E.G., CAMPING, ORIENTEERING, ROPES COURSES, GROUPINITIATED ACTIVITIES)

SKILL 22.1 Recognizing skills, rules, strategies, and performance assessment techniques for activities such as camping, orienteering, ropes courses, and group-initiated activities

RECREATIONAL ACTIVITIES AND OUTDOOR PURSUITS

Hiking – Instructors can take students on walking/hiking trips through nature reserves and national parks. Such trips can incorporate team-building activities and nature education.

Sail Training – Students taught to sail should display competence in the maintenance and piloting of a boat, including cooperative activities necessary to a successful sailing endeavor (e.g. working together to get the boat into and out of the water, paddling in rhythm, turning the boat, etc.). Prior to the start of sail training, students should understand all safety procedures and acceptable forms of behavior on a boat (e.g. only standing when necessary, no pushing, following instructions, wearing a life jacket, etc.). Students must also demonstrate swimming competence (i.e. ability to tread water, swim a distance continuously, and put on a life jacket while in the water).

Rope Challenge Courses – Good activity for team-building purposes. Challenges include personal physical challenges (climbing various structures), or group activities (e.g. requiring students to work together to coordinate the crossing of a course). Safety requirements include helmets, harnesses, spotters, trained supervisors, and strict adherence to all safety procedures and educator instructions.

Bicycling – In bicycling classes, students should learn proper bicycling form and how to gauge which gear is most appropriate for their current speed and level of inclination. Students should also become familiar with the proper way to maintain and care for their bicycles.

Bicycling strategy is similar to track events – learning to gauge the appropriate levels of energy expenditure relative to the length of the track and the fitness of the cyclist.

Safety practices while bicycling include seriousness in practice (no horseplay, which can result in injury) and attentiveness to the track so that students can avoid potentially dangerous bumps or cracks. Instructors should remind students not to race with each other, but rather to focus on their own physical activity.

Equipment required for bicycling with students includes proper gear (which includes clothing without loose appendages that can catch in bicycle gears), water for longer trips, and, of course, the bicycles themselves.

Cross-country skiing – Students in cross-country skiing classes will learn the proper form for cross-country skiing (e.g. herringbone, diagonal stride, double pole) and will greatly improve their fitness (as cross-country skiing is a very taxing activity on a very wide range of muscle groups).
Like most endurance activities, cross-country skiing strategy involves regulating the levels of energy expenditure relative to the length of the course and the fitness level of the athlete.

Safety practices in cross-country skiing include ensuring the availability of first aid and instructor attentiveness to the students (as it is easier to 'lose track' of a student who is having trouble). Instructors should also instruct students not to wander away from the group – a good solution is the implementation of a buddy system.

Equipment required for cross-country skiing trips includes appropriate dress (make sure students dress warmly), cross-country skis, and poles.

Canoeing – Students in canoeing classes will learn the various forms of paddling strokes, how to manage their weight, and how to work as a team to maneuver a canoe properly.

Strategies for effective canoeing include the clear delineation of members of a rowing team and the role that each individual serves. The 'captain' coordinates the efforts of the rowers on the canoe and should become familiar with the course and destination.

Safety practices for canoeing call for the instructor to ensure that the students are all able to swim and equipped with proper flotation equipment (e.g. lifejackets). First aid should be available and the instructor should see to it that he remains close enough to students in different canoes to be able to hear them and reach them if needed.

Equipment required for canoeing classes includes canoes, canoeing paddles, and proper flotation equipment. Instructors should advise students to have a change of clothes available in the event that they get wet.

Orienteering – Skills that students will acquire during orienteering activities include the ability to read a map, critical thinking stemming from practice identifying locations, navigation ability, and strategic thinking for selection of efficient movement patterns between several points.

Strategies for orienteering include ascertaining early the destination points and mapping an efficient course to pass through all of them.

Safety practices include ensuring the availability and accessibility of first aid, properly instructing the students in emergency procedures (e.g. blow the whistle and remain where you are), and selecting an area small enough so the instructor can hear the whistle from any position.

Equipment required for orienteering with students includes proper outdoor clothing and a whistle for use in emergency situations. Students will also need a map and possibly a compass.

Fishing – Students studying fishing will learn the correct technique for casting a line and will learn to identify spots where fish are most likely to congregate. Fishing also teaches patience to students.

Strategies for effective fishing with groups of students include deploying students in such a way that one will not interfere with another's fishing activities. Students should also learn about the habits of the fish that they are after, to allow them to tailor their approaches accordingly.

Safety practices for fishing call for instructors to remind students that their equipment does not consist of toys and they should not play with it. Students should definitely handle fishing rods and hooks carefully around other students.

Equipment required for fishing includes fishing rods, hooks, bait, gear (e.g. boots), and a bucket or other receptacle for the fish.

Inline skating – Skills that students in inline skating class will acquire include skating techniques (e.g. braking and stopping, skating backwards, skating downhill) and improved balance. Students should also learn to care for their skating equipment.

The focus during inline skating is to maintain proper form during the activity.

Safety practices in inline skating include requiring students to wear appropriate protective gear and ensuring that first aid is available. Instructors should instruct students not to attempt stunts, especially without supervision.

Equipment required for inline skating includes skates and appropriate protective gear (e.g. helmets, kneepads, elbow pads).

Rock climbing – Students studying rock climbing will gain proficiency in climbing techniques (including body positioning and learning to find proper toeholds and handholds in the rock face) belaying, and managing the climbing and harness equipment.

Strategies in rock climbing require the climber to remain aware not only of the current 'next step' of the climbing process, but to also remain aware of the entire rock face, and to plan on a course that she can follow through to completion (so as to prevent climbing to a dead-end area). Safety practices include explaining all safety practices so students understand, ensuring that students wear all safety gear (protective gear and harnesses) properly, and that all students have spotters monitoring their activities.

Equipment required for rock climbing activities includes proper attire, suitable footwear, protective equipment, and harnessing equipment.

Alpine skiing (downhill skiing) – The skills that students of alpine skiing will gain center on learning to control the direction and speed of their descent; novices will begin by learning the "snow plough" technique to turn, and will learn to point their skis inward to stop. More advanced technique will center on "carving", which allows the skis to turn without skidding or slowing down.

Alpine skiing strategy calls for awareness of the practitioner's current level of skill and avoiding over-reaching (i.e. attempting courses that are too advanced and thus dangerous). Instructors should teach students to be aware of the course ahead of them, allowing them to better plan their movements.

Safety practices in alpine skiing include proper inspection of the equipment to ensure that everything is in order and instructing the students in appropriate safety procedures. Most importantly, instructors should not allow students to attempt courses that are beyond their current skill levels.

Equipment required for alpine skiing includes appropriate dress that is adequately warm (hats, gloves, and goggles), skis, and poles.

Camping – Camping imparts a wide range of skills, from tent pitching to fire building to outdoor cooking.

Successful camping strategy focuses on planning and preparing the students (mentally, physically, and in terms of their equipment) for the camping experience.

Safety practices for camping include packing a first aid kit and emergency supplies (e.g. a map, compass, and whistle), checking the weather before departure, avoiding areas of natural hazards, and putting out fires appropriately. Instructors should teach students to identify and avoid poisonous plants.

Camping equipment includes a tent, lean-to, or other shelter device, a sleeping bag and sleeping pad (or air mattress), a portable stove (where campfires are impractical or not allowed), a lantern or flashlight, a hatchet, axe or saw, ropes, and tarps.
AQUATICS

Swimming is an excellent cardiorespiratory activity that has the added benefit of working more of the body's muscles, more evenly than most other exercises, without excessive resistance to any one part of the body that could result in an overuse injury. To use swimming as an educational cardiorespiratory activity, there must be qualified lifeguards present, and all students must pass basic tests of swimming ability.

Water safety issues include student familiarity with appropriate medical responses to life-threatening situations. Students should recognize signs that someone needs medical attention (e.g. not moving, not breathing, etc.) and have knowledge of the proper response (e.g. who to contact and where to find them). With older children, the instructor can introduce rudimentary first aid. The instructor must also ensure that students are aware and observant of safety rules (e.g. no running near the water, no chewing gum while swimming, no swimming without a lifeguard, no roughhousing near or in the water, etc.).

Swimming strokes include Butterfly, Breast Stroke, Crawl, Sidestroke, Trudgen, Freestyle, Backstroke, and Dog Paddle. When teaching children how to dive, instructors should emphasize form (arm and body alignment) and safety procedures (e.g. no diving in the shallow end, no pushing students into the water).

Water fitness activities and games should place emphasis on generating a lot of movement in the pool (gross motor activities), and may also incorporate activities that require more coordinated manipulations, like catching a ball (fine motor). Sample games include:

- **Water Tag** – Children can attempt to catch each other in the pool. When someone is caught, he becomes 'it'. Variations include freeze tag (where a caught student isn't allowed to move until someone swims between their legs to free them) and base tag (where some sections of the pool, for example the ladders or the walls, are a safe 'base' – rules must be in place limiting the time that a student can spend on the base). Water tag emphasizes gross motor activities. Safety issue: students may not hold other students or grab other students in the water.
- **Water Dodgeball** – Students divide into two teams, one on either side of the pool. They play dodgeball, throwing a ball from one side to the other. The opposing team captures a student who is hit by the ball, but if the ball is caught, the thrower is captured instead. Safety issue: students may not throw the ball at another student's head at close range.
- **Relay Races** – Students divide into teams and perform relay races (i.e. one student swims the length of the pool and back, when he returns the next one does the same, repeating until the whole team has completed the task). This can incorporate various swimming strokes; either all team members use the same stroke or each team member uses a different stroke.

SKILL 22.2 Demonstrating knowledge of appropriate etiquette, interactions, care of equipment, injury prevention techniques, and safety practices for outdoor, adventure, and group-initiated activities

○   *See also Skill 20.2*

Rules, discipline, cooperation, etiquette, and safety practices have a vital role to play in personal performance and other movement-based activities. These activities, by their very nature, will often challenge individuals to push their limitations, both in terms of their current physical and psychological limitations, and in terms of what they might consider behaviorally acceptable in competitive situations. Rules and discipline are critical in competitive situations where there is a strong drive to "achieve at any cost" (at least in terms of personal sacrifice and dedication).

Rules and self-discipline are the lines that divide healthy athletes from those who engage in unsportsmanlike behavior and training practices that do not fit into a balanced lifestyle. Similarly, cooperation is the element that allows athletes in a hard-training situation, who are both physically and mentally exhausted, to rely on each other for support. This is a critical factor to healthy training practices. Etiquette is the formalization of these cooperative practices. In situations where individuals might try to push their personal limits beyond what they know they are capable of, safety practices are critical to prevent injuries and accidents.

GENERAL SAFETY CONCERNS

Safety education related to outdoor pursuits and recreation should emphasize the importance of planning and research. Students should consider in advance what the potential dangers of an activity might be and to prepare plans accordingly (students and instructors should also examine weather forecasts). Of course, educator supervision is required. First-aid equipment and properly trained educators must be present for outdoor education activities. Students should use proper safety gear when appropriate (e.g. helmets, harnesses, etc.). Parental consent is generally required for outdoor education activities.

SKILL 22.3 Identifying critical elements and environmental considerations related to outdoor, adventure, and group-initiated activities (e.g., checking weather, equipment safety)

○   *See Skills 22.1 and 22.2*

COMPETENCY 23.0   UNDERSTAND TECHNIQUES, SKILLS, RULES, STRATEGIES, ETIQUETTE, AND SAFETY PRACTICES FOR CREATIVE MOVEMENT AND DANCE (E.G., FOLK, SOCIAL, SQUARE, LINE, MODERN, AEROBIC)

SKILL 23.1   Recognizing skills, rules, strategies, sequences, and performance assessment techniques for creative movement and dance

DANCE CONCEPTS, FORMS, AND BASIC VOCABULARY – JAZZ AND BALLET

There are several forms of dance including modern, ballet, jazz, country, ballroom, and hip-hop. Though essentially very different from each other, they all have similarities. A sense of musicality is the one constant required for each of the dance forms. Along with that, we can add timing, coordination, flexibility, and, an interest in the concept of dance itself. We all know that we will probably experience greater success when we engage in activities that we are interested in and enjoy. Understanding of most dance forms requires knowledge of basic vocabulary. For example, in jazz, turns or kick ball turns; in tap dance, the shuffle or the flap, etc. Ballet has more specialized vocabulary than any other dance form. For example, plie, to bend; tendu, to stretch; degage, to disengage; fouette, to whip; fondu, to melt; ronde jambe, circle of the leg; pirouette, to turn on one leg; port de bras, movement of the arms; and assemble, to assemble.

Integral to dance and particularly ballet are the concepts of balance and counterbalance, pull-up and turnout, weight distribution and alignment, including shoulders down, hips square, legs turned out, and chest lifted.
In ballet, there are many different dance forms and techniques that a dancer can follow. Three of the larger ones are the Cecchetti, Russian Vaganova, and Royal Academy of Dance, (RAD), programmes. They all have levels for all dancers from beginner to advanced and they all have their advantages and disadvantages. The Cecchetti Society developed the Cecchetti technique from the teachings of the great ballet master Enrico Cecchetti. It is a full syllabus designed to train dancers for professional work. One notable emphasis in the Cecchetti syllabus is that the arms flow and blend from position to position more than any other technique. The Cecchetti technique has formed the core of the program at the National Ballet School of Canada.

The Russian Vaganova technique derives and takes its name from the teachings of Agrippina Vaganova, who was the artistic director of the Kirov Ballet for many years. In the Vaganova method, the dancers bring attention to their hands. The hands do not flow invisibly from one position to the next, as in the Cecchetti method, rather they are left behind and turn at the last moment. This is where the "flapping" look comes from that many dancers make with their hands. Unlike the RAD method, the Vaganova method does not have formally established exercises for each level. Each teacher choreographs his own class according to specialized guidelines and the students dance that class in their examinations. The Vaganova method forms the core of the program at the Royal Winnipeg Ballet School. The RAD syllabus is very common. It is well suited to dance classes in community dance schools where the students usually do no more than an average of one class per day. If you go to the ballet school in your community, there is a good chance they will use the RAD method.

The American School of Ballet teaches the Balanchine method. Created by George Balanchine in the American School of Ballet, the Balanchine method allows dancers to dance Balanchine's choreography much more easily than other dancers can. In the Balanchine method the hands are held differently again from any of the other systems.

DANCE CONCEPTS, FORMS, AND BASIC VOCABULARY – FOLK AND TAP

Folk dance is a term used to describe a large number of dances that originated in Europe and share several common characteristics. Most folk dances practiced today were created before the 20th century, and were practiced by people with little or no training. For this reason, folk dances are usually characterized by a spontaneous style, adaptable movements, and culturally distinctive steps representative of the dance's country of origin. Types of folk dancing include the contra dance, English country-dance, and Maypole dance.

Contra dance is a term used to describe folk dances in which couples dance in two facing lines. A pair of such lines is a set, and these sets generally run the length of a long hall. The head of a set is the end of the line closest to the band and caller. At contra dance events where dancers perform several different folk dances, the caller or dance leader teaches the movements of an individual dance to the dancers during the "walk through," a short period before the next type of dance begins. During the walk through, all dancers mark the movements following the caller's instructions. At contra dance events in North America, contra dancers traditionally change partners for every dance, while in the United Kingdom, dancers remain with the same partner for the entire evening.

Square dance refers to a type of folk dance in which four couples begin and end each sequence in a square formation. When four couples align themselves in such a manner, the formation is "sets-in-order," and we call dances that use such formations "quadrilles." Similar to folk dance, American square dance steps are based on traditional European dances. At every square dance event, the dance caller prompts participants through a sequence of steps to the beat throughout the entirety of each dance, but does not usually participate in the dancing. Steps common to many square dances include allemande left and allemande right, where couples face, take hands, and circle around one another; promenade, where partners cross hands and walk to a counter-clockwise position; and circle right and circle left, where all dancers grasp hands and move round in a circle. Traditionally, the caller explains the steps to each individual square dance at the beginning of a session.

Tap is a form of dance born in the United States during the 19th century in which the dancer sounds out the rhythm by clicking taps on the toes and heels of his shoes. This form of percussive music and dance evolved from a fusion of Irish and African Shuffle in New York City during the 1830s. One common characteristic of modern tap dance is "syncopation," where choreographies generally begin on the eighth music beat. Learning to tap dance is a cumulative process in which new information builds on previously learned steps and terms. To teach tap dance successfully, instructors must first teach simple steps that make up the foundation of tap before introducing complex movements. The most basic steps of tap include the walk, step, heel, step-heel, stamp, ball-change, brush, toe tap, shuffle, side shuffle, back shuffle, and cramp roll. Dance instructors can combine these steps to form simple routines for beginners. Once students have mastered these steps, dancers can move on to attempt movements such as the buffalo, Maxi Ford, Cincinnati, pullback, wings, toe clips, and riffs.

AEROBIC DANCE

Dance aerobics is any type of cardiovascular exercise that is put to music, ranging from country line dancing to hip-hop. Aerobic dance can be performed on three different levels, high-impact aerobics, in which movements such as jumping cause both feet to lose contact with the ground simultaneously; low-impact aerobics, in which one foot remains in contact with the ground at all times; and step aerobics, in which dancers move on and around a slightly raised platform. A beneficial aerobics session is composed of three stages. During the warm-up, which usually lasts for 5-10 minutes, slow movements such as walking in place and stretching will prepare participants for more vigorous activity. The high-impact stage of dance aerobics follows the warm-up. High impact should last 20-30 minutes, and include anything from a dance routine to a step class.

Moves common to many dance/aerobic classes include the grapevine combined with kicks and lunges, high kicks, jumping jacks, and forward and back double kicks. Step routines are generally composed of movements on and off a platform, and also include kicks, swats, and lunges. In between movements of the high-impact period, dancers should always maintain constant movement, walking or marching in place to keep up their heart rate and burn more calories. The last 5-10 minutes of a dance aerobics session should be a cool down period, during which participants again stretch all muscles and slowly lower their heart rate.

SKILL 23.2 Demonstrating knowledge of appropriate etiquette, interactions, injury prevention techniques, and safety practices for creative movement and dance

- *See Skill 20.2*

SKILL 23.3 Identifying critical elements essential to competent performance in creative movement and dance

- *See also Skill 23.1*

Integral to dance and particularly ballet are the concepts of balance and counterbalance, pull-up and turnout, weight distribution and alignment, including shoulders down, hips square, legs turned out, and chest lifted.

SKILL 23.4 Analyzing the effect of participation in dance in promoting personal expression and appreciation of cultural, ethnic, gender, and physical diversity

We can divide the benefits of lifelong participation in dance and aesthetic activities, personal performance activities, and outdoor and adventure activities into physical and psychological dimensions (which, of course, have a reciprocal relationship).

On a physical level, personal performance activities contribute to the health and physical fitness of the participating individual. Physical benefits include increased cardiorespiratory fitness, improved circulation, and an increase in muscle tone.

On a psychological level, these activities contribute to the individual's sense of accomplishment and ability to deal with adversity (which is a part of any personal performance activity). When participants become more involved in their personal performance activity of choice, it can contribute to their sense of positive personal identity.

Strategies for promoting enjoyment and participation in personal performance activities throughout life are centered on matching the right activity to the interests, lifestyle, availability, and physical capabilities of the individual. Individuals must enjoy personal performance activities to devote their time on a regular basis, and the time required has to fit into the lifestyle and schedule of the person in question. It is also important to consider the physical condition of the individual. The activity in question must be compatible with their capabilities and they should work their way into the activity gradually.

ENJOYMENT AND PERSONAL EXPRESSION

In addition to the previously discussed achievement benefits of physical activity, physical activity also provides many people with pure enjoyment and the opportunity for personal expression. Exercise promotes a sense of well-being and usually improves a person's mood. Sports also provide a venue for social interaction and enjoyment of nature. Finally, many sports and activities, especially freestyle activities like skateboarding, figure skating, dance, and surfing, allow for a high level of personal expression.

ENJOYMENT OF AESTHETIC AND CREATIVE ASPECTS OF SKILLED PERFORMANCE

Physical education instructors should instill in their students a respect for and appreciation of the aesthetic and creative aspects of skilled performances. Dance, gymnastics, and figure skating are examples of performance activities that have an obvious creative and expressive element. In addition, all sports require creativity and have aesthetic elements. For example, the ball control of an expert soccer player, the touch, control, and power of a professional tennis player, and the elegance and grace of a basketball player soaring for a slam-dunk are all aesthetically pleasing and awe inspiring to the trained eye. To truly appreciate the complexity and difficulty of skilled performances, one must have sufficient knowledge and understanding of the activity. Thus, the role of physical education is to introduce students to various physical activities so they can understand the aesthetic elements.

CREATIVE DANCE

Creative dance is one technique for applying fundamental concepts. A social benefit of creative dance is that it encourages an interactive environment where children share space as they explore movement together in their own way. Gradually, opportunities arise for children to observe different responses to movement ideas and the possibility of creating movements together becomes more appealing. The children can explore different scenarios and improvise to describe what happens along the way. The teacher can assign the starting place (e.g. a zoo) and the children can choose an animal and move like that animal across the floor. Music adds flavor and children are also able to work on tempo and beat while moving like their favorite animal. They can also add props of their choice. For example, after a group experienced a free flow snow dance with white streamers moving up, down, and around in the air, some of the children improvised a solid ice castle of connected body shapes. In addition, after stomping around in a friendly dinosaur dance, some of the children decided to line up and take big steps together while dragging the last child along lying flat, as the tail!

The instructor can ask the children to solve a particular problem between two animals – perhaps a dog and a cat – that cannot seem to get along. One seems to want to eat the others food all the time. One child can play the cat, which eats most of his food and leaves some for the dog to taste and vice versa. Other students can take turns playing different animals that can solve their problems, work together, and still be friends. They can also move across the floor playing different colors, shapes, or other objects. This freedom to explore and create is a joyful and freeing experience for children of all ages.

Annotated List of Resources

This list identifies some resources that may help candidates prepare to take the Physical Education examination. While not a substitute for coursework or other types of teacher preparation, these resources may enhance a candidate's knowledge of the content covered on the examination. The references listed do not represent a comprehensive listing of all potential resources. Candidates need not read all of the materials listed below, and passage of the examination will not require familiarity with these specific resources. When available, we have provided a brief summary for the reference cited. We have organized the resources alphabetically and by content domain in subtest order.

GROWTH, MOTOR DEVELOPMENT, AND MOTOR LEARNING

Colvin, A. Vonnie; Nancy J.; and Walker, Pamela. (2000). *Teaching the Nutes and Bolts of Physical Education: Building Basic Movement Skills.* Champaign, IL: Human Kinetics.

> Provides foundational content knowledge in locomotor and manipulative skills. Topics include rolling, throwing, catching, passing, dribbling, striking, kicking, and punting.

Fronske, H. (2001). *Teaching Cues for Sports Skills* (2nd edition). San Francisco, CA: Pearson/Cummings.

> Designed to provide verbal and alternate teaching cues and point out common errors in a variety of sports.

Graham, George. (1992). *Teaching Children Physical Education: Becoming a Master Teacher.* Champaign, IL: Human Kinetics.

> Includes the skills and techniques that successful teachers use to make their classes more interesting and developmentally appropriate. A reference for K-5 teachers and physical education department chairs and administrators.

Lawson, H.A. (1984). *Invitation to Physical Education.* Champaign IL: Human Kinetics.

> Shows students and practitioners how to apply basic business management principles to a variety of health promotion programs.

Pangrazi, Robert. (2004). *Dynamic Physical Education for Elementary School Children* (14th edition). San Francisco, CA: Pearson/Cummings.

> Provides step-by-step techniques for teaching physical education while navigating through today's challenging educational terrain.

Powers, S.K., and Howley, E.T. (2003). *Exercise Physiology* (5th edition). New York, NY: McGraw Hill.

> Explains theory of exercise science and physical education with application and performance models to increase understanding of classroom learning.

Schmidt, R.A., and Lee, T.D. (1999). *Motor Control Learning: A Behavioral Emphasis* (3rd Edition). Champaign: IL: Human Kinetics.

> Addresses many factors that affect the quality of movement behaviors and the ease with which students can learn them.

Sherrill, C. (1998). *Adapted Physical Activity, Recreation and Sport: Cross-disciplinary and Lifespan* (5th edition). Dubuque, IA: WCB McGraw Hill.

> Emphasizes attitude change, inclusion, and psychosocial perspectives for understanding individual differences.

Siedentop, D. (1994). *Sport Education.* Champaign, IL: Human Kinetics.

> Shows how sport can help students learn fair play, leadership skills, and self-responsibility, in addition to becoming competent players. Also shows physical educators how to implement effective sport education programs to achieve these goals.

Summers, J.J. (1992). *Approaches to the Study of Motor Control and Learning.* Amsterdam: Elsevier Science.

> Provides analysis of research with particular emphasis on the methods and paradigms employed and the future direction of their work.

Thomas, Katherine, et al. (2003). *Physical Education Methods for Elementary Teachers.* Champaign, IL: Human Kinetics.

> Takes a research approach and offers a user-friendly technique to applicable teaching modalities for physical education for grades K-12.

Winnick, J.P. (2000). *Adapted Physical Education and Sport* (3rd edition). Champaign, IL: Human Kinetics.

> Provides a thorough introduction for students preparing to work with individuals with disabilities in a variety of settings.

THE SCIENCE OF HUMAN MOVEMENT

Birrell, S., and Cole, C.L. (1994). *Women, Sport, and Culture.* Champaign, IL: Human Kinetics.

> A collection of essays that examine the relationship between sport and gender.

Grantham, W.C.; Patton, R.W.; Winick, M.L.; and York, T.D. (1998). *Health Fitness Management.* Champaign, IL: Human Kinetics.

> Brings conventional business management principles and operational guidelines to the unconventional business of health and fitness.

Hall, S. (2003). *Basic Biomechanics.* Boston, MA: McGraw-Hill.

Hamill, J., and Knutzen, K. (1995). *Biomechanical Basis of Human Movement.* Hagerstown, MD: Lippincott, Williams & Wilkins.

> Integrates aspects of functional anatomy, physics, calculus, and physiology into a comprehensive discussion of human movement.

Hopper, Chris; Fisher, Bruce; and Muniz, Kathy. (1997). *Health-Related Fitness: Grades 1-2, 3-4, 5-6.* Champaign, IL: Human Kinetics.

> These three books provide a wealth of health and fitness information and are an excellent resource for classroom teachers with limited backgrounds in physical education.

Lawson, H.A. (1984). *Invitation to Physical Education.* Champaign, IL: Human Kinetics.

> Shows students and practitioners how to apply basic business management principles to a variety of health promotion programs.

Sample Test

DIRECTIONS: Read each item and select the best response.

1. **Which of the following is not characteristic for children ages 3-5?**
(Rigorous) (Skill 1.1)

   A. energy

   B. rest

   C. developing bones

   D. focus

2. **What of the following can not be said about adolescent development?**
(Rigorous) (Skill 1.1)

   A. girls will reach their full height

   B. acne is common

   C. gender related physical characteristics appear

   D. sexual activity is a concern

3. **Which of the following is true about visceral muscles?**
(Rigorous) (Skill 2.1)

   A. They attach to the bone.

   B. They are voluntary.

   C. They are associated with an internal body structure.

   D. They make up the heart.

4. **Which bodily system is responsible for the exchange of oxygen and carbon dioxide in the body?**
(Average Rigor) (Skill 2.1)

   A. Immune System

   B. Cardiovascular System

   C. Endocrine System

   D. Digestive System

5. This type of immune response occurs because the human body is repeatedly subjected to a microorganism and recognizes it.
(Rigorous) (Skill 2.1)

A. Specific

B. Non-specific

C. Inflammatory

D. Passive Immunity

6. Cilia, bronchioles and alveoli belong to what body system?
(Rigorous) (Skill 2.1)

A. Immune System

B. Cardiovascular System

C. Endocrine System

D. Respiratory System

7. Which of the following childhood illnesses might require antibiotics?
(Easy) (Skill 2.2)

A. Allergies

B. Pink eye

C. Asthma

D. Pediculosis

8. Complete this sentence: Hyperglycemia _____.
(Rigorous) (Skill 2.2)

A. occurs when the blood sugar level is low

B. occurs when the blood sugar level is high

C. is the correct balance of sugar within the body

D. results from physical exertion.

9. Which of the following conditions is not associated with a lack of physical activity?
(Average Rigor) (Skill 2.3)

A. Atherosclerosis

B. Longer life expectancy

C. Osteoporosis

D. Certain cancers

10. The most important nutrient the body requires, without which life can only be sustained for a few days, is:
(Easy) (Skill 3.1)

A. Vitamins

B. Minerals

C. Water

D. Carbohydrates

11. **With regard to protein content, foods from animal sources are usually:**
(Average Rigor) (Skill 3.1)

A. Complete

B. Essential

C. Nonessential

D. Incidental

12. **The healthiest form of fat to consume is:**
(Rigorous) (Skill 3.1)

A. Monounsaturated

B. Polyunsaturated

C. Hydrosaturated

D. Saturated

13. **An adequate diet to meet nutritional needs consists of:**
(Rigorous) (Skill 3.1)

A. No more than 30% caloric intake from fats, no more than 50 % caloric intake from proteins, and at least 20% caloric intake from carbohydrates.

B. No more than 30% caloric intake from fats, no more than 40% caloric intake from proteins, and at least 30% caloric intake from carbohydrates.

C. No more than 30% caloric intake from fats, no more than 15% caloric intake from proteins, and at least 55% caloric intake from carbohydrates.

D. No more than 30 % caloric intake from fats, no more than 30% caloric intake from proteins, and at least 40% caloric intake from carbohydrates.

14. **Most high-protein diets:**
(Average Rigor) (Skill 3.2)

A. Are high in cholesterol

B. Are high in saturated fats

C. Require vitamin and mineral supplements

D. All of the above

15. **Which one of the following statements about low-calorie diets is false?**
(Easy) (Skill 3.2)

   A. Most people who "diet only" regain the weight they lose.

   B. They are the way most people try to lose weight.

   C. They make weight control easier.

   D. They lead to excess worry about weight, food, and eating.

16. **Maintaining body weight is best accomplished by:**
(Easy) (Skill 3.4)

   A. Dieting

   B. Aerobic exercise

   C. Lifting weights

   D. Equalizing caloric intake relative to output

17. **Which of the following is true about sleep and children?**
(Average Rigor) (Skill 4.4)

   A. 7-8 hours daily is adequate

   B. the immune system cleanses the body during sleep

   C. good sleep corresponds with focus and control

   D. all of the above

18. **A physical education instructor anticipates and prevents potential injuries, watches for hidden injuries, and takes an injury evaluation of the entire class. Which of the following strategies to prevent injuries is the teacher demonstrating?**
(Average Rigor) (Skill 4.5)

   A. Maintaining hiring standards

   B. Proper use of equipment

   C. Proper procedures for emergencies

   D. Participant screening

19. **Which of the following pieces of exercise equipment best applies the physiological principles?**
(Rigorous) (Skill 4.7)

A. Rolling machine

B. Electrical muscle stimulator

C. Stationary Bicycle

D. Motor-driven rowing machine

20. **All of the following actions help avoid lawsuits except:**
(Easy) (Skill 4.7)

A. Ensuring equipment and facilities are safe

B. Getting exculpatory agreements

C. Knowing each students' health status

D. Grouping students with unequal competitive levels

21. **Which of the following actions does not promote safety?**
(Easy) (Skill 4.7)

A. Allowing students to wear the current style of shoes

B. Presenting organized activities

C. Inspecting equipment and facilities

D. Instructing skill and activities properly

22. **Which of the following is a negative coping strategy for dealing with stress?**
(Easy) (Skill 6.4)

A. Recreational diversions

B. Active thinking

C. Alcohol use

D. Imagery

23. **Which is not a common negative stressor?**
(Easy) (Skill 7.6)

A. Loss of significant other.

B. Personal illness or injury.

C. Moving to a new state.

D. Landing a new job.

24. Which is not a sign of stress?
(Rigorous) (Skill 8.2)

A. Irritability

B. Assertiveness

C. Insomnia

D. Stomach problems

25. Physiological benefits of exercise include all of the following except:
(Rigorous) (Skill 8.2)

A. Reducing mental tension

B. Improving muscle strength

C. Cardiac hypertrophy

D. Quicker recovery rate

26. Psychological benefits of exercise include all of the following except:
(Rigorous) (Skill 8.2)

A. Improved sleeping patterns

B. Improved energy regulation

C. Improved appearance

D. Improved quality of life

27. The most effective way to promote the physical education curriculum is to:
(Rigorous) (Skill 8.2)

A. Relate physical education to higher thought processes

B. Relate physical education to humanitarianism

C. Relate physical education to the total educational process

D. Relate physical education to skills necessary to preserve the natural environment

28. Which of the following body types is the most capable of motor performance involving endurance?
(Rigorous) (Skill 9.2)

A. Endomorph

B. Ectomorph

C. Mesomorph

D. Metamorph

29. **Which of the following is not a consideration for the selection of a facility?** *(Average Rigor) (Skill 11.2)*

    A. Community involvement

    B. Custodial staff

    C. Availability to women, minorities, and the handicapped

    D. Bond issues

30. **A subjective, observational approach to identifying errors in the form, style, or mechanics of a skill is accomplished by:** *(Rigorous) (Skill 12.3)*

    A. Product assessment

    B. Process assessment

    C. Standardized norm-referenced tests

    D. Criterion-referenced tests

31. **What type of assessment objectively measures skill performance?** *(Rigorous) (Skill 12.3)*

    A. Process assessment

    B. Product assessment

    C. Texas PE Test

    D. Iowa Brace Test

32. **Process assessment does not identify which of the following errors in skill performance:** *(Rigorous) (Skill 12.3)*

    A. Style

    B. Form

    C. End result

    D. Mechanics

33. **Determining poor performance of a skill using process assessment can best be accomplished by:** *(Rigorous) (Skill 12.3)*

    A. Observing how fast a skill is performed.

    B. Observing how many skills are performed.

    C. Observing how far or how high a skill is performed.

    D. Observing several attributes comprising the entire performance of a skill.

34. Which of the following principles is not a factor to assess to correct errors in performance for process assessment?
(Rigorous) (Skill 12.3)

A. Inertia

B. Action/Reaction

C. Force

D. Acceleration

35. Which of the following methods measures fundamental skills using product assessment?
(Rigorous) (Skill 12.3)

A. Criterion-referenced tests

B. Standardized norm-referenced tests

C. Both A and B

D. Neither A nor B

36. Product assessment measures all of the following except:
(Rigorous) (Skill 12.3)

A. How the student performs the mechanics of a skill.

B. How many times the student performs a skill.

C. How fast the student performs a skill.

D. How far or high the student performs a skill.

37. Instructors can evaluate skill level of achievement in archery by:
(Easy) (Skill 12.3)

A. Giving students a written exam on terminology.

B. Having students demonstrate the correct tension of arrow feathers.

C. Totaling a student's score obtained on the target's face.

D. Time how long a student takes to shoot all arrows.

38. Instructors can determine skill level achievement in golf by:
(Easy) (Skill 12.3)

A. The number of "birdies" that a student makes.

B. The number of "bogies" a student makes.

C. The score obtained after several rounds

D. The total score achieved throughout the school year.

39. **Instructors can determine skill level achievement in swimming by:**
(Easy) (Skill 12.3)

A. How long a student can float

B. How many strokes it takes a student to swim a specified distance.

C. How long a student can stay under the water without moving.

D. How many times a student can dive in five minutes.

40. **Instructors can assess skill level achievement in bowling by:**
(Easy) (Skill 12.3)

A. Calculating a student's average score.

B. Calculating how many gutter-balls the student threw.

C. Calculating how many strikes the student threw.

D. Calculating how many spares the student threw.

41. **Although they are still hitting the target, the score of some students practicing archery has decreased as the distance between them and the target has increased. Which of the following adjustments will improve their scores?**
(Rigorous) (Skill 12.3)

A. Increasing the velocity of their arrows.

B. Increasing the students' base of support.

C. Increasing the weight of the arrows.

D. Increasing the parabolic path of the arrows.

42. **Some students practicing basketball are having difficulty with "free throws," even though the shots make it to and over the hoop. What adjustment will improve their "free throws?"**
(Rigorous) (Skill 12.3)

A. Increasing the height of release (i.e. jump shot).

B. Increasing the vertical path of the ball.

C. Increasing the velocity of the release.

D. Increasing the base of support.

43. An instructor used a similar movement from a skill learned in a different activity to teach a skill for a new activity. The technique used to facilitate cognitive learning was:
(Average Rigor) (Skill 12.3)

A. Conceptual thinking

B. Transfer of learning

C. Longer instruction

D. Appropriate language

44. To enhance skill and strategy performance for striking or throwing objects, for catching or collecting objects, and for carrying and propelling objects, students must first learn techniques for:
(Easy) (Skill 12.4)

A. Offense

B. Defense

C. Controlling objects

D. Continuous play of objects

45. Using tactile clues is a functional adaptation that can assist which type of students?
(Easy) (Skill 12.4)

A. Deaf students

B. Blind students

C. Asthmatic students

D. Physically challenged students

46. What is the proper order of sequential development for the acquisition of locomotor skills?
(Rigorous) (Skill 12.4)

A. Creep, crawl, walk, jump, run, slide, gallop, hop, leap, skip; step-hop.

B. Crawl, walk, creep, slide, walk, run, hop, leap, gallop, skip; step-hop.

C. Creep, crawl, walk, slide, run, hop, leap, skip, gallop, jump; step-hop.

D. Crawl, creep, walk, run, jump, hop, gallop, slide, leap, skip; step-hop.

47. **Having students pretend they are playing basketball or trying to catch a bus develops which locomotor skill?**
(Average Rigor) (Skill 12.4)

A. Galloping

B. Running

C. Leaping

D. Skipping

48. **Having students play Fox and Hound develops:**
(Average Rigor) (Skill 12.4)

A. Galloping

B. Hopping

C. Stepping-hopping

D. Skipping

49. **Having students take off and land with both feet together develops which locomotor skill?**
(Average Rigor) (Skill 12.4)

A. Hopping

B. Jumping

C. Leaping

D. Skipping

50. **What is the proper sequential order of development for the acquisition of nonlocomotor skills?**
(Rigorous) (Skill 12.4)

A. Stretch, sit, bend, turn, swing, twist, shake, rock & sway, dodge; fall.

B. Bend, stretch, turn, twist, swing, sit, rock & sway, shake, dodge; fall.

C. Stretch, bend, sit, shake, turn, rock & sway, swing, twist, dodge; fall.

D. Bend, stretch, sit, turn, twist, swing, sway, rock & sway, dodge; fall.

51. **Activities such as pretending to pick fruit off a tree or reaching for a star develop which nonlocomotor skill?**
(Average Rigor) (Skill 12.4)

A. Bending

B. Stretching

C. Turning

D. Twisting

52. Picking up coins, tying shoes, and petting animals develop this nonlocomotor skill.
(Average Rigor) (Skill 12.4)

A. Bending

B. Stretching

C. Turning

D. Twisting

53. Having students collapse in their own space or lower themselves as though they are a raindrop or snowflake develops this nonlocomotor skill.
(Average Rigor) (Skill 12.4)

A. Dodging

B. Shaking

C. Swinging

D. Falling

54. Which is the proper sequential order of development for the acquisition of manipulative skills?
(Rigorous) (Skill 12.4)

A. Striking, throwing, bouncing, catching, trapping, kicking, ball rolling; volleying.

B. Striking, throwing, kicking, ball rolling, volleying, bouncing, catching; trapping.

C. Striking, throwing, catching, trapping, kicking, ball rolling, bouncing; volleying.

D. Striking, throwing, kicking, ball rolling, bouncing; volleying.

55. Having students hit a large balloon with both hands develops this manipulative skill.
(Average Rigor) (Skill 12.4)

A. Bouncing

B. Striking

C. Volleying

D. Trapping

56. Progressively decreasing the size of a target that balls are projected at develops which manipulative skill.
    (Average Rigor) (Skill 12.4)

    A. Throwing

    B. Trapping

    C. Volleying

    D. Kicking

57. Hitting a stationary object while in a fixed position, then incorporating movement, develops this manipulative skill.
    (Average Rigor) (Skill 12.4)

    A. Bouncing

    B. Trapping

    C. Throwing

    D. Striking

58. Coordinated movements that project a person over an obstacle is:
    (Rigorous) (Skill 13.1)

    A. Jumping

    B. Vaulting

    C. Leaping

    D. Hopping

59. Using the same foot to take off from a surface and land is which locomotor skill?
    (Rigorous) (Skill 13.1)

    A. Jumping

    B. Vaulting

    C. Leaping

    D. Hopping

60. Which nonlocomotor skill entails movement around a joint where two body parts meet?
    (Rigorous) (Skill 13.1)

    A. Twisting

    B. Swaying

    C. Bending

    D. Stretching

61. A sharp change of direction from one's original line of movement is which nonlocomotor skill?
    (Rigorous) (Skill 13.1)

    A. Twisting

    B. Dodging

    C. Swaying

    D. Swinging

62. **Which manipulative skill uses the hands to stop the momentum of an object?**
(Easy) (Skill 13.1)

A. Trapping

B. Catching

C. Striking

D. Rolling

63. **Playing "Simon Says" and having students touch different body parts applies which movement concept?**
(Rigorous) (Skill 13.1)

A. Spatial Awareness

B. Effort Awareness

C. Body Awareness

D. Motion Awareness

64. **Which movement concept involves students making decisions about an object's positional changes in space?**
(Rigorous) (Skill 13.1)

A. Spatial Awareness

B. Effort Awareness

C. Body Awareness

D. Motion Awareness

65. **There are two sequential phases to the development of spatial awareness. What is the order of these phases?**
(Rigorous) (Skill 13.1)

A. Locating more than one object in relation to each object; the location of objects in relation to one's own body in space.

B. The location of objects in relation to one's own body in space; locating more than one object in relation to one's own body.

C. Locating more than one object independent of one's body; the location of objects in relation to one's own body.

D. The location of objects in relation to one's own body in space; locating more than one object in relation to each object and independent of one's own body.

66. **Applying the mechanical principles of balance, time, and force describes which movement concept?**
(Rigorous) (Skill 13.4)

A. Spatial Awareness

B. Effort Awareness

C. Body Awareness

D. Motion Awareness

67. Having students move on their hands and knees, move on lines, and/or hold shapes while moving develops which quality of movement?
(Easy) (Skill 13.4)

A. Balance

B. Time

C. Force

D. Inertia

68. Students that paddle balls against a wall or jump over objects with various heights are demonstrating which quality of movement?
(Easy) (Skill 13.4)

A. Balance

B. Time

C. Force

D. Inertia

69. Having students move in a specific pattern while measuring how long they take to do so develops which quality of movement?
(Easy) (Skill 13.4)

A. Balance

B. Time

C. Force

D. Inertia

70. Equilibrium is maintained as long as:
(Rigorous) (Skill 13.4)

A. Body segments are moved independently.

B. The center of gravity is over the base of support

C. Force is applied to the base of support.

D. The center of gravity is lowered.

71. Which of the following does not enhance equilibrium?
(Rigorous) (Skill 13.4)

A. Shifting the center of gravity away from the direction of movement.

B. Increasing the base of support.

C. Lowering the base of support.

D. Increasing the base of support and lowering the center of support.

72. All of the following affect force except:
(Rigorous) (Skill 13.4)

A. Magnitude

B. Energy

C. Motion

D. Mass

73. For a movement to occur, applied force must overcome inertia of an object and any other resisting forces. What concept of force does this describe?
    (Rigorous) (Skill 13.4)

    A. Potential energy

    B. Magnitude

    C. Kinetic energy

    D. Absorption

74. The energy of an object to do work while recoiling is which type of potential energy?
    (Rigorous) (Skill 13.4)

    A. Absorption

    B. Kinetic

    C. Elastic

    D. Torque

75. Gradually decelerating a moving mass by utilization of smaller forces over a long period of time is:
    (Rigorous) (Skill 13.4)

    A. Stability

    B. Equilibrium

    C. Angular force

    D. Force absorption

76. The tendency of a body/object to remain in its present state of motion unless some force acts to change it is which mechanical principle of motion?
    (Rigorous) (Skill 13.4)

    A. Acceleration

    B. Inertia

    C. Action/Reaction

    D. Linear motion

77. The movement response of a system depends not only on the net external force, but also on the resistance to movement change. Which mechanical principle of motion does this definition describe?
    (Rigorous) (Skill 13.4)

    A. Acceleration

    B. Inertia

    C. Action/Reaction

    D. Air Resistance

78. **Which of the following mechanical principles of motion states that every motion has a similar, contrasting response? (Rigorous) (Skill 13.4)**

A. Acceleration

B. Inertia

C. Action/Reaction

D. Centripetal force

79. **Examples of tumbling include all of the following except _____. (Easy) (Skill 14.5)**

A. Cartwheel

B. Straddle roll

C. Uneven bars

D. Back Tuck

80. **Through physical activities, John has developed self-discipline, fairness, respect for others, and new friends. John has experienced which of the following? (Easy) (Skill 15.1)**

A. Positive cooperation psycho-social influences

B. Positive group psycho-social influences

C. Positive individual psycho-social influences

D. Positive accomplishment psycho-social influences

81. **Activities that enhance team socialization include all of the following except: (Easy) (Skill 15.2)**

A. Basketball

B. Soccer

C. Golf

D. Volleyball

82. **Social skills and values developed by activity include all of the following except:**
    (Easy) (Skill 15.5)

    A. Winning at all costs

    B. Making judgments in groups

    C. Communicating and cooperating

    D. Respecting rules and property

83. **The ability for a muscle(s) to repeatedly contract over a period of time is:**
    (Average Rigor) (Skill 16.3)

    A. Cardiovascular endurance

    B. Muscle endurance

    C. Muscle strength

    D. Muscle force

84. **Working at a level that is above normal is which exercise training principle?**
    (Easy) (Skill 16.4)

    A. Intensity

    B. Progression

    C. Specificity

    D. Overload

85. **Students on a running program to improve cardio-respiratory fitness apply which exercise principle.**
    (Easy) (Skill 16.4)

    A. Aerobic

    B. Progression

    C. Specificity

    D. Overload

86. **Adding more reps to a weightlifting set applies which exercise principle.**
    (Easy) (Skill 16.4)

    A. Anaerobic

    B. Progression

    C. Overload

    D. Specificity

87. **Which of the following does not modify overload?**
    (Average Rigor) (Skill 16.4)

    A. Frequency

    B. Perceived exertion

    C. Time

    D. Intensity

88. **Prior to activity, students perform a 5-10 minute warm-up. Which is not recommended as part of the warm-up?**
(Average Rigor) (Skill 16.4)

A. Using the muscles that will be utilized in the following activity.

B. Using a gradual aerobic warm-up.

C. Using a gradual anaerobic warm-up.

D. Stretching the major muscle groups to be used in the activity.

89. **Which is not a benefit of warming up?**
(Average Rigor) (Skill 16.4)

A. Releasing hydrogen from myoglobin.

B. Reducing the risk of musculoskeletal injuries.

C. Raising the body's core temperature in preparation for activity.

D. Stretching the major muscle groups to be used in the activity.

90. **Which is not a benefit of cooling down?**
(Average Rigor) (Skill 16.4)

A. Preventing dizziness.

B. Redistributing circulation.

C. Removing lactic acid.

D. Removing myoglobin.

91. **Activities to specifically develop cardiovascular fitness must be:**
(Rigorous) (Skill 16.4)

A. Performed without developing an oxygen debt

B. Performed twice daily.

C. Performed every day.

D. Performed for a minimum of 10 minutes.

92. **Overloading for muscle strength includes all of the following except:**
(Rigorous) (Skill 16.4)

A. Raising heart rate to an intense level.

B. Lifting weights every other day.

C. Lifting with high resistance and low reps.

D. Lifting 60% to 90% of assessed muscle strength.

93. **Which of the following applies the concept of progression?**
(Average Rigor) (Skill 16.4)

   A. Beginning a stretching program every day.

   B. Beginning a stretching program with 3 sets of reps.

   C. Beginning a stretching program with ballistic stretching.

   D. Beginning a stretching program holding stretches for 15 seconds and work up to holding stretches for 60 seconds.

94. **Which of following overload principles does not apply to improving body composition?**
(Average Rigor) (Skill 16.4)

   A. Aerobic exercise three times per week.

   B. Aerobic exercise at a low intensity.

   C. Aerobic exercise for about an hour.

   D. Aerobic exercise in intervals of high intensity.

95. **Which of the following principles of progression applies to improving muscle endurance?**
(Average Rigor) (Skill 16.4)

   A. Lifting weights every day.

   B. Lifting weights at 20% to 30% of assessed muscle strength.

   C. Lifting weights with low resistance and low reps.

   D. Lifting weights starting at 60% of assessed muscle strength.

96. **Aerobic dance develops or improves each of the following skills or health components except...**
(Average Rigor) (Skill 16.5)

   A. Cardio-respiratory function

   B. Body composition

   C. Coordination

   D. Flexibility

97. **Rowing develops which health or skill related component of fitness?**
(Average Rigor) (Skill 16.5)

   A. Muscle endurance

   B. Flexibility

   C. Balance

   D. Reaction time

98. **Calisthenics develops all of the following health and skill related components of fitness except:**
(Average Rigor) (Skill 16.5)

A. Muscle strength

B. Body composition

C. Power

D. Agility

99. **Which health or skill related component of fitness is developed by rope jumping?**
(Average Rigor) (Skill 16.5)

A. Muscle Force

B. Coordination

C. Flexibility

D. Muscle strength

100. **Swimming does not improve which health or skill related component of fitness?**
(Average Rigor) (Skill 16.5)

A. Cardio-respiratory function

B. Flexibility

C. Muscle strength

D. Foot Speed

101. **Data from a cardio-respiratory assessment can identify and predict all of the following except:**
(Rigorous) (Skill 16.5)

A. Functional aerobic capacity

B. Genetic disposition for excessive fat

C. Running ability

D. Motivation

102. **Data from assessing _____ identifies an individual's potential of developing musculoskeletal problems and an individual's potential of performing activities of daily living.**
(Rigorous) (Skill 16.5)

A. Flexibility

B. Muscle endurance

C. Muscle strength

D. Motor performance

103. A 17-year-old male student performed 20 sit-ups, ran a mile in 8 minutes, and has a body fat composition of 17%. Which is the best interpretation of his fitness level?
(Rigorous) (Skill 16.5)

   A. Average muscular endurance, good cardiovascular endurance; appropriate body fat composition.

   B. Low muscular endurance, average cardiovascular endurance; high body fat composition.

   C. Low muscular endurance, average cardiovascular endurance; appropriate body fat composition.

   D. Low muscular endurance, low cardiovascular endurance; appropriate body fat composition.

104. Based on the information given in the previous question, what changes would you recommend to improve this person's level of fitness?
(Average Rigor) (Skill 16.5)

   A. Muscle endurance training and cardiovascular endurance training.

   B. Muscle endurance training, cardiovascular endurance training, and reduction of caloric intake.

   C. Muscle strength training and cardio-vascular endurance training.

   D. No changes necessary.

105. An obese student's fitness assessments were poor for every component of fitness. Which would you recommend first?
(Average Rigor) (Skill 16.5)

   A. A jogging program.

   B. A weight lifting program.

   C. A walking program.

   D. A stretching program.

106. **Which of the following psycho-social influences is <u>not</u> negative?**
(Easy) (Skill 16.5)

  A. Avoidance of problems

  B. Adherence to exercise

  C. Ego-centeredness

  D. Role conflict

107. **An instructor notices that class participation is much lower than expected. By making changes in equipment and rules, the instructor   applied which of the following concepts to enhance participation?**
(Average Rigor) (Skill 16.6)

  A. Homogeneous grouping

  B. Heterogeneous grouping

  C. Multi-activity designs

  D. Activity modification

108. **Using the Karvonean Formula, compute the 60% - 80% THR for a 16-year old student with a RHR of 60.**
(Rigorous) (Skill 17.2)

  A. 122-163 beats per minute

  B. 130-168 beats per minute

  C. 142-170 beats per minute

  D. 146-175 beats per minute

109. **Using Cooper's Formula, compute the THR for a 15 year old student.**
(Rigorous) (Skill 17.2)

  A. 120- 153 beats per minute

  B. 123-164 beats per minute

  C. 135-169 beats per minute

  D. 147-176 beats per minute

110. **Flexibility is _____.**
(Easy) (Skill 18.1)

  A. The range of motion possible.

  B. Static

  C. Dynamic

  D. All of the above.

111. **The affective domain of physical education contributes to all of the following except:**
(Average Rigor) (Skill 19.1)

  A. Knowledge of exercise, health, and disease

  B. Self-actualization

  C. An appreciation of beauty

  D. Good sportsmanship

112.   Educators can evaluate the cognitive domain by all of the following methods except:
       (Average Rigor) (Skill 19.1)

       A. Norm-Referenced Tests

       B. Criterion Referenced Tests

       C. Standardized Tests

       D. Willis Sports Inventory Tests

113.   Which of the following is not a skill assessment test to evaluate student performance?
       (Easy) (Skill 19.2)

       A. Harrocks Volley

       B. Rodgers Strength Test

       C. Iowa Brace Test

       D. AAHPERD Youth Fitness Test

114.   The ability to change rapidly the direction of the body is:
       (Easy) (Skill 19.2)

       A. Coordination

       B. Reaction time

       C. Speed

       D. Agility

115.   Students are performing the vertical jump. What component of fitness does this activity assess?
       (Average Rigor) (Skill 19.2)

       A. Muscle strength

       B. Balance

       C. Power

       D. Muscle endurance

116.   Students are performing trunk extensions. What component of fitness does this activity assess?
       (Easy) (Skill 19.2)

       A. Balance

       B. Flexibility

       C. Body Composition

       D. Coordination

117.   An archery student's arrow bounced off the red part of the target face. What is the correct ruling?
       (Average Rigor) (Skill 20.1)

       A. No score.

       B. Re-shoot arrow.

       C. 7 points awarded.

       D. Shot receives same score as highest arrow shot that did not bounce off the target.

118. A student playing badminton believed that the shuttlecock was going to land out-of-bounds. The shuttlecock landed on the line. What is the correct ruling?
(Average Rigor) (Skill 20.1)

   A. The shuttlecock is out-of-bounds.

   B. The shuttlecock is in-bounds.

   C. The point is replayed.

   D. That player is charged with a feint.

119. A mechanical pinsetter accidentally knocked down the only bowling pin left standing for a spare attempt after clearing all the other pins knocked down by the first ball thrown. What is the correct ruling?
(Average Rigor) (Skill 20.1)

   A. Foul

   B. Spare

   C. Frame is replayed

   D. No count for that pin

120. The ball served in racquetball hits the front line and lands in front of the short line. What is the ruling?
(Average Rigor) (Skill 20.1)

   A. Fault

   B. Reserve

   C. Out-of-bounds

   D. Fair ball

121. Two students are playing badminton. When receiving the shuttlecock, one student consistently stands too deep in the receiving court. What strategy should the server use to serve the shuttlecock?
(Average Rigor) (Skill 20.1)

   A. Smash serve

   B. Clear serve

   C. Overhead serve

   D. Short serve

122. A teacher who modifies and develops tasks for a class is demonstrating knowledge of which appropriate behavior in physical education activities.
(Average Rigor) (Skill 20.2)

A. Appropriate management behavior

B. Appropriate student behavior

C. Appropriate administration behavior

D. Appropriate content behavior

123. Two opposing soccer players are trying to gain control of the ball when one player "knees" the other. What is the ruling?
(Average Rigor) (Skill 21.1)

A. Direct free kick

B. Indirect free kick

C. Fair play

D. Ejection from the game

124. A basketball team has an outstanding rebounder. In order to keep this player near the opponent's basket, which strategy should the coach implement?
(Average Rigor) (Skill 21.1)

A. Pick-and-Roll

B. Give-and-Go

C. Zone defense

D. Free-lancing

125. Volleyball player LB on team A digs a spiked ball. The ball deflects off LB's shoulder. What is the ruling?
(Average Rigor) (Skill 21.1)

A. Fault

B. Legal hit

C. Double foul

D. Play over

Answer Key

1.	D	33.	D	65.	D	97.	A
2.	C	34.	C	66.	B	98.	C
3.	C	35.	C	67.	A	99.	B
4.	B	36.	A	68.	C	100.	D
5.	A	37.	C	69.	B	101.	B
6.	D	38.	C	70.	B	102.	A
7.	B	39.	B	71.	A	103.	C
8.	B	40.	A	72.	D	104.	A
9.	B	41.	D	73.	B	105.	C
10.	C	42.	B	74.	C	106.	B
11.	A	43.	B	75.	D	107.	D
12.	B	44.	C	76.	B	108.	D
13.	C	45.	B	77.	A	109.	B
14.	D	46.	D	78.	C	110.	A
15.	C	47.	B	79.	C	111.	A
16.	D	48.	A	80.	B	112.	D
17.	D	49.	B	81.	C	113.	A
18.	D	50.	C	82.	A	114.	D
19.	C	51.	B	83.	B	115.	C
20.	D	52.	A	84.	D	116.	B
21.	A	53.	D	85.	C	117.	C
22.	C	54.	B	86.	B	118.	B
23.	D	55.	C	87.	B	119.	D
24.	B	56.	A	88.	C	120.	A
25.	A	57.	D	89.	A	121.	D
26.	B	58.	B	90.	D	122.	D
27.	C	59.	D	91.	A	123.	A
28.	B	60.	C	92.	A	124.	C
29.	A	61.	B	93.	D	125.	B
30.	B	62.	B	94.	A		
31.	B	63.	C	95.	B		
32.	C	64.	A	96.	D		

Rigor Table

	Easy %24	Average Rigor %36	Rigorous %40
Question #	7, 10, 15, 16, 20, 21, 22, 23, 37, 38, 39, 40, 44, 45, 62, 67, 68, 69, 79, 80, 81, 82, 84, 85, 86, 106, 110, 113, 114, 116	4, 9, 11, 14, 17, 18, 29, 43, 47, 48, 49, 51, 52, 53, 55, 56, 57, 83, 87, 88, 89, 90, 93, 94, 95, 96, 97, 98, 99, 100, 104, 105, 107, 111, 112, 115, 117, 118, 119, 120, 121, 122, 123, 124, 125	1, 2, 3, 5, 6, 8, 12, 13, 19, 24, 25, 26, 27, 28, 30, 31, 32, 33, 34, 35, 36, 41, 42, 46, 50, 54, 58, 59, 60, 61, 63, 64, 65, 66, 70, 71, 72, 73, 74, 75, 76, 77, 78, 91, 92, 101, 102, 103, 108, 109

Rationales with Sample Questions

1. **Which of the following is not characteristic for children ages 3-5?**
   (Rigorous) (Skill 1.1)

   A. energy

   B. rest

   C. developing bones

   D. focus

(D). Small children (ages 3-5) have a propensity for engaging in periods of a great deal of physical activity, punctuated by a need for a lot of rest. Children at this stage lack fine motor skills and cannot focus on small objects for very long. Their bones are still developing. At this age, girls tend to be better coordinated while boys tend to be stronger.

2. **What of the following can not be said about adolescent development?**
   (Rigorous) (Skill 1.1)

   A. girls will reach their full height

   B. acne is common

   C. gender related physical characteristics appear

   D.. sexual activity is a concern

(C). As children proceed to the later stages of adolescence (ages 15-17), girls will reach their full height, while boys will still have some growth remaining. The increase in hormone levels will cause acne, which coincides with a slight decrease of preoccupation with physical appearance. At this age, children may begin to initiate sexual activity (boys generally are more motivated by hormones, and girls more by peer pressure). There is a risk of teen pregnancy and sexually transmitted diseases. Gender related physical characteristics appear in the pre-adolescent years (ages 9-11).

3.   **Which of the following is true about visceral muscles?**
      (Rigorous) (Skill 2.1)

   A. They attach to the bone.

   B. They are voluntary.

   C. They are associated with an internal body structure.

   D. They make up the heart.

(C). Muscles are classified in three categories: Skeletal (muscles that attach to the bone), Visceral (muscles that are associated with an internal body structure), and Cardiac (muscles that form the wall of the heart). Skeletal muscles are the only voluntary muscles.

4.   **Which bodily system is responsible for the exchange of oxygen and carbon dioxide in the body?**
      (Average Rigor) (Skill 2.1)

   A. Immune System

   B. Cardiovascular System

   C. Endocrine System

   D. Digestive System

(B). The immune system's function is to keep human beings healthy and free of disease and illness. The function of the cardiovascular system is to carry oxygenated blood and nutrients to all cells of the body and return carbon dioxide waste to the lungs for expulsion. The main function of the endocrine system is to aid in the regulation of body activities by producing chemical substances we know as hormones. The function of the digestive system is to break food down into nutrients, absorb them into the blood stream, and deliver them to all cells of the body for use in cellular respiration.

5. **This type of immune response occurs because the human body is repeatedly subjected to a microorganism and recognizes it.**
   (Rigorous) (Skill 2.1)

   A. Specific

   B. Non-specific

   C. Inflammatory

   D. Passive Immunity

(A). Non-specific immune mechanisms include skin and mucous membranes, or, alternatively, the white blood cells and the inflammatory response. Specific immune mechanism is aptly named because it recognizes specific foreign material and responds by destroying the invader. Passive immunity can be passed between mother and breastfed infant or by the use of antibiotics.

6. **Cilia, bronchioles and alveoli belong to what body system?**
   (Rigorous) (Skill 2.1)

   A. Immune System

   B. Cardiovascular System

   C. Endocrine System

   D. Respiratory System

(D). The process of respiration is as follows: air enters the mouth and nose, where it is warmed, moistened and filtered of dust and particles. Cilia in the trachea trap and expel unwanted material in mucus. The trachea splits into two bronchial tubes and the bronchial tubes divide into smaller and smaller bronchioles in the lungs. The internal surface of the lung is composed of alveoli, which are thin walled air sacs. These allow for a large surface area for gas exchange. Capillaries line the alveoli. Oxygen diffuses into the bloodstream and carbon dioxide diffuses out of the capillaries and is exhaled from the lungs due to partial pressure. Hemoglobin, a protein containing iron, carries the oxygenated blood to the heart and all parts of the body.

7. **Which of the following childhood illnesses might require antibiotics?**
    (Easy) (Skill 2.2)

    A. Allergies

    B. Pink eye

    C. Asthma

    D. Pediculosis

(B). Of the common ailments listed, only pink-eye, or conjunctivitis, is ever treated with antibiotics. Allergies have a wide range of treatment plans, the most severe of which include the use of an epi-pen. Asthma is typically treated with an inhaler and Pediculosis, or lice, must be quarantined and treated with over the counter medication.

8. **Complete this sentence: Hyperglycemia _____.**
    (Rigorous) (Skill 2.2)

    A. occurs when the blood sugar level is low

    B. occurs when the blood sugar level is high

    C. is the correct balance of sugar within the body

    D. results from physical exertion.

(B). Diabetics control their disease by keeping the level of sugar (glucose) in the blood as close to normal as possible. Most children with diabetes self-monitor blood glucose levels to track their condition and respond to changes. Exercise and insulin make the body's glucose level fall. Hypoglycemia occurs when the blood sugar level is low. Hyperglycemia occurs when the blood sugar level is high.

9. **Which of the following conditions is not associated with a lack of physical activity?**
   (Average Rigor) (Skill 2.3)

   A. Atherosclerosis

   B. Longer life expectancy

   C. Osteoporosis

   D. Certain cancers

(B.) A lack of physical activity can contribute to atherosclerosis, osteoporosis, and certain cancers. Conversely, regular physical activity can contribute to longer life expectancy.

10. **The most important nutrient the body requires, without which life can only be sustained for a few days, is:**
    (Easy) (Skill 3.1)

    A. Vitamins

    B. Minerals

    C. Water

    D. Carbohydrates

(C.) Although the body requires vitamins, minerals, and carbohydrates to achieve proper growth and shape, water is essential. Without it, the body gets dehydrated and death is a possibility. Water should be pure, as seawater can cause kidney failure and death.

11. **With regard to protein content, foods from animal sources are usually:**
    (Average Rigor) (Skill 3.1)

    A. Complete

    B. Essential

    C. Nonessential

    D. Incidental

(A.) Animal protein is complete, meaning it provides all of the amino acids that the human body requires. Although animal meat is not essential to a person's diet, it is an excellent source of protein.

12. **The healthiest form of fat to consume is:**
    (Rigorous) (Skill 3.1)

    A. Monounsaturated

    B. Polyunsaturated

    C. Hydrosaturated

    D. Saturated

(B.) Polyunsaturated fatty acids contain multiple carbon-carbon double bonds. Thus, there is room for two or more hydrogen atoms. Polyunsaturated fats are healthier than saturated fats.

13.   **An adequate diet to meet nutritional needs consists of:**
        (Rigorous) (Skill 3.1)

        A. No more than 30% caloric intake from fats, no more than 50 % caloric intake from proteins, and at least 20% caloric intake from carbohydrates.

        B. No more than 30% caloric intake from fats, no more than 40% caloric intake from proteins, and at least 30% caloric intake from carbohydrates.

        C. No more than 30% caloric intake from fats, no more than 15% caloric intake from proteins, and at least 55% caloric intake from carbohydrates.

        D. No more than 30 % caloric intake from fats, no more than 30% caloric intake from proteins, and at least 40% caloric intake from carbohydrates.

(C.) General guidelines for nutritionally sound diets are 30% caloric intake from fats, no more than 15% caloric intake from proteins, and at least 55% caloric intake from carbohydrates.

14.   **Most high-protein diets:**
        (Average Rigor) (Skill 3.2)

        A. Are high in cholesterol

        B. Are high in saturated fats

        C. Require vitamin and mineral supplements

        D. All of the above

(D.) High-protein diets are high in cholesterol, saturated fats, and they require vitamin and mineral supplements.

15. **Which one of the following statements about low-calorie diets is false?**
    (Easy) (Skill 3.2)

    A. Most people who "diet only" regain the weight they lose.

    B. They are the way most people try to lose weight.

    C. They make weight control easier.

    D. They lead to excess worry about weight, food, and eating.

(C.) People who participate in low-calorie diets do not control their weight easily. They must work more and utilize their bodies in many other ways (e.g., walking) to keep themselves fit.

16. **Maintaining body weight is best accomplished by:**
    (Easy) (Skill 3.4)

    A. Dieting

    B. Aerobic exercise

    C. Lifting weights

    D. Equalizing caloric intake relative to output

(D.) The best way to maintain a body weight is by balancing caloric intake and output. Extensive dieting (caloric restriction) is not a good option as this would result in weakness. Exercise is part of the output process that helps balance caloric input and output.

17. **Which of the following is true about sleep and children?**
    (Average Rigor) (Skill 4.4)

    A. 7-8 hours daily is adequate

    B. the immune system cleanses the body during sleep

    C. good sleep corresponds with focus and control

    D. all of the above

(D). Sleep gives the body a break from the normal tasks of daily living. During sleep, the body performs many important cleansing and restoration tasks. The immune and excretory systems clear waste and repair cellular damage that accumulates in the body each day. Similarly, the body requires adequate rest and sleep to build and repair muscles. Without adequate rest, even the most strenuous exercise program will not produce muscular development. Finally, lack of rest and sleep leaves the body vulnerable to infection and disease. The recommended amount of sleep is 7-8 hours per night.

18. **A physical education instructor anticipates and prevents potential injuries, watches for hidden injuries, and takes an injury evaluation of the entire class. Which of the following strategies to prevent injuries is the teacher demonstrating?**
    (Average Rigor) (Skill 4.5)

    A. Maintaining hiring standards

    B. Proper use of equipment

    C. Proper procedures for emergencies

    D. Participant screening

(D.) In order for the instructor to know each student's physical status, she takes an injury evaluation. Such surveys are one way to know the physical status of an individual. It chronicles past injuries, tattoos, activities, and diseases the individual may have or had. It helps the instructor to know the limitations of each individual. Participant screening covers all forms of surveying and anticipation of injuries.

19. **Which of the following pieces of exercise equipment best applies the physiological principles?**
(Rigorous) (Skill 4.7)

   A. Rolling machine

   B. Electrical muscle stimulator

   C. Stationary Bicycle

   D. Motor-driven rowing machine

(C.) A stationary bicycle is the best option to support the body physically as it includes all of the operations related to an individual's body (e.g., movement of legs, position of arms, back exercise, stomach movement). Electrical muscle stimulators are very dangerous as they can cause muscles to loosen too much. Other machines may provide an unnecessarily extensive workout that is dangerous for muscle.

20. **All of the following actions help avoid lawsuits except:**
(Easy) (Skill 4.7)

   A. Ensuring equipment and facilities are safe

   B. Getting exculpatory agreements

   C. Knowing each students' health status

   D. Grouping students with unequal competitive levels

(D.) Grouping students with unequal competitive levels is not an action that can help avoid lawsuits. Such a practice could lead to injury because of the inequality in skill, size, and strength.

21.   **Which of the following actions does not promote safety?**
       (Easy) (Skill 4.7)

       A. Allowing students to wear the current style of shoes

       B. Presenting organized activities

       C. Inspecting equipment and facilities

       D. Instructing skill and activities properly

(A.) Shoes are very important in physical education and the emphasis on current shoe styles does not promote safety because they focus more on the look of the clothing, rather than functionality.

22.   **Which of the following is a negative coping strategy for dealing with stress?**
       (Easy) (Skill 6.4)

       A. Recreational diversions

       B. Active thinking

       C. Alcohol use

       D. Imagery

(C.) The use of alcohol is a negative coping strategy for dealing with stress. Alcohol causes the brain to lose the stressful data thus soothing the individual, but it can be highly detrimental in the long run. Positive ways to deal with stress include active thinking, imagery, and recreational diversions.

23.   **Which is not a common negative stressor?**
       (Easy) (Skill 7.6)

       A. Loss of significant other.

       B. Personal illness or injury.

       C. Moving to a new state.

       D. Landing a new job.

(D.) Landing a new job is generally not a cause of worry or stress. In fact, it is usually a positive event. Personal illness, loss of a significant other, or moving to a strange state can cause negative stress.

24. **Which is not a sign of stress?**
(Rigorous) (Skill 8.2)

A. Irritability

B. Assertiveness

C. Insomnia

D. Stomach problems

(B.) Assertiveness is not a sign of stress. Irritability, insomnia, and stomach problems are all related to stress.

25. **Physiological benefits of exercise include all of the following except:**
(Rigorous) (Skill 8.2)

A. Reducing mental tension

B. Improving muscle strength

C. Cardiac hypertrophy

D. Quicker recovery rate

(A). Physical exercises can help improve muscle strength by making the body move and they can help provide quicker recovery between exercise sessions and from injuries. However, physical activity does not directly relieve mental tension. It might reduce tension temporarily, but chances are the tension will persist.

26. **Psychological benefits of exercise include all of the following except:**
(Rigorous) (Skill 8.2)

A. Improved sleeping patterns

B. Improved energy regulation

C. Improved appearance

D. Improved quality of life

(B.) The psychological benefits of exercise include improved sleeping patterns, improved appearances, and an improved quality of life. Improved energy regulation is a physical benefit, not a psychological one.

27. **The most effective way to promote the physical education curriculum is to:**
(Rigorous) (Skill 8.2)

   A. Relate physical education to higher thought processes

   B. Relate physical education to humanitarianism

   C. Relate physical education to the total educational process

   D. Relate physical education to skills necessary to preserve the natural environment

(C.) The government treats the physical education curriculum as one of the major subjects. Because of all of the games that we now participate in, many countries have focused their hearts and set their minds on competing with rival countries. Physical education is now one of the major, important subjects and instructors should integrate physical education into the total educational process.

28. **Which of the following body types is the most capable of motor performance involving endurance?**
(Rigorous) (Skill 9.2)

   A. Endomorph

   B. Ectomorph

   C. Mesomorph

   D. Metamorph

(B.) Characteristically, ectomorphs are lean and slender with little body fat and musculature. Ectomorphs are usually capable of performing at high levels in endurance events.

29. **Which of the following is not a consideration for the selection of a facility?**
    (Average Rigor) (Skill 11.2)

    A. Community involvement

    B. Custodial staff

    C. Availability to women, minorities, and the handicapped

    D. Bond issues

(A.) While community involvement positively impacts the communities where individuals live and work, it is not a major consideration in facility selection. Factors that are more important are staffing, accessibility, and financial considerations.

30. **A subjective, observational approach to identifying errors in the form, style, or mechanics of a skill is accomplished by:**
    (Rigorous) (Skill 12.3)

    A. Product assessment

    B. Process assessment

    C. Standardized norm-referenced tests

    D. Criterion-referenced tests

(B.) Process assessment is one way to identify errors in the skills of an individual. It is one way to know the limitations and skills that every individual possesses.

31.   **What type of assessment objectively measures skill performance?**
      (Rigorous) (Skill 12.3)

      A. Process assessment

      B. Product assessment

      C. Texas PE Test

      D. Iowa Brace Test

(B.) Product assessment measures the skills of an individual. This process is a methodical evaluation of the characteristics of your product or service in the eyes of potential users and customers. The two principle types of assessments are principle-based assessments and usability testing.

32.   **Process assessment does not identify which of the following errors in skill performance:**
      (Rigorous) (Skill 12.3)

      A. Style

      B. Form

      C. End result

      D. Mechanics

(C.) Process assessment does not evaluate end results. Process assessment emphasizes analysis of style, form, and mechanics.

33. **Determining poor performance of a skill using process assessment can best be accomplished by:**
    (Rigorous) (Skill 12.3)

    A. Observing how fast a skill is performed.

    B. Observing how many skills are performed.

    C. Observing how far or how high a skill is performed.

    D. Observing several attributes comprising the entire performance of a skill.

(D.) To determine the source of the error in the poor performance of an individual, we use observations of several attributes that compromise the entire performance of a skill. Instructors should observe limitations and mistakes and determine how to best address these problems to improve future performance.

34. **Which of the following principles is not a factor to assess to correct errors in performance for process assessment?**
    (Rigorous) (Skill 12.3)

    A. Inertia

    B. Action/Reaction

    C. Force

    D. Acceleration

(C.) Force is not a factor one would consider in process assessment.

35. **Which of the following methods measures fundamental skills using product assessment?**
     (Rigorous) (Skill 12.3)

     A. Criterion-referenced tests

     B. Standardized norm-referenced tests

     C. Both A and B

     D. Neither A nor B

(C.) Criterion-referenced tests and standardized norm-referenced tests are both methods that can prove and measure skills in product assessment. They can help to prevent or lessen errors.

36. **Product assessment measures all of the following except:**
     (Rigorous) (Skill 12.3)

     A. How the student performs the mechanics of a skill.

     B. How many times the student performs a skill.

     C. How fast the student performs a skill.

     D. How far or high the student performs a skill.

(A.) Product assessment evaluates student performance and gives insight into how students can correct errors. Product assessment measures results. Thus, how the student performs the mechanics of a skill is not relevant to product assessment.

37.   Instructors can evaluate skill level of achievement in archery by: *(Easy) (Skill 12.3)*

      A. Giving students a written exam on terminology.

      B. Having students demonstrate the correct tension of arrow feathers.

      C. Totaling a student's score obtained on the target's face.

      D. Time how long a student takes to shoot all arrows.

(C.) Archery is the practice of using a <u>bow</u> to shoot <u>arrows</u>. Totaling a student's score is the only method, of the possible choices, that evaluates skill level. Choices A and B test knowledge and choice D is an arbitrary measure.

38.   Instructors can determine skill level achievement in golf by: *(Easy) (Skill 12.3)*

      A. The number of "birdies" that a student makes.

      B. The number of "bogies" a student makes.

      C. The score obtained after several rounds

      D. The total score achieved throughout the school year.

(C.) Instructors can determine skill level in golf by evaluating a golfer's score after several rounds. The number of bogies or birdies is not necessarily indicative of skill level because they are isolated events (i.e. the score on one hole). The player who consistently scores the lowest likely has the most impressive golf skills. Therefore, a player's score is the best way to determine his/her skill level. Finally, several rounds is a sufficient sample to determine skill level. An entire year's worth of scores is not necessary.

39. **Instructors can determine skill level achievement in swimming by:**
    (Easy) (Skill 12.3)

    A. How long a student can float

    B. How many strokes it takes a student to swim a specified distance.

    C. How long a student can stay under the water without moving.

    D. How many times a student can dive in five minutes.

(B.) Instructors can determine skill level in swimming by counting the strokes a swimmer takes when covering a certain distance. The arm movement, the strength, and the tactic to move quickly gives the swimmer an ability to swim faster. The ability to float, stay under water, and dive quickly are not relevant to swimming ability.

40. **Instructors can assess skill level achievement in bowling by:**
    (Easy) (Skill 12.3)

    A. Calculating a student's average score.

    B. Calculating how many gutter-balls the student threw.

    C. Calculating how many strikes the student threw.

    D. Calculating how many spares the student threw.

(A.) Instructors can determine the skill level of a bowler by calculating the student's average game score. There is a possibility that some coincidences take place (e.g., bowling a strike). To check the consistency, we determine the average instead of looking at only the score from a single game.

41.   Although they are still hitting the target, the score of some students practicing archery has decreased as the distance between them and the target has increased. Which of the following adjustments will improve their scores?
        (Rigorous) (Skill 12.3)

        A. Increasing the velocity of their arrows.

        B. Increasing the students' base of support.

        C. Increasing the weight of the arrows.

        D. Increasing the parabolic path of the arrows.

(D.) Increasing the parabolic path of the arrows will increase accuracy and precision at greater distances.

42.   Some students practicing basketball are having difficulty with "free throws," even though the shots make it to and over the hoop. What adjustment will improve their "free throws?"
        (Rigorous) (Skill 12.3)

        A. Increasing the height of release (i.e. jump shot).

        B. Increasing the vertical path of the ball.

        C. Increasing the velocity of the release.

        D. Increasing the base of support.

(B.) In this case, increasing the vertical path of the ball will help the students make more free throws. Increased vertical path provides greater margin for error, allowing the ball to drop more easily through the hoop. Increasing the velocity cannot work due to common sense. Finally, increasing the height of release and base of support are not viable options in this case because the students are having no problem getting the ball to the basket.

43. **An instructor used a similar movement from a skill learned in a different activity to teach a skill for a new activity. The technique used to facilitate cognitive learning was:**
(Average Rigor) (Skill 12.3)

A. Conceptual thinking

B. Transfer of learning

C. Longer instruction

D. Appropriate language

(B.) Using a previously used movement to facilitate a new task is a transfer of learning. The individual relates the past activity to the new one, enabling him/her to learn it more easily. Conceptual thinking is related to the transfer of learning, but it does not give the exact idea. Rather, it emphasizes the history of all learning.

44. **To enhance skill and strategy performance for striking or throwing objects, for catching or collecting objects, and for carrying and propelling objects, students must first learn techniques for:**
(Easy) (Skill 12.4)

A. Offense

B. Defense

C. Controlling objects

D. Continuous play of objects

(C.) For enhancing the catching, throwing, carrying, or propelling of objects, a student must learn how to control the objects. The control gives the player a sense of the object. Thus, offense, defense, and continuous play come naturally, as they are part of the controlling process.

45. **Using tactile clues is a functional adaptation that can assist which type of students?**
    (Easy) (Skill 12.4)

    A. Deaf students

    B. Blind students

    C. Asthmatic students

    D. Physically challenged students

(B.) Blind people use tactile clues to identify colors. Instructors should use tactile clues to help students see or hear targets by adding color, making them larger, or moving them closer.

46. **What is the proper order of sequential development for the acquisition of locomotor skills?**
    (Rigorous) (Skill 12.4)

    A. Creep, crawl, walk, jump, run, slide, gallop, hop, leap, skip; step-hop.

    B. Crawl, walk, creep, slide, walk, run, hop, leap, gallop, skip; step-hop.

    C. Creep, crawl, walk, slide, run, hop, leap, skip, gallop, jump; step-hop.

    D. Crawl, creep, walk, run, jump, hop, gallop, slide, leap, skip; step-hop.

(D.) The sequential steps are defined below in their appropriate order.

LOCOMOTOR SKILL: A skill that utilizes the feet and moves you from one place to another.

CRAWL: A form of locomotion where the person moves in a prone position with the body resting on or close to the ground or on the hands and knees.

CREEP: A slightly more advanced form of locomotion in which the person moves on the hands and knees.

WALK: A form of locomotion in which body weight is transferred alternately from the ball (toe) of one foot to the heel of the other. At times one foot is on the ground and during a brief phase, both feet are on the ground. There is no time when both feet are off the ground.

RUN: A form of locomotion much like the walk except that the tempo and body lean may differ. At times one foot is on the ground and during a brief phase both feet are off the ground. There is no time when both feet are on the ground simultaneously.

JUMP: A form of locomotion in which the body weight is projected from one or two feet and lands on two feet. Basic forms: for height, from height, distance, continuous, and rebounding.

HOP: A form of locomotion in which the body is projected from one foot to the same foot.

GALLOP: A form of locomotion that is a combination of an open step by the leading foot and a closed step by the trailing foot. The same foot leads throughout. The rhythm is uneven.

SLIDE: The same action as the gallop except that the direction of travel is sideways instead of forward. The rhythm is uneven.

LEAP: An exaggerated running step. There is a transfer of weight from one foot to the other and a phase when neither foot is in contact with the ground.

SKIP: A locomotor skill that combines a hop and a step (walk or run). The rhythm is uneven.

47. **Having students pretend they are playing basketball or trying to catch a bus develops which locomotor skill?**
    (Average Rigor) (Skill 12.4)

    A. Galloping

    B. Running

    C. Leaping

    D. Skipping

(B.) Playing basketball involves near constant running up and down the court. In addition, chasing is a good example to use with children to illustrate the concept of running.

48. **Having students play Fox and Hound develops:**
    (Average Rigor) (Skill 12.4)

    A. Galloping

    B. Hopping

    C. Stepping-hopping

    D. Skipping

(A.) Fox and Hound is an activity that emphasizes rapid running. The form of the exercise most closely resembles a gallop, especially in rhythm and rapidity. It can develop or progress at an accelerated rate.

49. **Having students take off and land with both feet together develops which locomotor skill?**
(Average Rigor) (Skill 12.4)

   A. Hopping

   B. Jumping

   C. Leaping

   D. Skipping

(B.) Jumping is a skill that most humans and many animals share. It is the process of getting one's body off of the ground for a short time using one's own power, usually by propelling oneself upward via contraction and then forceful extension of the legs. One can jump up to reach something high, jump over a fence or ditch, or jump down. One can also jump while dancing and as a sport in track and field.

50. **What is the proper sequential order of development for the acquisition of nonlocomotor skills?**
(Rigorous) (Skill 12.4)

   A. Stretch, sit, bend, turn, swing, twist, shake, rock & sway, dodge; fall.

   B. Bend, stretch, turn, twist, swing, sit, rock & sway, shake, dodge; fall.

   C. Stretch, bend, sit, shake, turn, rock & sway, swing, twist, dodge; fall.

   D. Bend, stretch, sit, turn, twist, swing, sway, rock & sway, dodge; fall.

(C.) Each skill in the progression builds on the previous skills.

51. **Activities such as pretending to pick fruit off a tree or reaching for a star develop which nonlocomotor skill?**
(Average Rigor) (Skill 12.4)

   A. Bending

   B. Stretching

   C. Turning

   D. Twisting

(B.) Stretching is the activity of gradually applying tensile force to lengthen, strengthen, and lubricate muscles, often performed in anticipation of physical exertion and to increase the range of motion within a joint. Stretching is an especially important accompaniment to activities that emphasize controlled muscular strength and flexibility. These include ballet, acrobatics or martial arts. Stretching also may help prevent injury to tendons, ligaments, and muscles by improving muscular elasticity and reducing the stretch reflex in greater ranges of motion that might cause injury to tissue. In addition, stretching can reduce delayed onset muscle soreness (DOMS).

52. **Picking up coins, tying shoes, and petting animals develop this nonlocomotor skill.**
(Average Rigor) (Skill 12.4)

   A. Bending

   B. Stretching

   C. Turning

   D. Twisting

(A.) Bending is the action of moving the body across a skeletal joint. In each of the sample activities, one must bend from the waist or knees to reach a low object.

53. **Having students collapse in their own space or lower themselves as though they are a raindrop or snowflake develops this nonlocomotor skill.**
(Average Rigor) (Skill 12.4)

    A. Dodging

    B. Shaking

    C. Swinging

    D. Falling

(D.) Falling is a major cause of personal injury in athletics. Athletic participants must learn how to fall in such a way as to limit the possibility of injury.

54. **Which is the proper sequential order of development for the acquisition of manipulative skills?**
(Rigorous) (Skill 12.4)

    A. Striking, throwing, bouncing, catching, trapping, kicking, ball rolling; volleying.

    B. Striking, throwing, kicking, ball rolling, volleying, bouncing, catching; trapping.

    C. Striking, throwing, catching, trapping, kicking, ball rolling, bouncing; volleying.

    D. Striking, throwing, kicking, ball rolling, bouncing; volleying.

(B.) Striking, throwing, kicking, ball rolling, volleying, bouncing, catching, and trapping is the proper sequential order of development for the acquisition of manipulative skills. Each skill in this progression builds on the previous skill.

55.   Having students hit a large balloon with both hands develops this manipulative skill.
        (Average Rigor) (Skill 12.4)

    A. Bouncing

    B. Striking

    C. Volleying

    D. Trapping

(C.) In a number of <u>ball games</u>, a volley is the ball that a player receives and delivers without touching the ground. The ability to volley a ball back and forth requires great body control and spatial awareness.

56.   Progressively decreasing the size of a target that balls are projected at develops which manipulative skill.
        (Average Rigor) (Skill 12.4)

    A. Throwing

    B. Trapping

    C. Volleying

    D. Kicking

(A.) Children develop throwing skills (the ability to propel an object through the air with a rapid movement of the arm and wrist) by projecting balls at progressively smaller targets.

57. **Hitting a stationary object while in a fixed position, then incorporating movement, develops this manipulative skill.** *(Average Rigor) (Skill 12.4)*

    A. Bouncing

    B. Trapping

    C. Throwing

    D. Striking

(D.) Striking is the process of hitting something sharply, as with the hand, the fist, or a weapon.

58. **Coordinated movements that project a person over an obstacle is:** *(Rigorous) (Skill 13.1)*

    A. Jumping

    B. Vaulting

    C. Leaping

    D. Hopping

(B.) Vaulting is the art of acrobatics on horseback. Vaulting is an internationally recognized, competitive sport that is growing in popularity. At the most basic level vaulting enhances riding skills. At any skill-level, this ancient dance between horse and rider deepens the sense of balance, timing, and poise for the rider, as well as a sensitivity to and respect for the horse-rider relationship. Participants can vault in competition individually or on a team of 8 people with up to 3 people on the horse at once.

59.   **Using the same foot to take off from a surface and land is which locomotor skill?**
      (Rigorous) (Skill 13.1)

      A. Jumping

      B. Vaulting

      C. Leaping

      D. Hopping

(D.) Hopping is a move with light, bounding skips or leaps. Basically, it is the ability to jump on one foot.

60.   **Which nonlocomotor skill entails movement around a joint where two body parts meet?**
      (Rigorous) (Skill 13.1)

      A. Twisting

      B. Swaying

      C. Bending

      D. Stretching

(C.) Bending is a deviation from a straight-line position. It is also means to assume a curved, crooked, or angular form or direction, to incline the body, to make a concession, yield, to apply oneself closely, or to concentrate (e.g., *she bent to her task).*

61.   **A sharp change of direction from one's original line of movement is which nonlocomotor skill?**
      (Rigorous) (Skill 13.1)

      A. Twisting

      B. Dodging

      C. Swaying

      D. Swinging

(B.) Dodging is the ability to avoid something by moving or shifting quickly aside.

62.   **Which manipulative skill uses the hands to stop the momentum of an object?**
       (Easy) (Skill 13.1)

       A. Trapping

       B. Catching

       C. Striking

       D. Rolling

(B.) The ability to use the hands to catch an object is a manipulative skill. Catching stops the momentum of an object. A successful catch harnesses the force of the oncoming object to stop the object's momentum.

63.   **Playing "Simon Says" and having students touch different body parts applies which movement concept?**
       (Rigorous) (Skill 13.1)

       A. Spatial Awareness

       B. Effort Awareness

       C. Body Awareness

       D. Motion Awareness

(C.) Body Awareness is a method that integrates European traditions of movement and biomedical knowledge with the East Asian traditions of movement (e.g. Tai chi and Zen meditation).

64. **Which movement concept involves students making decisions about an object's positional changes in space?**
(Rigorous) (Skill 13.1)

A. Spatial Awareness

B. Effort Awareness

C. Body Awareness

D. Motion Awareness

(A.) Spatial awareness is an organized awareness of objects in the space around us. It is also an awareness of our body's position in space. Without this awareness, we would not be able to pick food up from our plates and put it in our mouths. We would have trouble reading, because we could not see the letters in their correct relation to each other and to the page. Athletes would not have the precise awareness of the position of other players on the field and the movement of the ball, which is necessary to play sports effectively.

65. **There are two sequential phases to the development of spatial awareness. What is the order of these phases?**
(Rigorous) (Skill 13.1)

A. Locating more than one object in relation to each object; the location of objects in relation to one's own body in space.

B. The location of objects in relation to one's own body in space; locating more than one object in relation to one's own body.

C. Locating more than one object independent of one's body; the location of objects in relation to one's own body.

D. The location of objects in relation to one's own body in space; locating more than one object in relation to each object and independent of one's own body.

(D.) The order of the two sequential phases to develop spatial awareness are as follows: the location of objects in relation to one's own body in space, and locating more than one object in relation to each object and independent of one's own body.

66. **Applying the mechanical principles of balance, time, and force describes which movement concept?**
     (Rigorous) (Skill 13.4)

     A. Spatial Awareness

     B. Effort Awareness

     C. Body Awareness

     D. Motion Awareness

(B.) Effort Awareness is the knowledge of balance, time, and force and how they relate to athletic movements and activities.

67. **Having students move on their hands and knees, move on lines, and/or hold shapes while moving develops which quality of movement?**
     (Easy) (Skill 13.4)

     A. Balance

     B. Time

     C. Force

     D. Inertia

(A.) Balance is one of the <u>physiological</u> <u>senses</u>. It allows <u>humans</u> and <u>animals</u> to <u>walk</u> without falling. Some animals are better at this than humans. For example, a <u>cat</u> (as a <u>quadruped</u> using its <u>inner ear</u> and <u>tail</u>) can walk on a thin <u>fence</u>. All forms of equilibrioception are essentially the detection of acceleration.

68.   Students that paddle balls against a wall or jump over objects with various heights are demonstrating which quality of movement? *(Easy) (Skill 13.4)*

    A. Balance

    B. Time

    C. Force

    D. Inertia

(C.) Force is the capacity to do work or create physical change, energy, strength, or active power. It is a classical force that causes a free body with <u>mass</u> to <u>accelerate</u>. A net (or resultant) force that causes such acceleration may be the non-zero additive sum of many different forces acting on a body.

69.   Having students move in a specific pattern while measuring how long they take to do so develops which quality of movement? *(Easy) (Skill 13.4)*

    A. Balance

    B. Time

    C. Force

    D. Inertia

(B.) Time is a sequential arrangement of all events or the interval between two events in such a sequence. We can discuss the concept of time on several different levels: physical, psychological, philosophical, scientific, and biological. Time is the non-spatial continuum in which events occur, in apparently irreversible succession, from the past through the present to the future.

70. **Equilibrium is maintained as long as:**
    (Rigorous) (Skill 13.4)

    A. Body segments are moved independently.

    B. The center of gravity is over the base of support

    C. Force is applied to the base of support.

    D. The center of gravity is lowered.

(B.) Equilibrium is a condition in which all acting influences are canceled by others, resulting in a stable, balanced, or unchanging system. It allows <u>humans</u> and <u>animals</u> to <u>walk</u> without falling. An object maintains equilibrium as long as its center of gravity is over its base of support.

71. **Which of the following does not enhance equilibrium?**
    (Rigorous) (Skill 13.4)

    A. Shifting the center of gravity away from the direction of movement.

    B. Increasing the base of support.

    C. Lowering the base of support.

    D. Increasing the base of support and lowering the center of support.

(A.) Equilibrium is a state of balance. When a body or a system is in equilibrium, there is no net tendency toward change. In mechanics, equilibrium has to do with the forces acting on a body. When no force acts to make a body move in a line, the body is in translational equilibrium. When no force acts to make the body turn, the body is in rotational equilibrium. A body in equilibrium while at rest is in static equilibrium. Increasing the base of support, lowering the base of support, and increasing the base of support and lowering the center of support all enhance equilibrium by balancing forces.

72. **All of the following affect force except:**
(Rigorous) (Skill 13.4)

   A. Magnitude

   B. Energy

   C. Motion

   D. Mass

(D.) Mass is a property of a <u>physical</u> object that quantifies the amount of <u>matter</u> and <u>energy</u> it contains. Unlike <u>weight</u>, the mass of something stays the same regardless of location. Every object has a unified body of matter with no specific shape.

73. **For a movement to occur, applied force must overcome inertia of an object and any other resisting forces. What concept of force does this describe?**
(Rigorous) (Skill 13.4)

   A. Potential energy

   B. Magnitude

   C. Kinetic energy

   D. Absorption

(B.) Speaking of magnitude in a purely relative way states that nothing is large and nothing small. If everything in the universe increased in bulk one thousand diameters, nothing would be any larger than it was before. However, if one thing remained unchanged, all of the others would be larger than they had been. To a person familiar with the relativity of magnitude and distance, the spaces and masses of the astronomer would be no more impressive than those of the microscopist would. To the contrary, the visible universe may be a small part of an atom, with its component ions floating in the life-fluid (luminiferous ether) of some animal.

74. **The energy of an object to do work while recoiling is which type of potential energy?**
(Rigorous) (Skill 13.4)

    A. Absorption

    B. Kinetic

    C. Elastic

    D. Torque

(C.) In <u>materials science</u>, the word <u>elastomer</u> refers to a material that is very elastic (like <u>rubber</u>). We often use the word elastic colloquially to refer to an elastomeric material such as <u>rubber</u> or cloth/rubber combinations. It is capable of withstanding stress without injury. Elastic potential energy describes the energy inherent in flexible objects.

75. **Gradually decelerating a moving mass by utilization of smaller forces over a long period of time is:**
(Rigorous) (Skill 13.4)

    A. Stability

    B. Equilibrium

    C. Angular force

    D. Force absorption

(D.) Force absorption is the gradual deceleration of a moving mass by utilization of smaller forces over a long period of time.

76. **The tendency of a body/object to remain in its present state of motion unless some force acts to change it is which mechanical principle of motion?**
(Rigorous) (Skill 13.4)

    A. Acceleration

    B. Inertia

    C. Action/Reaction

    D. Linear motion

(B.) Inertia is a term used in physics that describes the resistance of a body to any alteration in its state of <u>motion</u>. Inertia is a property common to all matter. Galileo first observed this property and Newton later restated it. Newton's first law of motion is sometimes called the law of inertia. Newton's second law of motion states that the external force required to affect the motion of a body is proportional to that acceleration. The constant of proportionality is the <u>mass</u>, which is the numerical value of the inertia. The greater the inertia of a body, the less acceleration is needed for a given, applied force.

77. **The movement response of a system depends not only on the net external force, but also on the resistance to movement change. Which mechanical principle of motion does this definition describe?**
(Rigorous) (Skill 13.4)

    A. Acceleration

    B. Inertia

    C. Action/Reaction

    D. Air Resistance

(A.) Acceleration is the change in the <u>velocity</u> of a body with respect to time. Since velocity is a <u>vector</u> quantity involving both magnitude and direction, acceleration is also a vector. In order to produce acceleration, a <u>force</u> must on a body. The magnitude of the force (*F*) must be directly proportional to both the mass of the body (*m*) and the desired acceleration (*a*), according to Newton's second law of motion (*F=ma*). The exact nature of the acceleration depends on the relative directions of the original velocity and force. A force acting in the same direction as the velocity changes only the <u>speed</u> of the body. An appropriate force, acting always at right angles to the velocity, changes the direction of the velocity but not the speed.

78. **Which of the following mechanical principles of motion states that every motion has a similar, contrasting response?** *(Rigorous) (Skill 13.4)*

   A. Acceleration

   B. Inertia

   C. Action/Reaction

   D. Centripetal force

(C.) The principle of action/reaction is an assertion about the nature of motion from which we can determine the trajectory of an object subject to forces. The path of an object yields a stationary value for a quantity called the action. Thus, instead of thinking about an object accelerating in response to applied forces, one might think of them as picking out the path with a stationary action.

79. **Examples of tumbling include all of the following except _____.** *(Easy) (Skill 14.5)*

   A. Cartwheel

   B. Straddle roll

   C. Uneven bars

   D. Back Tuck

(C). Floor exercise and tumbling can include somersaults, backward and frontward rolls, cartwheels, forward straddle rolls, back tucks, back handsprings, and handstands. Gymnasts perform apparatus work on the vaulting horse, balance beam, and uneven bars.

80. **Through physical activities, John has developed self-discipline, fairness, respect for others, and new friends. John has experienced which of the following?**
(Easy) (Skill 15.1)

   A. Positive cooperation psycho-social influences

   B. Positive group psycho-social influences

   C. Positive individual psycho-social influences

   D. Positive accomplishment psycho-social influences

(B.) Through physical activities, John developed his social interaction skills. Social interaction is the sequence of social actions between individuals (or groups) that modify their actions and reactions due to the actions of their interaction partner(s). In other words, they are events in which people attach meaning to a situation, interpret what others mean, and respond accordingly. Through socialization with other people, John feels the influence of the people around him.

81. **Activities that enhance team socialization include all of the following except:**
(Easy) (Skill 15.2)

   A. Basketball

   B. Soccer

   C. Golf

   D. Volleyball

(C.) Golf is mainly an individual sport. Though golf involves social interaction, it generally lacks the team element inherent in basketball, soccer, and volleyball.

82. **Social skills and values developed by activity include all of the following except:**
     (Easy) (Skill 15.5)

     A. Winning at all costs

     B. Making judgments in groups

     C. Communicating and cooperating

     D. Respecting rules and property

(A.) Winning at all costs is not a desirable social skill. Instructors and coaches should emphasize fair play and effort over winning. Answers B, C, and D are all positive skills and values developed in physical activity settings.

83. **The ability for a muscle(s) to repeatedly contract over a period of time is:**
     (Average Rigor) (Skill 16.3)

     A. Cardiovascular endurance

     B. Muscle endurance

     C. Muscle strength

     D. Muscle force

(B.) Muscle endurance gives the muscle the ability to contract over a period of time. Muscle strength is a prerequisite for the endurance of muscle. Cardiovascular endurance involves aerobic exercise.

84. **Working at a level that is above normal is which exercise training principle?**
(Easy) (Skill 16.4)

   A. Intensity

   B. Progression

   C. Specificity

   D. Overload

(D.) Overloading is exercising above normal capacities. Intensity and progression are supporting principles in the process of overload. Overloading can cause serious issues within the body, either immediately or after some time.

85. **Students on a running program to improve cardio-respiratory fitness apply which exercise principle.**
(Easy) (Skill 16.4)

   A. Aerobic

   B. Progression

   C. Specificity

   D. Overload

(C.) Running to improve cardio-respiratory fitness is an example of specificity. Specificity is the selection of activities that isolate a specific body part or system. Aerobics is also a good option, but it deals with the entire body, including areas not specific to cardio-respiratory fitness.

86. **Adding more reps to a weightlifting set applies which exercise principle.**
(Easy) (Skill 16.4)

   A. Anaerobic

   B. Progression

   C. Overload

   D. Specificity

(B.) Adding more repetitions (reps) to sets when weightlifting is an example of progression. Adding reps can result in overload, but the guiding principle is progression.

87. **Which of the following does not modify overload?**
(Average Rigor) (Skill 16.4)

   A. Frequency

   B. Perceived exertion

   C. Time

   D. Intensity

(B.) Time extension, frequency of movement, and intensity are all indicators of overload. However, exertion is not a good indicator of overload, because measuring exertion is subjective and difficult to monitor.

88. **Prior to activity, students perform a 5-10 minute warm-up. Which is not recommended as part of the warm-up?**
(Average Rigor) (Skill 16.4)

A. Using the muscles that will be utilized in the following activity.

B. Using a gradual aerobic warm-up.

C. Using a gradual anaerobic warm-up.

D. Stretching the major muscle groups to be used in the activity.

(C.) Warm-up is always necessary, but it should not be an anaerobic warm-up. The muscle exercises, the stretching, and even the aerobics are all helpful and athletes should complete these exercises within the normal breathing conditions. In fact, athletes should focus more closely on proper breathing. Athletes should engage in anaerobic stretching after activity, when muscles are loose and less prone to injury.

89. **Which is not a benefit of warming up?**
(Average Rigor) (Skill 16.4)

A. Releasing hydrogen from myoglobin.

B. Reducing the risk of musculoskeletal injuries.

C. Raising the body's core temperature in preparation for activity.

D. Stretching the major muscle groups to be used in the activity.

(A.) Warm-up can reduce the risk of musculoskeletal injuries, raise the body's temperature in preparation for activity, and stretch the major muscle groups. However, a warm-up does not release hydrogen from myoglobin. Myoglobin binds oxygen, not hydrogen.

90. **Which is not a benefit of cooling down?**
     (Average Rigor) (Skill 16.4)

A. Preventing dizziness.

B. Redistributing circulation.

C. Removing lactic acid.

D. Removing myoglobin.

(D.) Cooling down helps the body to regain blood circulation and to remove lactic acid. It also prevents dizziness, which may occur after extensive exercises. The only thing that cooling down does not support is removing myoglobin. However, it can help myoglobin get a strong hold in the muscles.

91. **Activities to specifically develop cardiovascular fitness must be:**
     (Rigorous) (Skill 16.4)

A. Performed without developing an oxygen debt

B. Performed twice daily.

C. Performed every day.

D. Performed for a minimum of 10 minutes.

(A.) The development of cardiovascular fitness is not dependent on specific time limits or routine schedules. Participants should perform aerobic activities without developing an oxygen debt.

92. **Overloading for muscle strength includes all of the following except:**
     (Rigorous) (Skill 16.4)

A. Raising heart rate to an intense level.

B. Lifting weights every other day.

C. Lifting with high resistance and low reps.

D. Lifting 60% to 90% of assessed muscle strength.

(A.) Overloading muscle strength is possible by lifting weights every other day or by lifting weights with high resistance and low repetition. Overloading does not cause or require an intense increase in heart rate. However, overloading has many other possibilities.

93. **Which of the following applies the concept of progression?**
(Average Rigor) (Skill 16.4)

 A. Beginning a stretching program every day.

 B. Beginning a stretching program with 3 sets of reps.

 C. Beginning a stretching program with ballistic stretching.

 D. Beginning a stretching program holding stretches for 15 seconds and work up to holding stretches for 60 seconds.

(D.) Progression is the process of starting an exercise program slowly and cautiously before proceeding to more rigorous training. Answer D is the only answer that exemplifies progression.

94. **Which of following overload principles does not apply to improving body composition?**
(Average Rigor) (Skill 16.4)

 A. Aerobic exercise three times per week.

 B. Aerobic exercise at a low intensity.

 C. Aerobic exercise for about an hour.

 D. Aerobic exercise in intervals of high intensity.

(A.) To improve body composition, a person should engage in aerobic exercise daily, not three times per week. However, an individual can do aerobics for at least half an hour daily, he/she can exercise at a low intensity, or he/she can train with intervals of high intensity.

95. **Which of the following principles of progression applies to improving muscle endurance?**
    (Average Rigor) (Skill 16.4)

    A. Lifting weights every day.

    B. Lifting weights at 20% to 30% of assessed muscle strength.

    C. Lifting weights with low resistance and low reps.

    D. Lifting weights starting at 60% of assessed muscle strength.

(B.) To improve muscle endurance, a person should lift weights at 20 to 30% of the assessed muscle strength. Lifting weights daily is counterproductive because it does not allow for adequate rest. In addition, lifting at 60% of the assessed muscle strength can damage the muscle.

96. **Aerobic dance develops or improves each of the following skills or health components except...**
    (Average Rigor) (Skill 16.5)

    A. Cardio-respiratory function

    B. Body composition

    C. Coordination

    D. Flexibility

(D.) Aerobic dance does not develop flexibility, as flexibility results from stretching and not aerobic exercise. Ballet dancing, however, does develop flexibility. Aerobic dance develops cardio-respiratory function due to the unusual body movements performed. It also improves body composition and coordination due to the movement of various body parts.

97. **Rowing develops which health or skill related component of fitness?**
    (Average Rigor) (Skill 16.5)

    A. Muscle endurance

    B. Flexibility

    C. Balance

    D. Reaction time

(A.) Rowing helps develop muscle endurance because of the continuous arm movement against the force of the water. However, flexibility, balance, and reaction time are not important components of rowing. Rowing also develops the lower abdominal muscles while the individual is in the sitting position when rowing.

98. **Calisthenics develops all of the following health and skill related components of fitness except:**
    (Average Rigor) (Skill 16.5)

    A. Muscle strength

    B. Body composition

    C. Power

    D. Agility

(C.) Calisthenics is a sport that actually helps to keep a body fit in by combining gymnastic and aerobic activities. Calisthenics develop muscle strength and agility and improves body composition. However, calisthenics do not develop power because they do not involve resistance training or explosiveness.

99. **Which health or skill related component of fitness is developed by rope jumping?**
(Average Rigor) (Skill 16.5)

   A. Muscle Force

   B. Coordination

   C. Flexibility

   D. Muscle strength

(B.) Rope jumping is a good mental exercise and it improves coordination. Many athletes (e.g. boxers, tennis players) jump rope to improve coordination and quickness. Muscle strength is secondary to that.

100. **Swimming does not improve which health or skill related component of fitness?**
(Average Rigor) (Skill 16.5)

   A. Cardio-respiratory function

   B. Flexibility

   C. Muscle strength

   D. Foot Speed

(D.) Swimming involves every part of the body. It works on the cardio-respiratory system and it develops flexibility because of the intense body movement in the water. It also improves muscle strength as swimmers must move their bodies against the force of water. Increased foot speed is not an outcome of swimming.

101. **Data from a cardio-respiratory assessment can identify and predict all of the following except:**
     (Rigorous) (Skill 16.5)

     A. Functional aerobic capacity

     B. Genetic disposition for excessive fat

     C. Running ability

     D. Motivation

(B.) The data from cardio-respiratory assessment can identify and predict running ability, motivation, and functional aerobic capacity. However, it cannot predict natural over-fatness, as natural over-fatness is a part of the human body. It is not artificially developed like running ability and motivation.

102. **Data from assessing _____ identifies an individual's potential of developing musculoskeletal problems and an individual's potential of performing activities of daily living.**
     (Rigorous) (Skill 16.5)

     A. Flexibility

     B. Muscle endurance

     C. Muscle strength

     D. Motor performance

(A.) Flexibility is more important than any of the other choices when determining an individual's potential of developing musculoskeletal problems and an individual's potential of performing activities of daily living.

103. **A 17-year-old male student performed 20 sit-ups, ran a mile in 8 minutes, and has a body fat composition of 17%. Which is the best interpretation of his fitness level?**
(Rigorous) (Skill 16.5)

   A. Average muscular endurance, good cardiovascular endurance; appropriate body fat composition.

   B. Low muscular endurance, average cardiovascular endurance; high body fat composition.

   C. Low muscular endurance, average cardiovascular endurance; appropriate body fat composition.

   D. Low muscular endurance, low cardiovascular endurance; appropriate body fat composition.

(C.) A 17-year-old male who performs 20 sit-ups, runs a mile in 8 minutes, has 17% fat composition, has low muscular endurance, average cardiovascular endurance, and appropriate fat composition. 20 sit-ups is a relatively low number. An 8-minute mile is an average time for a 17-year-old male. Finally, a body fat composition of 17% is appropriate.

104. **Based on the information given in the previous question, what changes would you recommend to improve this person's level of fitness?**
(Average Rigor) (Skill 16.5)

   A. Muscle endurance training and cardiovascular endurance training.

   B. Muscle endurance training, cardiovascular endurance training, and reduction of caloric intake.

   C. Muscle strength training and cardio-vascular endurance training.

   D. No changes necessary.

(A.) The person requires both muscle endurance and cardiovascular training while keeping the other bodily intakes normal. An appropriate program would include moderate weightlifting and regular aerobic activity.

105. **An obese student's fitness assessments were poor for every component of fitness. Which would you recommend first?** *(Average Rigor) (Skill 16.5)*

    A. A jogging program.

    B. A weight lifting program.

    C. A walking program.

    D. A stretching program.

(C.) An obese person should begin by walking and then progress to jogging. Weightlifting and stretching are not as important initially. They are also dangerous because the student may not have the ability to complete such strenuous tasks safely.

106. **Which of the following psycho-social influences is <u>not</u> negative?** *(Easy) (Skill 16.5)*

    A. Avoidance of problems

    B. Adherence to exercise

    C. Ego-centeredness

    D. Role conflict

(B.) The ability of an individual to adhere to an exercise routine due to her/his excitement, accolades, etc. is not a negative psycho-social influence. Adherence to an exercise routine is healthy and positive.

107. **An instructor notices that class participation is much lower than expected. By making changes in equipment and rules, the instructor applied which of the following concepts to enhance participation?** *(Average Rigor) (Skill 16.6)*

    A. Homogeneous grouping

    B. Heterogeneous grouping

    C. Multi-activity designs

    D. Activity modification

(D.) Activity modification involves changing rules and equipment to fit the needs of students of different ability levels and physical development levels. Activity modification can encourage participation by making games and activities more enjoyable and allowing for more student success.

108. **Using the Karvonean Formula, compute the 60% - 80% THR for a 16-year old student with a RHR of 60.** *(Rigorous) (Skill 17.2)*

    A. 122-163 beats per minute

    B. 130-168 beats per minute

    C. 142-170 beats per minute

    D. 146-175 beats per minute

(D.) Solution is as follows:
220 – 16 (age) = 204, 204 – 60 (RHR) = 144, 144 x .60 (low end of heart range) = 86, 86 + 60 (RHR) = 146 (bottom of THR)
220 – 16 (age) = 204, 204 – 60 (RHR) = 144, 144 x 0.80 (high end of heart range) = 115, 115 + (RHR) = 175 (top of THR)
146-175 beats per minute is the 60%-80% THR.

109. **Using Cooper's Formula, compute the THR for a 15 year old student.**
(Rigorous) (Skill 17.2)

   A. 120- 153 beats per minute

   B. 123-164 beats per minute

   C. 135-169 beats per minute

   D. 147-176 beats per minute

(B.) Cooper's Formula to determine target heart range is:
THR = (220 - AGE) x .60 to (220 - AGE) x .80.
Therefore, the answer is 123-164 beats per minute.

110. **Flexibility is _____.**
(Easy) (Skill 18.1)

   A. The range of motion possible.

   B. Static

   C. Dynamic

   D. All of the above.

(A.) Flexibility is the range of motion around a joint or muscle. Flexibility has two major components: static and dynamic. Static flexibility is the range of motion without a consideration for speed of movement. Dynamic flexibility is the use of the desired range of motion at a desired velocity. These movements are useful for most athletes.

111. **The affective domain of physical education contributes to all of the following except:**
(Average Rigor) (Skill 19.1)

   A. Knowledge of exercise, health, and disease

   B. Self-actualization

   C. An appreciation of beauty

   D. Good sportsmanship

(A.) The affective domain encompasses emotions, thoughts, and feelings related to physical education. Knowledge of exercise, health, and disease is part of the cognitive domain.

112. **Educators can evaluate the cognitive domain by all of the following methods except:**
(Average Rigor) (Skill 19.1)

   A. Norm-Referenced Tests

   B. Criterion Referenced Tests

   C. Standardized Tests

   D. Willis Sports Inventory Tests

(D.) The Willis Sports Inventory Test is not a cognitive evaluation tool.

113. **Which of the following is not a skill assessment test to evaluate student performance?**
(Easy) (Skill 19.2)

   A. Harrocks Volley

   B. Rodgers Strength Test

   C. Iowa Brace Test

   D. AAHPERD Youth Fitness Test

(A.) Harrocks Volley is a volleyball code, not an assessment tool.

114. **The ability to change rapidly the direction of the body is:**
(Easy) (Skill 19.2)

    A. Coordination

    B. Reaction time

    C. Speed

    D. Agility

(D.) Agility is the ability of the body to change position quickly. Reaction time, coordination, and speed are not the right words to describe the ability to move quickly, as we always say that the goalkeeper is agile.

115. **Students are performing the vertical jump. What component of fitness does this activity assess?**
(Average Rigor) (Skill 19.2)

    A. Muscle strength

    B. Balance

    C. Power

    D. Muscle endurance

(C.) Vertical jumping assesses the power of the entire body. It shows the potential of the legs to hold the upper body and the strength in the joints of the legs. Balance and muscle strength are secondary requirements. Power automatically ensures these secondary requirements.

116. **Students are performing trunk extensions. What component of fitness does this activity assess?**
(Easy) (Skill 19.2)

    A. Balance

    B. Flexibility

    C. Body Composition

    D. Coordination

(B.) The core component of trunk extensions is flexibility. Trunk extensions also indicate the body's capacity for full expansion and emphasizes areas such as the stomach, arms, and shoulder joints.

117. **An archery student's arrow bounced off the red part of the target face. What is the correct ruling?**
(Average Rigor) (Skill 20.1)

    A. No score.

    B. Re-shoot arrow.

    C. 7 points awarded.

    D. Shot receives same score as highest arrow shot that did not bounce off the target.

(C.) When an arrow bounces off the red area of a target, the archer receives 7 points, the value of the shot had the arrow stuck in the target.

118. **A student playing badminton believed that the shuttlecock was going to land out-of-bounds. The shuttlecock landed on the line. What is the correct ruling?**
(Average Rigor) (Skill 20.1)

    A. The shuttlecock is out-of-bounds.

    B. The shuttlecock is in-bounds.

    C. The point is replayed.

    D. That player is charged with a feint.

(B.) If a shuttlecock lands on the line, it is in-bounds by the rules of badminton.

119. **A mechanical pinsetter accidentally knocked down the only bowling pin left standing for a spare attempt after clearing all the other pins knocked down by the first ball thrown. What is the correct ruling?**
(Average Rigor) (Skill 20.1)

   A. Foul

   B. Spare

   C. Frame is replayed

   D. No count for that pin

(D.) When the mechanical pin setter touches a pin and knocks it down, there is no count for the pin. This is because the pin's fall resulted from a mechanical fault and not from the player's skill. The other pins count and there is no foul for the player.

120. **The ball served in racquetball hits the front line and lands in front of the short line. What is the ruling?**
(Average Rigor) (Skill 20.1)

   A. Fault

   B. Reserve

   C. Out-of-bounds

   D. Fair ball

(A.) If a served ball falls in front of the short line, it is a fault according to a rule that states that a ball must fall within the short line frame at the time of serving. It is not out-of-bounds, as it is still within the limits of the pitch. However, it is also not a fair ball due to the service rule.

121. **Two students are playing badminton. When receiving the shuttlecock, one student consistently stands too deep in the receiving court. What strategy should the server use to serve the shuttlecock?**
(Average Rigor) (Skill 20.1)

   A. Smash serve

   B. Clear serve

   C. Overhead serve

   D. Short serve

(D.) The short serve would give land short in the court so the opponent would not be able to reach the shuttlecock. Therefore, the short serve would win the point. A clear or overhead serve enables the opponent to hit the shuttlecock and continue the game. A smash serve runs a higher risk of falling out-of-bounds. Neither of these scenarios are goals of the server.

122. **A teacher who modifies and develops tasks for a class is demonstrating knowledge of which appropriate behavior in physical education activities.**
(Average Rigor) (Skill 20.2)

   A. Appropriate management behavior

   B. Appropriate student behavior

   C. Appropriate administration behavior

   D. Appropriate content behavior

(D.) In this case, the teacher is demonstrating knowledge of a behavior in reference to physical activity. It is known as appropriate content behavior. The other options are not related to physical activities.

123. **Two opposing soccer players are trying to gain control of the ball when one player "knees" the other. What is the ruling?**
(Average Rigor) (Skill 21.1)

    A. Direct free kick

    B. Indirect free kick

    C. Fair play

    D. Ejection from the game

(A.) Assuming that the soccer player didn't intentionally hit the other player's knee, the result would be a direct free kick. If the foul was intentional, the referee can eject the offender from the game. Minor offenses and offenses not involving contact result in indirect free kicks.

124. **A basketball team has an outstanding rebounder. In order to keep this player near the opponent's basket, which strategy should the coach implement?**
(Average Rigor) (Skill 21.1)

    A. Pick-and-Roll

    B. Give-and-Go

    C. Zone defense

    D. Free-lancing

(C.) A zone defense, where each player guards an area of the court rather than an individual player, allows an outstanding rebounder to remain near the basket. The give-and-go, pick-and-roll, and free-lancing are offensive strategies that do not affect rebounding.

125. **Volleyball player LB on team A digs a spiked ball. The ball deflects off LB's shoulder. What is the ruling?**
(Average Rigor) (Skill 21.1)

   A. Fault

   B. Legal hit

   C. Double foul

   D. Play over

(B.) Since the spiked ball does not touch the ground and instead deflects off LB's shoulder, it is a legal hit. In order for a point to end, the ball must touch the ground. In this instance, it does not.

Sample Written Assignments

Sample Written Assignment #1

This sample written assignment consists of a brief scenario followed by a sequence of questions or topics to discuss. You should draft an essay of 200-400 words addressing all of the topics or questions. It is important that you organize your response and demonstrate a thorough understanding of the subject matter. Content is more important than writing style, though poor grammar, punctuation, spelling, and sentence structure can detract from your response.

Use the information below to complete the exercise that follows.

Evan is a 10-year-old fifth grade student who recently completed a physical fitness evaluation in his physical education class. Evan was able to perform 6 push-ups and no pull-ups. He completed the mile run in 6:58. The evaluation also showed that Evan had below average flexibility.

Evan is a physically active child, participating in tennis and soccer outside of school. Evan is a very talented athlete looking to improve his performance in his sporting activities. Evan is also a very reserved, shy child who does not make friends easily or interact much with other children. In addition, Evan's parents feel Evan is an unusually gifted tennis player and should stop playing soccer to focus on tennis.

Based on your knowledge of physical fitness construct a written response that addresses the following:

- interpret the results of Evan's fitness evaluation; determine the components of fitness that Evan needs to address

- identify two age-appropriate fitness activities that will help Evan achieve his goals

- advise Evan's parents on their desire to have Evan focus on tennis taking into account the social and psychological aspects of participation in sports and fitness activities

Strong Response to the Sample Written Assignment #1

The results of Evan's physical fitness assessment show that he has a high level of cardiovascular endurance (good mile run time), a low level of muscular endurance (poor results on push-up and pull-up test), and a low level of flexibility. Thus, a fitness program for Evan should focus on developing muscular endurance and flexibility. In addition, because Evan participates in soccer and tennis, he likely receives more than enough aerobic activity in these aerobically intensive sports.

Flexibility and muscular endurance are important, and often overlooked, aspects of tennis and soccer. Thus, developing these areas will improve Evan's athletic performance. Because Evan is only 10-years-old, I would recommend he engage in body support exercises, rather than resistance training exercises, to increase his muscular endurance. Such exercises include push-ups, pull-ups, sit-ups, lunges, and squats. I would not recommend weight training for a 10-year-old because lifting weights is dangerous and possibly detrimental for developing bodies. Evan should also engage in a regular stretching program after his tennis and soccer practices and matches. Stretching improves flexibility and stretching after physical activity is safest and most effective.

Finally, I would advise Evan's parents that he should continue to play both soccer and tennis. Sport specialization is not necessary at Evan's age to maximize performance and asking Evan to give up soccer could have other detrimental effects. Because Evan is shy and reserved, the social aspects of a team sport like soccer are important to his development. Participation in team sports promotes the development of social skills, leadership, teamwork, and interpersonal relationships. Evan will benefit from such interaction with other children and will improve his self-esteem, especially because he is a talented player. While tennis is an excellent sport, it is mainly an individual sport, and the opportunity for socialization and the development of friendships is limited.

Sample Written Assignment #2

This sample written assignment requires you to respond to a question about human health and development. You should draft an essay of 200-400 words addressing the topic. It is important that you organize your response and demonstrate a thorough understanding of the subject matter. Content is more important than writing style, though poor grammar, punctuation, spelling, and sentence structure can detract from your response.

Participation in physical activities can enhance the development of many social skills. Choose <u>one</u> of the following social skills enhanced by physical activity: collaboration/cooperation/teamwork, loyalty, compassion/consideration for others, leadership, valuing/respecting diversity and individual differences.

- **discuss how participation in physical activity can affect the development of the social skill you chose**

- **identify strategies for encouraging development of the skill in the physical education classroom**

- **discuss how the acquired skill will benefit students later in life**

Strong Response to Sample Written Assignment #2

Participation in physical activities and sports can greatly enhance the development of collaboration, cooperation, and teamwork skills. Many physical activities require some degree of cooperation, most notably team sports. Team sports require participants to work together to achieve a common goal. Participants learn to pool the talents and minimize the weaknesses of different team members. Students will quickly learn that individualism can destroy the team concept and damage the team's performance. In addition, students will learn that a lack of respect or dissension between teammates will hurt the team. Students will learn to respect their teammates, value their contributions, and encourage them to perform their best.

Physical educators can encourage development of teamwork skills by including team-oriented activities in their lesson plans. Common examples include basketball, softball, volleyball, and soccer. In addition, instructors should watch closely for and discipline students that blatantly disrupt the team concept by bullying or belittling teammates.

Teamwork, collaboration, and cooperation skills are important in many walks of life. Students will use teamwork skills in their academic careers, in the workplace, and at home. For example, many academic classes from elementary school through college require group work. Most jobs require employees to work with others to achieve goals. Finally, we can view a family unit as a team. Students will have to play many roles on their family team (e.g. child, sibling, spouse, and parent) throughout their lives.